Also by Barrie C. Bartulski

The Red Schwinn Bicycle
"A Sentimental Journey"

ISBN: 978-0-595-89106-1 Hardcover

ISBN: 978-0-595-41094-1 Paperback

ISBN: 978-0-595-85453-0 E-book Format

Visit Barrie's website, www.redschwinn.com.

Where the Hell Is
TURTLE CREEK?

A Memoir of Days Gone By

BARRIE C. BARTULSKI

iUniverse, Inc.
Bloomington

Where the Hell Is Turtle Creek?
A Memoir of Days Gone By

iUniverse books may be ordered through booksellers or by contacting:

iUniverse
1663 Liberty Drive
Bloomington, IN 47403s
www.iuniverse.com
1-800-Authors (1-800-288-4677)

ISBN: 978-1-4620-4109-1 (sc)
ISBN: 978-1-4620-4111-4 (hc)
ISBN: 978-1-4620-4110-7 (ebk)

Printed in the United States of America

iUniverse rev. date: 11/16/2011

To:

The struggling working families of the past who helped make America what it is and stands for, and to the families and young children of today who hold America's future in their hands.

Saint Colman's Sisters of Mercy, priests, and public schoolteachers, who had their hands full with all of us children.

CONTENTS

**Read below about Barrie C. Bartulski's
forthcoming first suspenseful novel**

THE ZEALOTS

A story about a high tech Corporation, Guidance Development Inc. with headquarters located in Calabasas, California. All is going well and business is extremely good, until fraud and malfeasance is uncovered. The unauthorized removal of a "characterized" or best of the lot tested Gyroscope, from a government bonded store room is discovered!

This gyroscope is now suspect in an armed and deadly confrontation between an Iranian submarine and United States aircraft carrier.

World peace is at stake, threats of nuclear retaliation and Saber rattling coming from Russia, Syria, and Iraq all friendly to Iran is not helping the situation!

PREFACE

The stories in this book reflect the adventures of a group of children, from mixed ethnic and religious backgrounds, growing up in the 1940s and '50s in Turtle Creek, a small town in western Pennsylvania, near Pittsburgh. In addition, the stories also address the hardships of quite a few of the parents and the local townsfolk during these times.

As one of these young children, now grown up and living in California, I am always presented with an outcry of "Where the hell is Turtle Creek?" coming from the mouths of people after they ask me where I grew up. I soon came to realize that folks from the Pittsburgh area have a distinct and recognizable accent.

My California neighbors in the various cities I have lived in over the years often made fun of a town called Turtle Creek. They would ask me to describe what it was like living there. Some would even refer to it, due to its name, as perhaps being a "hick place."

Many would even comment that it sounded like it might have been a dull place, not where someone would like to live and grow up. I always interpreted comments like this as meaning there were not a lot of exciting and fun things to do.

Contrary to their expressed opinions, I never thought about it that way. Turtle Creek had churches of different denominations, a movie theater, a soda fountain in the drugstore, and a G. C. Murphy five-and-ten store. We even had a White Tower, a small hamburger, soda, and coffee restaurant that became overcrowded with ten people gathered inside it. From the outside, its décor of black and white ceramic tiles resembled that of a White Castle hamburger establishment.

Many of the children in town were affiliated with a Cub, Boy, or Girl Scout troop, or some church group that provided a great deal of things for them to do and become involved in. As the children grew older, there were many other things to do, commensurate with becoming a teenager and young adult. Community halls and school gymnasiums were the social meeting places for large clusters of children. They were where many of them learned how to dance, play games, watch movies, become involved in sports, and socially interact with one another.

A dip in the indoor pool at the local high school offered some cooling relief during the long, hot, humid summer months. It seemed but a short time before that many of these children's parents had also played together, belonged to the same organizations, and used these same facilities. It also seemed as if no one wanted to leave the town, even as they got older.

I don't want to stereotype anyone, but getting married and going to work for Westinghouse, U.S. Steel, Westinghouse Air Brake, or the Union Railroad and owning a home, was the set plan for most of the young people. I have to include myself in this category.

Turtle Creek also had a post office, a fire and police station, a poolroom, two bowling alleys, a few restaurants and bars, and a portion of the largest Westinghouse manufacturing facility in the United States. A state-run store for adults to purchase wine and hard liquor was located in the center of town.

It seems like a very antiquated thing in this modern age, but Pennsylvania still has an old blue law that requires everybody to purchase their alcohol from a state-run store! I personally believe the law is a state-controlled monopoly. Under today's laws, a *private* business cannot monopolize a certain product and eliminate its competition!

However, beer can be purchased in the local bars or at an independent beer distributor facility. It is unlike California, where one can buy all types of booze, such as liquor, wine, and beer, twenty-four hours a day. It can be purchased in just about every major food market, convenience store, and drugstores, but all of them must adhere to state liquor-control laws and the restricting of sales to minors.

I can remember as a young boy observing many people entering and leaving our "state liquor store." Some of them had a look of what I will call guilt or humiliation. Men would often turn up their coat collars or shield their faces in some manner to avoid being recognized. Perhaps they did not want to be seen by some of the local residents, or perhaps even a priest or minister, as doing something evil and sinful.

I ask myself why they even cared, since stopping off at the local bars for a shot of whiskey and a beer chaser before and after work was a daily ritual. For some of the men, too much liquor often led to verbal and physical abuse in the household and caused the wife or children to run out and seek safety and comfort with other relatives. Especially Grandma and Granddad.

Females entering and leaving the same liquor store would often do the same thing with their coat collars. In addition, they would conceal their faces with a tightly wrapped head scarf, a *babushka* as we would say in Polish. Many other adults, such as my father, would walk in and out of this state-controlled liquor store feeling no sense of guilt or remorse. They acted very cavalier and as if they were entering or leaving the local Giant Eagle grocery market or a drugstore.

Living in such a small town allowed many neighbors to personally know one another on a first-name basis. The majority of them would often come to the aid of families with the offering of help and food baskets during hard times or periods of long unemployment. Everyone knew what family the small children playing and bouncing along the streets belonged to and was always watchful of them.

House doors were often left open during the day, weather permitting, and there were not many families living in Turtle Creek who could classify themselves as "upper-crust."

It is my belief that there are still thousands of lovely little Turtle Creeks scattered across the United States today. They would be places where children can grow up and enjoy a slower country-style pace of life, without the benefits of—or the drawbacks of—a big-city environment. Many towns like Turtle Creek are disappearing and have become blighted over time. Unemployment is high as it is in the rest of the country, and it is due to an industrial slowdown, factories closing, and the high-technology world we live in today.

The stories you are about to read are a presentation of what we children in Turtle Creek, and the children of the area's other small towns, did to keep busy, the games we played and the things we did while growing up, and our close camaraderie with one another. Some of the events described in my days-gone-by stories reflect upon the unique and special social interaction during this time period that helped children fully understand and learn about tolerance and respect for one another.

This social acceptance was learned and developed by most children at an early age while playing games with one another, mostly outdoors! Of course, Mom and Dad's influence and guidance helped also. In addition, perhaps feeling the sting from their parents' hands or the sting of a belt on the buttocks regarding "right from wrong" was a prevailing factor in building the moral value and character of such children. My mother was not bashful about slapping us children across the face from time to time if our back talk got out of hand.

Somehow it seems to me that today, much of this childhood social interaction and way of life is diminishing very quickly. Television, iPods, Nintendos, Xboxes, and other electronic games are becoming the new social nexus and playtime pals for a lot of children. Homeschooling programs of today and courses without the proper supervised educated adult guidance, in my opinion, disallow such needed social interaction.

My childhood was a time of youthful and exuberant innocence, with timeless values, where children got along happily with one another without our government's current mandates and laws with regard to race, creed, and color. However, there were many times when minor disputes arose among us children to cause an exchange of some name-calling and a few tears being shed.

About the worst and most hateful things most kids would ever say when they got really mad at one another was "I hate you" or "I wish you were dead." Or maybe "I am never going to be your friend or play with you ever again."

Soon afterward, the disagreements, arguing, sniveling, and name-calling would stop as quickly as they had started. Then a lot of "I am sorry" exchanges and other words of regretfulness could be heard. It did not take very long for children to become mad at someone and then quickly make up with each other and get over any incidents. Afterward, some would even share their penny Tootsie Roll with those they offended or hurt, or who may have offended or hurt them.

The cultures of each child or group, although different, were rarely discussed. There was always a fervent respect for one another, even when a comment or joke might be made by children or even adults about one's ethnicity. In fact, many of the comments expressed by one child to another were openly received and gladly accepted as signs of friendship and love. However, it was also a time when most families in town—although they did not express it openly—expected their children to marry within their group.

Laws in effect today prohibit one from saying things that were never considered distasteful or offensive during my growing up when done in a pleasant way. Today, federal, state, and local authorities, fearful of unfavorably perceived ethnic remarks and the potential for a lawsuit, are often standing on "thin ice." You will also find the business community and educational institutions reacting in the same fearful way.

A wink of the eye years ago toward a young female by a young man often led to the start of a lovely and beautiful romance and perhaps even marriage. However, in today's society, it could lead to a sexual harassment complaint. What some of these idiotic laws have done, as I put it, is "broken the string on Cupid's bow."

Someone interpreting an ethnic remark being made by an individual as being off-color or not politically correct can result in serious consequences. It could even lead to sanctions, such as job dismissal or suspension, and possibly destroy an individual's character and reputation. I personally do not condone any individuals or organizations that blatantly use and make derogatory, off-color, and hateful ethnic remarks. However, some ethnic remarks, as distasteful as they may seem, must be tempered according to the attitude of the person expressing them, and the individual on the receiving end!

During the time of days gone by, comments such as those you are about to read were always made in jest, while playing with one another or even greeting someone.

They could be said while walking down the street or school hallway, passing a house or business, or visiting the local grocery store. They were considered "quite acceptable" and even showed how well people liked you.

This was because both children and adults were uninhibited and felt free to tease you. It was nothing more than another form of personal camaraderie and, I believe, still goes on today in many regions, especially where generation after generation of families have grown up, lived, and played together.

A person of Polish descent, such as me, walking into the local butcher shop would find it quite pleasing to hear someone shout out loud, "Hey, Hunky, how are you doing, and what can I get for you today?" The word *hunky* was initially used to define people of Slavic extraction. It can also be recognized as a vulgar term, one of hostility and contempt, and was used quite often during the 1890s and 1900s against many of the Eastern European Caucasians immigrating into America.

It was used in America's great steel mills, on the railroad, and in the coal mines, by the early Irish, Johnny Bulls, and Scottish immigrants, who considered themselves better and wanted to demean those working under them. It was also a way of not giving good jobs to hunkies, since they were not considered as capable of doing anything else but hard labor.

One must ask oneself why any human being could be so cruel and have such disregard for people's feelings. What most immigrants wanted when they came to America was to live proudly, keep their dignity, and maintain their customs and ancestry.

A reply to the loud shout coming from the butcher might have been "a pound of jumbo (Turtle Creek slang terminology for bologna), hamburger, or kielbasa, you greasy Sicilian." Or the butcher might say to my mother, Mary Byrne and of Irish descent, "How is my Green Isle Lace Curtain Irish gal doing today?" On other occasions, my father, after being greeted with a "Hello, Hunky," might have said back to the butcher, who was Italian, "Some hamburger and pork chops, Wop."

Sometimes he might have even addressed the butcher as a "guinea," slang terminology used to describe Italians. Local athletes and grown adults would find it pleasing to hear someone greet them with a "Hey, Bo-Hunk." Again, this was considered a nasty term of derision for Eastern European Caucasians.

One might even shout out and say to an Italian, "Hey, Dago, why don't you swim back to Italy, and take a few of your buddies with you on your back?" Irish individuals could even be addressed as "Lace Curtain" or "Shanty House."

At other times, one might hear them referred to as "Pig Shit Irish." The German kid could be called "the big dumb German," or the Jewish kid "Jew boy." The Greeks were known simply as the Greeks, and the Albanians as Albanians. But always, people of Slavic ethnicity were addressed and known as hunkies.

During my youthful days, there were very few Asian, Mid-Eastern, and African American ethnic people living in Turtle Creek. Therefore, it would be difficult and very presumptuous of me to describe how they might have jokingly interacted with one another or other ethnic groups.

This type of dialogue was carried on every day between neighbors, schoolchildren, and people who cared for and knew one another; and no one, to my knowledge, considered it offensive or distasteful! While skipping rope at school or other play areas, younger and older girls, of different ethnic makeup, could be heard laughing, giggling, and singing a song with the following lyrics in good fun:

"Hunky, Dago, Sheeny, Wop, I eat spaghetti, you eat slop"!

In all of my youthful years, while playing with my friends, not once did I ever hear them refer to African Americans in a derogatory, hateful, or racist manner. They were known to be colored or black and were always called by their given name or whatever nickname they had when we played together.

I would be remiss, however, if I did not point out that I knew of and on occasion did hear the inflammatory word *nigger* used by several adults inside their households and on the open street.

Offering no excuses for this, I must also say that during this age of innocence, all of us children were quite naïve and had very little knowledge of or understanding as to its connotation. To draw a parallel to how such a word can cause inflammatory situations, in our age of innocence, we children were not taught, familiar with, or had ever heard words such as cracker, redneck, honky, or kike which can be considered equally inflammatory today.

The series of stories presented in this book revolve around Turtle Creek's Saint Colman's Catholic elementary school and the public junior and senior high school students and friends. The book also contains some of the young age, mischievous antics of my brother, Richard, and me years ago—and in the days gone by since then!

Most of these children came from depression-era parents, who would always help out one another during difficult times. They also had very little money, and there were some with limited educations, due to difficult times and other hardships. Because of this situation, the majority of the Turtle Creek and other area parents were employed in a mix of hard labor and blue-collar jobs.

Many parents had immigrated to America from Europe and other parts of the world; and like many other immigrants, they came to America seeking a better way of life. Families were responsible for helping one another in a time of need, without the expectation of a government dole. It was also a time when all churches played a major role in helping down-and-out families.

This same scenario existed for a great deal of children and parents throughout the other small towns and industrial enclaves surrounding the Pittsburgh area.

Some of these enclaves were manufacturing plants, belching out noxious smoke and other industrial waste from their tall mill stacks or dumping toxic coolant and raw sewage into the local rivers and streams. The sight of dirty-looking smoke or the blowing of factory whistles meant good times and prosperity.

The whistles also could mean it was time for a lunch break, a work shift change, an accident, or fire. After a while, the local residents recognized what each whistle, or series of short whistles, stood for. For many, it was their Morse code.

Jokingly some people would say that the steel mill hunkies or bo-hunks did not need watches, since they could only tell what time it was by listening to the whistles blowing. However, the most important whistle of the day or night for the hardworking mill hands was the one signifying it was time to end work. Perhaps, they might even have time to stop off at a local bar for a three-finger shot of Corby's or Four Roses whiskey and an Iron City beer chaser afterward! For some, they might even request that a few raw eggs also be dropped into their beer glass!

During the time of days gone by, no one ever wanted to see the steel-mill smoke disappear or the whistles stop blowing, since most often it would mean a strike. The strikes were generally brought about due to disagreements between management and labor.

Strikes often turned out to be bitter and long, and scab workers were brought in to fill the jobs of striking union workers. Fights between the striking union workers and the scabs often resulted in Pennsylvania state troopers, mounted on horseback, being called in to quell rioting.

The U.S. Steel Homestead plant strike of 1892 was one of the most bitterly fought industrial disputes in the history of US labor. The displaced workers opened fire on a barge loaded with three hundred Pinkerton agents being brought in as strikebreakers. Three Pinkerton agents and seven strikebreakers were killed; later, several other men died from their wounds. This strike was a total defeat for the workers and unionism as a whole!

Fifteen years earlier, another traumatic industrial labor dispute, the great railroad strike of 1877, cannot be overlooked. Railroad owners and strikers disagreeing over the cutting of wages caused havoc all around, and Pittsburgh, Pennsylvania, became the site of the worst violence.

Thomas Alexander Scott of the Pennsylvania Railroad, often considered one of the first robber barons, suggested that the strikers should be given "a rifle diet for a few days and see how they like that kind of bread." However, local law enforcement officers refused to fire on the strikers.

Nonetheless, his request came to pass on July 21, when militiamen bayoneted and fired on rock-throwing strikers, killing twenty people and wounding twenty-nine others. Rather than quell the uprising, however, this action merely infuriated the strikers, who then forced the militiamen to take refuge in a railroad roundhouse and then set fires that razed thirty-nine buildings and destroyed 104 locomotives and 1,245 freight and passenger cars. On July 22, the militiamen mounted an assault on the strikers, shooting their way out of the roundhouse and killing twenty more people on their way out of the city. After over a month of constant rioting and bloodshed, President Rutherford B. Hayes sent in federal troops to end the strike.

When the bellowing smoke from the outside mill stacks finally disappeared, it meant that the plants were shut down completely, except for needed maintenance and management personnel. Soon after the shutdown, many struggling and hardworking people would be without work for months to come. No one ever saw or cared about the harm and health issues that would someday surface from this unregulated industrial, putrid, smoking giant.

Turtle Creek and the East Pittsburgh Westinghouse Electric Plant, employing twenty thousand workers in the 1940s, was dismantled years later, and many other towns also succumbed to factory shutdowns and work curtailments. Towns like Braddock, Homestead, and Clairton, with their mighty steel mills producing the steel for great bridges, tanks, and battleships that made Pittsburgh famous, were always the hardest hit.

Other neighboring towns that suffered after providing a great deal of the mill and other industrial workers, such as Munhall, North Braddock, Duquesne, Trafford, East Pittsburgh, Wilmerding, Pitcairn, Rankin, Swissvale, Wilkinsburg, McKeesport, and New Kensington, to mention a few, will forever remain in my treasured memories.

As time passed, plant relocations, such as the Westinghouse East Pittsburgh/Turtle Creek facilities, to different parts of the country, to improve efficiency and reap the benefits of cheaper labor, began to take their toll on the workforce. This same practice is still being employed by major American corporations around the United States today.

However, it has now migrated into other parts of the global business world and has become known as outsourcing. Unfortunately, this sad story of industrial decline over the years has taken its toll on many other small towns of America, especially in those areas described as the "rust belt of the east" and the once-mighty shoe manufacturing industry.

Partial view of Turtle Creek, 2002.

Penn Avenue, main street, 1960s.

Penn Avenue, main street, 1960s, Continued.

Penn Avenue, main street, 1960s, Continued.

Penn Avenue, main street, 1960s, Continued.

Original Westinghouse plant, 1894.

ACKNOWLEDGMENTS

Writing these stories was not a difficult task, since I still retain the everlasting fond memories of my childhood in Turtle Creek, Pennsylvania. I feel as if it were yesterday and I had used a video camera and tape recorder to help me recall some of the events and antics I remember and write about.

I can still see clearly the faces of all my school friends, teachers, priests, nuns, local residents, business establishments, and factories; I can still recall all of their names. The beautiful trees and woods of Pennsylvania and the other small, adjacent towns that I once played in or traveled through are also still embedded deeply in my mind.

I can recall the wonderful times I had going to school and playing exciting games with the boys and girls. Especially those games played during the summer, the harshest rainfall, and those great snow—and ice-filled days of winter.

I give special acknowledgment to these wonderful childhood friends and other people, many of whom are now deceased, whom I was privileged to know. Without my memories of these fine people, the age of youthful innocence and happy times in "days gone by" could never have been written down and told about.

I SHALL NOT PASS THIS WAY AGAIN

Through this toilsome world, alas!

Once and only once I pass;

If a kindness I may show,

If a good deed I may do

To a suffering fellow man,

Let me do it while I can.

No delay, for it is plain

I shall not pass this way again.

—Author Unknown

SPECIAL THANKS

To Turtle Creek Individuals, for copies of the following:

Rosie Divens—Town photos

Joseph Martinelli—Saint Colman School and Church photos

HISTORY OF SAINT COLMAN'S SCHOOL

Saint Colman's was formed in September 1882. The twenty-eight-family congregation drew from Wall, which is now known as Pitcairn, Wilmerding, and East Pittsburgh. During peak times, the flock grew into several thousand families. Until the church was built, the holy sacrifice of the Mass was offered up on Sundays and holy days in the public school located on Church Street and during the week in a rented parochial residence.

How simple life was during days gone by when people were so busy just trying to survive and take care of their families. Little time was left for meddling and novices attempting to impose their wishes or to interpret the Constitution and what our founding fathers meant by separation of church and state. On reading this book and having something of a religious background, one can only imagine what would happen today if someone were to hold a religious service of any kind or say a prayer in a public school!

The American Civil Liberties Union (ACLU) would most assuredly be filing a lawsuit to prevent it. As a personal note, I believe, "As long as there are standardized tests in a public school, unknowingly, there will always be some individual, in some schoolroom, who will be saying a prayer to pass."

After forming the parish and having sufficient funds to begin, a wooden church, the "old church," was erected around 1884. The walls were undressed, the pews plain, and the vestments only such as were absolutely needed. There was no choir, nor did an organ or an organ loft appear among the embellishments of the building. One Low Mass was said every Sunday, and a sermon was preached. This constituted the services for several months.

A considerable amount of discussion took place between the various outlying town congregations regarding their participation in starting a school in Turtle Creek. Finally one was opened in 1887. This undertaking was accomplished by renovating and using the lower story of the old wooden church to make four large classrooms and a small apartment to be used by the nuns as a reception and community room.

The building was not plastered, and nothing but the weatherboards protected the interior from the outside elements. There were times during the harsh cold months when the hot air furnaces were not working properly, so students or parishioners were often cold. Many times the priest saying Mass above or on the second floor discovered the wine and water frozen when he was about to pour them into the chalice at the offertory.

Due to these conditions, Saint Colman's congregation decided to start a separate and distinct school for its local Catholic children in 1888. A building was rented, the doors were opened, and 120 pupils were enrolled. In charge of their education were two Sisters of Mercy who came direct from Dublin, Ireland, and resided in the Saint Thomas Convent, located in the nearby town of Braddock.

The Sisters continued to travel back and forth from Braddock during the years between 1888 and April 1892, during which time the enrollment grew to 210 pupils and another Sister was added to the teaching staff. When Saint Colman's new Romanesque-style church was completed in 1903, the upper story of the old wooden church was renovated to add additional classrooms, which brought the school to a total of eight classrooms, 398 pupils, and five Sisters.

During the celebration of Saint Colman's Silver Jubilee in its twenty-fifth year in 1907, Pastor William Cunningham pleaded with the parishioners to help liquidate the old debt so that a new school could be built. His pleas were answered, and a new modern school incorporating some of the building materials and Romanesque design of the new church was finally built and opened in 1928.

The old combined wooden church and school that provided religious training and education for so many children during the early years at Saint Colman's was torn down after completion of the new school. Most of the exterior styling of the school was completed in 1928 and still stands today.

My mother, Mary Byrne, and her siblings attended Saint Colman's School, as did I, my sisters, Joy and Judy, and my brother, Richard. After a lot of interior remodeling and a brand-new addition in 1954, it was referred to as the Junior High.

Sadly and with much regret, I must now write that due to financial considerations, Saint Colman's, the "gold standard" in a Catholic school for educational and religious teachings, has been closed.

There were approximately 120 children attending the school when a diocese decision was made to close it. Today the classrooms are leased out by the Pittsburgh Diocese to the state of Pennsylvania as an alternative or continuation public school for many students.

Saint Colman's School, Grades 1-8, 1950.

HISTORY OF SAINT COLMAN'S CHURCH

The third bishop of the Pittsburgh Diocese, Right Reverend John Tuigg, appointed Father Thomas Neville in 1882 to take charge and to erect a new church to replace the small old wooden church. He labored at this task for two years, and through fairs, lawn fetes, picnics, bazaars, teas, raffles, concerts, and other forms of entertainment, raised sufficient funds to ensure there would be a permanent Saint Colman's Church in Turtle Creek.

Shortly after achieving this goal, he was appointed by the bishop as pastor of Saint Malachy Church in Pittsburgh. The reverend father W. A. Cunningham was then assigned by the bishop to replace Father Neville as Saint Colman's pastor and begin the process of constructing the church.

Five hundred little wooden box savings banks were ordered and distributed to the good parishioners of Turtle Creek in order to continue fund-raising. A brass identification plate was riveted to the box. The inscription on the box, in bold letters, read: "ST. COLMAN DEBT SOCIETY, TURTLE CREEK, PA. You are a Member, or a Friend of a Member. 'God Loveth a Cheerful Giver,' 2 Cor. Ix, 7. W. A. Cunningham, Pastor."

The banks were locked, and only the priests retained the keys so that no other person could have access to the contents. They were brought into the rectory from time to time to be emptied. A simple philosophy was employed to encourage saving. Pennies, nickels, dimes, quarters, half dollars, and dollars were to be deposited in the banks.

A penny a day meant $3.65 a year. Multiply this by the 450 families in the parish, and you have a handsome sum of $1,642.50. Now, if everyone were to place a nickel in the box instead of a penny daily, the aggregate at the end of the year from all families would be five times $1,642.50, or $8,212.50.

This scheme worked over time to liquidate the debt on the acquired lots and properties. When construction was sufficient, the cornerstone for Saint Colman's was laid on Sunday, June 2, 1901.

The church construction was of a Romanesque design, with lofty steeples and opulent stained-glass windows. The windows were copied from religious masterpieces, and several stained-glass windows were of notable individuals, such as the Holy Father Pope Leo XIII.

It was a magnificent structure for all around to see. Built on a frontage of almost six hundred feet on paved streets, its foundation was formed on a plot one hundred feet wide and two hundred feet deep. The church structure was 136 feet long with a front of seventy feet and was located in a prime and convenient location for most of the parishioners to access.

Saint Colman's Church had a nave (a long central section or narrow sanctuary leading to the main altar) of fifty-six feet and a transept (section that cut horizontally through the nave) of sixty-six feet. The intersection of nave and transept crossing at right angles was located under the high arched ceiling above the main altar and decorated with rose and light blue winged angels and other colorful religious figures. It was said to be the heart of the church.

The building materials of terra-cotta brick, Indiana and Cleveland blue stone trimmings, and all construction costs (including the renovation of the old wooden school) and the furnishings totaled up to a final amount of $118,369.87. The new Saint Colman's church was officially dedicated on May 10, 1903.

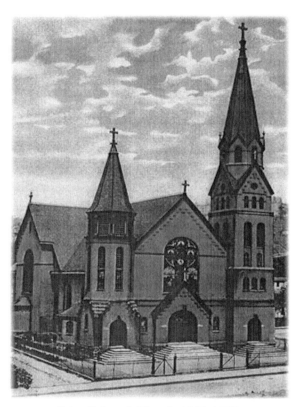

Saint Colman's Church, 1903-1977.

ST. COLMAN'S DEBT SOCIETY,

TURTLE CREEK, PA.

You are a Member, or a Friend of a Member.

"God Loveth a Cheerful Giver," 2 Cor. ix, 7.

W.A. Cunningham, Pastor.

"Our Little Box"

The little box collections started about 1886.

THE PUBLIC SCHOOLS

The Turtle Creek Penn Avenue Elementary Public School was opened in 1898 and had fifteen rooms; Turtle Creek High School, formerly called Union High, was opened in 1919. Both of these fine institutions had a mix of Protestant and Catholic students along with an ethnic makeup of English, Irish, Scottish, Italian, Polish, German, Scandinavian, Slovak, Hungarian, Czechoslovakian, Russian, Greek, and a very small population of African Americans.

Some of the Russian students practiced the Jewish faith, and the Greek population was mainly Eastern Orthodox. Diversity and affirmative action were not required nor heard of during this period. Most, if not all, of these students mixed together in a harmonious fashion and became good friends, playing with one another without regard to race, creed, or color.

These different nationalities found comfort in their churches and did not try to impose their religion or culture on anyone else. The children's innocence during days gone by allowed them to mix and play naturally with people of other nationalities and to respect their religious beliefs without any prejudices.

Both of these public schools had a high enrollment of Catholic children, some of whom had previously attended Saint Colman's up to eight grades. Discussions between adults over the years regarding private schooling versus public schooling often led to heated but civil arguments. I personally believe the arguments were foolish and that the children who attended the public schools during days gone by received an education equal to that of any Catholic or other private institution.

One might ask why I believe the educational system of the early years for both institutions was comparatively equal; from my viewpoint, the answer is simple. The Sisters and public schoolteachers and administrators were highly respected and looked up to, and the schools had strict educational requirements and rules. If you disobeyed the rules, you were disciplined and punished accordingly at school. In addition, further punishment was usually administered at home.

The discipline could be in the form of physical paddling or restrictions as to what you could do during school, after school, and in free playtime hours. Failing to meet and pass some of the required educational courses, such as reading, writing, English, history, chemistry, typing, civics, mathematics, and science courses, meant you would be held back or not allowed to graduate until they were made up or completed! A physical education class was also required during days gone by, unless you had some disability or sickness that prevented it.

At times, a doctor's or a parent's written note was required if you needed to be excused from class. An elective Latin or Spanish class, homemaking, auto shop, and mechanical drawing class were also available if you wanted to enroll. These classes, along with the aforementioned classes, recorded your personal ability and willingness to learn under a grading system from A to F; a pass/fail criterion was a nonexistent option.

There was no reward for laziness and goofing off. Promoting a failing student to a higher grade just to pass them along was never allowed. Some of these failing students would eventually come around and bear down on their studies if they wanted to graduate. I must confess that I fell into a lazy mode, enjoyed the party way of life, and did no homework assignments for history and geometry during my sophomore year. Because of this, I failed the required tests and did not receive a grade for the courses!

During days gone by, two major tests, known as the mid and final exams, were given for each course to determine, along with other academic assignments, how well a student was doing and comprised part of a student's final grade. Needless to say, I got very busy in my senior year when I was told I would not be graduating without making up and taking the required classes that I had failed. My final courses and the makeup classes were a heavy workload, but I got through them, passed the tests, made the honor roll one time that year, and graduated.

The school principal's phone call to my parents and my parents' long discussion about failing and other mischievous deeds were also very instrumental in my graduating. My father's scolding, along with a physical beating coming from his razor strap, also made me get busy and pay more attention to my schoolwork. His own failure, as he put it and his lack of a high school diploma were often emphasized by him; he constantly said,

"If it is the last thing I do, I will make sure all of you kids graduate from high school."

This was a man who spoke fluent Polish, Russian, and German, but refused to teach his children the languages. He would say to us, "This is America, and English is what you must speak, not some foreign language." I am sure that there were many other parents who would not speak to their children in their native language also. Today I am very envious of those nations whose educational systems mandate foreign language courses and the children and adults who not only speak their native language, but English also!

My father was knowledgeable enough at this time to recognize that without a high school education and diploma, one's chances of obtaining a good job were diminished. He knew that very few companies would hire you without one. He would often say that my brother and I would never be allowed to work in the steel mill.

His statement was not meant to degrade mill workers, since he was one himself, but only to emphasize that a solid education would make it easier for us to seek employment in a profession we would like to enter. In the highly technological world of today, most parents have probably changed my father's philosophy and statements a little and are telling their children that without a college education and degree, or respected trade, they will not be able to find a well-paying job or become globally competitive.

In a few years, a mechanical robot (most likely conceptually developed by a school like Carnegie Mellon) or a voice-activated reality program, with no human dialogue or interaction whatsoever, will be used in the screening of individuals' qualifications during a job interview. The computer has also taken a lot of the human element out of applying for work, since resume exchange and looking for a job is now done in a lot of cases via the Internet. Craigslist, an Internet site operating out of San Francisco, California, are very good examples of this!

In these days gone by, those students who did not want to learn, unfortunately, would eventually quit school. In some cases, there were bright students who met all of their course requirements but due to economic conditions at home, had to quit school early. They had to go to work and help out with the household finances. Some, as a last resort, would even join the military, as many still do today!

Graduates of these fine schools, (Saint Colman's, the Turtle Creek public system) due to the grim days of the depression, felt that college was out of the question. A "good job" for the men might lead them into the mill stoking open-hearth furnaces or winding copper armatures in the Westinghouse Electric plant. Other good jobs might be landed at the Union Railroad or the Westinghouse Air Brake facility.

Many, however, would put on a military uniform, serve their country, and after the war, go on to further their education under the G.I. Bill. They, along with many women, would go on in life to become engineers, psychologists, microbiologists, pharmacists, entomologists, physicists, teachers, professors, social workers, journalists, accountants, stockbrokers, law enforcement officers, doctors, nurses, lawyers, judges, and corporate CEOs. Some of these graduates would also become priests, nuns, and ministers. Some would even become authors!

One of the most notable graduates among this list would be Leon Hart, who was born November 2, 1928, in Turtle Creek and passed away on September 24, 2002. Hart, the product of a Polish mother and Ukrainian father, was a coach's dream. He went on to play four years at right tight end for Notre Dame, from 1946 to 1949. Notre Dame went 36-0-2 and won three national championships. 1946, 1947 and 1949. Hart was All-America three times, won the 1949 Heisman and Maxwell Awards, and was 1949 Associated Press Male Athlete of the Year. He was the second lineman to win the Heisman and Maxwell. Notre Dame Coach Frank Leahy remembered Hart best for his spectacular touchdown that tied Southern California in a fourteen-point battle in 1948. In his college career, he caught forty-nine passes for 742 yards and thirteen touchdowns. Hart was the Detroit Lions number one draft choice in 1950 and earned All-Pro defensive laurels the following season. In 1951, he became the last player selected All-Pro on both offense and defense. During his eight years with the Lions, Detroit won four division and three league titles. When his football-playing days ended, Hart used his mechanical engineering degree from Notre Dame and entered the business world. His marriage took place inside Saint Colman's Church in 1950 and drew a spectacular crowd of people.

Michael Estocin, born April 27, 1931, in Turtle Creek, Pennsylvania, attended Saint Colman's Grade School and graduated in 1949 from Turtle Creek High School. He attended Slippery Rock State College and graduated in 1954 with a BS in physical education. Upon his graduation, he enlisted in the Navy pilot training program. Mike was a member of the Navy Drill Team that performed at the Naval Academy football games at half time. He served three terms in Vietnam. During Mike's third tour of duty, he was recommended for the Congressional Medal of Honor.

Mike was shot down on his last mission on April 26, 1967, fifty miles north of Hanoi. In July 1967, he was listed as a prisoner of war. Mike is still unaccounted for from the Vietnam War. Captain Michael Estocin is the highest decorated hero from the Vietnam War, a Congressional Medal of Honor recipient, and has a Navy ship named in his honor—the USS *Estocin-FFG-15*.

Mike's citation for the Medal of Honor reads:

"For conspicuous gallantry and intrepidity at the risk of his life above and beyond the call of duty on 20 April and 26 April, 1967 as a pilot in attack squadron 192. Leading a three plane group of aircraft in support of a coordinated strike against the thermal power plants in Haiphong, North Vietnam, on 20 April, 1967, Captain Estocin provided continuous warnings to the strike group leaders of the surface to air missile (SAM) threats and personally neutralized three SAM sites. Captain Estocin's aircraft was severely damaged by an exploding missile, he re-entered the target area and relentlessly prosecuted a strike attack in the face of anti-aircraft fire. With less than five minutes of fuel remaining, he departed the target area and commenced in-flight refueling which continued for over one hundred miles. Three miles aft of the Ticonderoga and without enough fuel for a second approach, he disengaged from the tanker and executed a precise approach to a fiery arrested landing. On 26 April, 1967 in support of a strike against vital fuel facilities in Haiphong, he led an attack on a threatening SAM site, during which his aircraft was seriously damaged by an exploding SAM: nevertheless, Captain Estocin regained control of his aircraft and courageously launched his strike missiles before departing the area. By his inspiration and courage and unswerving devotion to duty in the face of grave danger, Captain Estocin upheld the highest traditions of the United States Navy".

Mike's wife Marie and their three daughters now reside in California.

Mike was a good friend and taught me how to execute a half gainer off the diving board at the Blue Dell swimming pool.

Colonel Patrick Fallon is another Saint Colman's and 1939 Turtle Creek High School graduate. He was born and raised on Sixth Street and was one of nine children in a typical Irish family. He went on to the US

Military Academy and joined the US Air Force. Pat graduated with honors from the University of Pittsburgh, and received his MA in International Relations and doctorate from Georgetown University in Washington, DC. In 1953 he was voted one of Pittsburgh's 100 Leaders of Tomorrow" by the Pittsburgh Press, Chamber of Commerce, and *Time Weekly News* magazine.

He served his country during World War II, the Korean and Vietnam wars. He is a highly decorated Air Force figure earning many decorations, including a Distinguished Flying Cross.

Pat was a command pilot navigator, earned paratrooper wings and in Korea he flew 125 combat missions and as a forward air controller parachuted behind enemy lines. Here he earned many more medals, one being a Purple Heart and was personally awarded by General Dwight Eisenhower. He trained Italian pilots and served in Greenland, Germany, and Turkey. He was a part-time instructor for the University of Maryland overseas and planned to teach after retiring from the Air Force in 1974. It is highly likely that Colonel Fallon would have made general before he retired.

While vice wing commander at Nakhon Phanom, Thailand, he flew over 100 missions again in his A-1, flying low to check enemy positions. He was shot down on July 4, 1969, in Laos while on a Skyraider mission to check out enemy activity. He made radio contact with other planes after getting hit, but was forced to bail out. The area was surrounded and too close to the enemy for him to be rescued.

Based on radio contact between supporting Skyraider aircraft, while he lay wounded on the floor of a Laos valley, he told them, "there are guys coming down the hill towards me." Then he orders them to "put it all around me. I'm hit." They radio back to him after identifying the bombing sight with a marking rocket and "tell him OK, duck your head". After this wave after wave of bombs obliterate the ridge lines and the A-1s continue attacking with rockets and 20mm cannon. He either died or was wounded and captured. His actions on this day earned him more medals and a second Purple Heart.

Based on information about Colonel Fallon's last mission and unselfish heroic act, I feel our top-ranking U.S. Air Force military leaders and the Department of Defense, should reevaluate what he did on this day and award him the Congressional Medal of Honor posthumously.

To really understand the dangers pilots faced while flying the World War II-vintage Douglas A-1 Skyraider and searching for downed pilots, one must read George J. Marrett's book titled *Cheating Death*. It tells of the dangerous combat air rescues in Vietnam and Laos.

Both Mike's and Pat's status were changed over the years by the military from prisoner of war (POW) and missing in action (MIA). They have both now been declared killed in action (KIA). This is due to the issuance of a government policy stating that after ten years of not being accounted for, all missing military personnel are considered KIA.

Even with this information the U.S. Air force is still looking for signs of Colonel Fallon in Laos, where he was shot down. This would include DNA analysis of any findings. However, one has to be wary of unscrupulous individuals, preying on family members of missing U.S. military personnel, who offer to provide bone fragments for money!

Colonel Fallon's wife Jean lives in Atlanta, Georgia and has two wonderful daughters Jean Elizabeth and Mary Catherine or "Cappie" and six grandchildren who are always there for her. It has been forty two years since Jean's husband was shot down and unaccounted for. However, since there is no proof he is dead, she continues to remain positive and has never given up hope that Pat will return home to her and their children one day.

Many other students from these schools went on to proudly serve their country in various U.S military branches during peace and war. Some of them returned home with serious wounds, both physical and emotional, and some, like Mike and Patrick, would never return.

The schools also produced a proud generation of hardworking mill hands, railroad workers, electrical and mechanical assemblers, secretaries, and other blue-collar laborers for America's corporations. These same people, many of them affiliated with labor unions and striking through the years for well-deserved benefits, paved the way for the medical, vacation, and pension benefits that many of us receive today.

A new working generation now sees these benefits dwindling and having to pay a considerable amount of money, on their own, to obtain a much lesser degree of coverage. Many workers are also seeing the health benefits they once received either free or at a minimal cost diminishing. In addition, company contributions toward an employee's health plan are being considered by the government as a form of income to be taxed.

Jobs are also disappearing at an alarming rate due to the outsourcing of work overseas and US companies struggling to remain competitive in a global economy and stay in business. Corporate greed, fraud, and malfeasance have also taken a toll on the American economy and job market. In addition, computers have replaced a lot of people in the workforce.

New technology and software are now manipulating many physical components that were once used in large manufacturing and test processes and have resulted in eliminating the once used physical labor content! This leading-edge technology is being applied continuously in just about every industrial plant owned by US firms (including those located offshore), thus creating a ripple effect on job losses and unemployment throughout the United States.

The parents of today must continue to emphasize the importance of a good education to their children and its importance in their becoming employed in today's challenging technical and global business environment. Today's educational system must also adapt itself to teaching and preparing such children for the high-technical and green-technology job challenges that await them in the future.

Oh, how I, and many others, long for the return of "days gone by."

Turtle Creek High School, grades 10-12, 1950s.

Turtle Creek Public Elementary School, grades 1-9, 1950s.

Leon Hart.

Colonel Patrick Fallon, US Air Force.

Captain Michael Estocin, US Navy.

CHAPTER 1

A DAY AT SCHOOL

It was a beautiful summer day when the dismissal bell rang out loud like a fire alarm on a Friday afternoon at Saint Colman's two-story, stone-and-brick Catholic elementary school. The early morning regimentation of children waking up, having a quick bowl of oatmeal, a cup of hot chocolate or Ovaltine, and a piece of hard crusty toast taken off the oven rack and smothered with Oleo and jelly would stop after today's school day.

Soon there would be two days they would not have to wake up early, dash off to school, get to the classroom, and remove loose clothing to hang up in the cloakroom. Hanging up their clothing was just a starter before saying the Pledge of Allegiance to the flag and kneeling down on the hardwood oak floors to begin reciting their morning prayers.

Grades one and two would be learning how to say the Our Father and Hail Mary prayers, practicing their numbers and the alphabet and doing block printing, reading, and spelling in the morning. In the afternoon after lunch, it would be more prayers and saying the rosary, simple adding and subtracting of numbers, English sentence structure, and Palmer cursive writing practice. Catechism study, first Holy Communion preparation (which included learning how to make a confession to the priest), and a good "act of contrition" would soon follow.

Catechism instruction was aimed at presenting the essential and fundamental contents of Catholic doctrine regarding both faith and morals. A precursor to these teachings is for every Catholic child to have been baptized, which is one of the seven sacraments of the church. Many descriptions of baptism can be found in the Bible, but simply put, it is necessary for salvation and assures entry into eternal beatitude.

By being baptized, all sins are forgiven, such as original sin and all personal sins, as well as all punishment for such sins. The church has done away with the belief that Catholics are born with original sin due to the disobedience of Adam and Eve to God's command. The remaining six sacraments are confirmation, the Eucharist (Communion), penance, the anointing of the sick, holy orders, and matrimony.

The next big thing in a Catholic child's life was to frequently receive Holy Communion, where one believes they swallow the body and blood of Jesus Christ. Early church doctrine would not allow Catholic children under the age of twelve to receive Communion. This rule has been done away with, and today the sacrament is generally provided for in the second grade of school. Also, Communion could only be administered by an ordained priest! This too has changed, and today many lay personnel, including women and known as Eucharistic ministers, are allowed to administer Communion. These individuals must be recommended by a priest and take two classes of theology (Catholic teachings) and one class of practicum for the teaching of such administration.

During my early Catholic teachings about receiving Holy Communion, some of us children were led to believe that if an individual regurgitated the Communion wafer, the priest had to pick it up and swallow it! I sincerely doubt that this act ever did or would take place anywhere Communion was being served. I know that procedures are in place within the church to see that any Communion wafers dropped on the floor are disposed of in the most holy manner.

Prior to receiving Communion, if children believed they had sinned, they would confess such sins to a priest. This act would be the sacrament of penance, also known as confession. After the confessing of sins, each child would tell the priest, through their "act of contrition," how sorry they were for offending God. They would go on to tell the priest about detesting their sins, dreading the loss of heaven, and fearing the pains of hell, and they would promise to do penance and amend their lives. "Amen."

The sacrament of anointing of the sick, also known as extreme unction or the last rites is when a priest is called to anoint and pray for a critically injured person. Family members and the ecclesial community may be invited to surround the sick in a special way through their prayers.

The ordination of a priest is the sacrament of holy orders, whereby the priest is enabled to act in the name of Jesus Christ. The priest also takes a vow of celibacy, devotes his life to God and men, and serves as Christ's instrument for his church.

Grades three through eight would also be saying their prayers and rosaries at different times during the day and in the morning working on their multiplication tables, percentages, fractions, decimals, and geometry, history, and geography lessons. In the afternoon, it would be more English sentence structure and Palmer cursive writing lessons, reading, catechism lessons, and confirmation study.

Confirmation is a renewal of baptismal promises and the act of reaffirming one's faith at a later age. Adults can, after taking the required studies, receive both baptism and confirmation at the same time.

In each class, an individual would be selected by Sister to approach the front of the classroom and talk about homework, or go to the blackboard and begin writing down a problem, religious question, or other parts of the homework assignment and explain it to Sister and the class.

This would go on for a while until several children had taken their place in front of the class, including those who obviously had not completed their homework assignment. Sister would deal with these children later!

Some of the boys called to take their position and stand by the blackboard would look for a new piece of white chalk lying on the ledge. The longer the better, since there was a unique way that the chalk stick could be placed on the blackboard while beginning to write so that it would emit a shriek that would irritate everyone, including Sister.

Depending on Sister's mood, this mischievous deed could earn you a slap with her hand on the head, arms, or back, or a trip to the cloakroom. One did not want to upset Sister and have her order you to "the evil cloakroom," which in most cases also meant there would be a thick wooden paddle dangling from her hand for further discipline.

The homework assignment papers would be exchanged between the students for correction and grading. If you were lucky, someone you knew who had your paper might even erase and put in the correct answers, numbers, or words to the questions or problems. Then, rather than getting a B or a C, you could get an A+ or an A.

Heaven forbid if Sister were to catch someone doing this! It would mean both parties had to stay after school, and all recess activities would be stopped for a long time. Below a C was D or F (there was no such thing as pass/fail criteria), and getting too many Ds or Fs in any subject would result in Sister making a phone call (to those parents who had one) or writing a note to the parents.

The worst thing that could happen was having Sister tell a disruptive or failing student in front of the whole class that, since there was nothing else they could do with you, they would have one of the priests talk to you. Now I do not know about your Catholic school days, but during my time at Saint Colman's, a threat like this would put the fear of death in most Catholic schoolchildren.

A wrong arithmetic calculation, misspelled word, or answer to a question could be disastrous for the individual. A lot of children trembled and shook, especially those who had not studied, as they got up very slowly and approached the blackboard. Especially if they were unsure if they would know the answer to what Sister might ask.

If you wrote the wrong answer on the board, Sister would quickly scold you, grab an eraser to scrub it off, and methodically explain what must be done to provide the right answer. If you still could not do it correctly, no matter how much Sister explained the subject, you could be scolded even more and sent back to your desk or to the cloakroom to think about what it was you were doing wrong!

There would be no talking back to Sister or challenging her in any way during this one-on-one exchange, since a mild paddling in the upper grades could also be administered by the Sisters. The failure of a child not learning was particularly hard on the Sisters, in that they considered themselves failures also if you were not learning what they were teaching.

Next would come the testing of our spelling, which was done by separating the class into teams on opposite sides of the classroom. Sometimes it would be the boys against the girls. Sister would call out a word to one side, and a child would spell it out. If he or she spelled it correctly, he or she stayed in the spelling test.

Then Sister would direct her next word to be spelled out to the other side of the classroom. Anyone misspelling a word was sent back to his or her desk. As for me, I liked sitting more than standing, and after a while I would deliberately misspell the word. The last person standing was declared the spelling king or queen.

Some of my closest school friends, such as Jean, Audrey, and Lois, were often designated the spelling queen, and Carmen, Marty, or Paul declared the spelling king.

Catechism lessons would soon follow, and Sister did not fool around and was very harsh with anyone providing wrong answers to her questions.

Extra homework would be handed out for sure, along with not being allowed to participate in recess school yard activities. No one really cared if it was raining or during the dead of winter and too cold to play outside, but we hated to have this punishment happen on a warm and beautiful day.

Recess lasted about twenty minutes, and generally, in addition to play, it produced nothing but a lot of yelling and screaming from us children. After recess, we were assembled and marched back into school and our classroom by an arm-waving and silver colored whistle-blowing Sister.

More papers would be handed out to do more arithmetic, spelling, and reading tests. When it was time for lunch, some of us children living close by the school would go home to eat. Many other children, who carried their lunch to school, went to the small school auditorium, located on the school's first floor, to eat it.

There was no cafeteria in Saint Colman's for serving hot or even cold food of any kind. No beverages could be obtained except for small bottles of milk. Depending on your family's financial situation, children either paid for or received the milk free. I, along with my brother and sisters, always went home for lunch, which for years consisted of nothing but Isaly's chocolate milk and maple rolls. We loved it.

The maple rolls came in the form of a slab of twelve from O'Neill's bakery, and you broke off what amount you could eat. On occasion, especially during those harsh and bitter cold Pennsylvania winter days, when my brother and sisters and I did take our lunch to school, we were provided with free milk.

After eating lunch and returning to the classroom, the saying of a rosary was always the first thing that had to be done. I, along with many other kids, hated saying a rosary and could not wait for it to end. We had to get down on both of our knees, on the hard wooden floor, to say it! Oh, what agony must one go through, especially small children, to prove their love for God? Many of us kneeling children, after a while and with grimacing facial features, would look like we were spastic, not in control of our nervous system.

With the palms and fingers of both of our hands pressed firmly together and arched straight up, we would twist and turn sideways, with locked elbows digging into our rib cages. Some of us would rock backward and forward to ease the pressure on our kneecaps, back, and spine. At the same time and when Sister was not looking, some of us would lift up our kneecaps from the floor to ease the pain.

One not acquainted with the Catholic religion would be surprised at how fast a bunch of Catholic schoolchildren can hurry up and say a complete rosary in record time to get up off their knees! We children always hoped that none of the priests would make a surprise classroom guest appearance.

They often did this, asked questions, and then led us in a few more prayers while still on our painful knees. I hated it when a priest would open the classroom door unexpectedly, enter the classroom, look at Sister, and say, "Don't let me disturb you."

At that very moment, in my mind I would call him "a dirty rat." I was always hopeful the priest would immediately say, "You can get up off your knees now, children." After awhile of continued agony he would let us get up.

After our afternoon prayer session, it was back to the basic academics of reading, writing, spelling, and blackboard guest appearances by random individuals in the classroom.

All during this time, there would be a lot of us children staring into space or looking out the big windows, anxious for the final school bell of the day to ring. We all wanted to be outside for the start of a long weekend, even if the weather was going to be bad. None of the children had a watch, and there was no clock in any of the classrooms. If there were, at this early age, most of us did not know how to tell time yet. You knew school was over for the day only when Sister said it was, regardless if the dismissal bell rang.

As the afternoon was wearing down and you could feel it was time for the school bell to ring and end the day, Sister would announce that we were to write down certain problems or some other assignment from our schoolbooks to work on as homework.

The children of grades one through eight sat straight up in their wooden desk seats, with arms resting on their small rectangular scarred wood desktops, waiting anxiously for the dismissal bell. The desk scarring was the result of children scratching the surface, and in some cases even adding an initial, with a sharp instrument or pen point. The desks were yellowed in color, by years of sun rays eating into their thick coats of varnish. Years of hardened bubble gum sneakily placed by some child, to avoid being caught with it by Sister, clung to the underside of every desk and seat in the classroom.

Even at such a young age, the children of Saint Colman's, like most children in every other school, during a summer day eagerly waited on this welcome sound of the bell. In each classroom on all three floors of the school, the children would breathe out a silent soft sigh of joy and relief when it finally rang out loud.

At the command and direction of their individual Sister, each child would quietly and slowly lift up their hinged desktop with one hand. With the other hand, they placed their books, pencils, writing paper, paper clips, rubber bands, white paste, and any other personal paraphernalia into the hollow desk cavity.

Then they would slowly lower the heavy hinged rectangular top back into place without making any noise. The glass-bottled black ink container, sunk into a small circular hole located on the top right-hand corner of the desk and away from the hinged desktop, would remain in place.

The only time the glass ink bottle was removed was to fill it back up or to clean it. There were times when the glass bottle, while being handled by a child, would accidentally fall to the floor. When this happened if it broke or the ink was spilled out, it would leave black ink shapes staring back at you. These images that only a child's mind could imagine, such as a spider, elephant, or perhaps even God or the devil, would begin to form from the running ink and appear on the varnished and oak-slatted wooden floor.

Most Sisters accepted this could happen, and a word of caution in handling the ink bottle was passed down with no discipline ever imposed. There was never any damage done to the wooden classroom floors. This was due to the heavy coats of varnish that had been applied to them every year; after a while, they matched the color of the desks.

Thinking about these images that would appear from the spilled ink is how I believe someone developed those ink cards that a psychiatrist may use in conducting the Rorschach Psychodiagnostic Test.

This test is done when they quickly flash a card in front of an individual and ask them what image they see while looking at the card. The individual interpretation of the pictorial forms perceived could be classified into those of a normal person and those suffering from hysteria, schizophrenia, and other mental disorders.

My writing about the fallen ink bottle took me back to a time and place I had not thought about for years. It was then that I recalled some of the images I had imagined while looking at the spilled ink on a classroom floor.

After suffering severe head, shoulder, and facial injuries during a "live fire" exercise while in the army, I was hospitalized for several months. During that time, I was given some electrical brain tests that measured wave patterns, in response to a question. After these tests, I was put through the Rorschach or a similar test and responded to what I saw in each card being shown to me.

Subconsciously all I could see—what the cards reminded me of—was a Sister of Mercy nun. All of the images on the cards were black with a white background, like the black clothing and white starched habit of the Sisters. I often thought of the Sisters' attire as that of a penguin.

Boys in the higher fourth through eighth grades, such as Ron (or "Lash," as he was called), I, and other close school friends Jimmy and Eddy, would sometimes let our desktops drop down very hard! This was done deliberately, so as to make a very loud and cracking noise.

The sound and mischievous act was a foolish thing to do on such a beautiful day. It created sporadic echoes throughout the classroom and caused some of the girls to scream out loud with fright!

The girls were never as mischievous as the boys, and none of them would ever give any thought to letting their desktop slip out of their hands and make a loud noise. This act could upset Sister very badly and result in the whole class being held back and not being dismissed on time.

The guilty parties, if noticed and caught in the act of doing this, would be punished. They could even be brought to the front of the classroom and beat on the buttocks with the hidden wooden paddle Sister removed from under her desk.

At times, Sister might pick up her wooden ruler and smack the guilty parties quite hard with it on their arms and hands, perhaps even catching a few knuckles in between. If Sister had an eraser in her hand, she might throw it at the closest guilty party. Sisters Gruff and Ruff were quite good at doing this and rarely missed what or who they were aiming at. Blackboards were especially vulnerable to having erasers thrown at them, since it would leave a very white chalky imprint on them. One could even call it a visible imprint alerting Sister as to someone being mischievous in the classroom.

The same ruler being used to inflict punishment and pain was also very instrumental in helping the children while learning and practicing their Palmer cursive penmanship. An incorrect position of the palm and wrist lying on the writing paper and desktop, or sloppiness in your practice letters, could bring a smack of the ruler from Sister on someone's knuckles.

It took a long time and several light taps with a ruler on the left-handed children to make them write right-handed. However, the kindly Sisters Hildergard and Mary David during first and second grade realized they were not going to be able to change me or my brother, Richard, from writing left-handed.

As we progressed up to the higher grades, the taps from the ruler became a little harder. Perhaps it was because we were a little bigger and could withstand more pain. By the fifth grade, there was never any more attempts made to have us write using only our right hand. Reading the book called "The Thorn birds" brought back memories of this and incident whereby, a small girl had her left arm tied behind her back, by Sister to stop her from writing with her left hand!

My mother initially started out being a left-handed writer, but during her school days at Saint Colman's, and with the help of a stinging ruler, she was converted to writing right-handed. She became ambidextrous. In later years as a Saint Colman's and high school graduate, she was one of the first outside temporary lay teachers to teach the Palmer cursive penmanship class, and she did it using her right hand. People would comment up until the day she passed away as to how beautiful her writing was.

Needless to say, the guilty boys dropping their desktops would draw the ire of and dart-like stares from the rest of the class, especially the girls, for their antics and bad behavior. On some days, when it was raining or snowing or very cold outside, it might have been all right for them to do it, and everyone would get a good chuckle out of it. However, it was not appreciated on this particular sunny and warm day.

The guilty boys would not be spoken to for several days afterward, and it was highly unlikely they would be asked to join in any after-school games. Even if Sister were to finally dismiss all of them! It was also highly unlikely, that the boys causing the disturbance would do any studying over the weekend. Come Monday morning, they should not be surprised when the girls who were temporarily held back refused to help them with the work assignments or show them the answers to the homework.

While all the children were being held back before being dismissed, one of the boys in the classroom would be directed by Sister to close the windows. These were three large, arched, oak-framed, small-paned French glass windows that tilted into the classroom and offered some relief from the heat and humidity. On several occasions, the windows had been accidentally left open, and severe thunderstorms carried the rain through the open windows and into the classroom.

The floors became very wet, along with those desks closest to the windows. As a result, both the desks and floor had to be dried out and sanded and a new coat of varnish applied. It did not take long for the refinished floor and desks to blend in with the yellowish and peeling aged varnish color of the other desks and the rest of the flooring. Due to all the mopping and maintenance required after this invading rain, Mister Clark, the resident janitor, would complain severely to Father Shields.

Father would not be bashful about approaching and chastising the Sister who failed to see that the windows were not closed securely. When something like this happened, we children knew there would be extra spelling, reading, writing, and arithmetic homework assignments and Sister would not be in a very good mood for quite a while.

Most of the boys, including myself and Ron, would recognize this and make every attempt to behave in class. We would not cause any problems during recess and would volunteer to help Sister empty the waste cans and clean the erasers and blackboards. On this Friday afternoon, Carmen, a close friend and neighbor and one of our altar boys of Italian descent, opened and closed his desktop properly and was selected to close the windows.

It was considered a great honor and privilege to be selected to perform this task of opening and closing the windows, and all the boys jumped at the chance when asked to do it. The physical aspects of doing this chore and balancing the long pole became complicated at times.

But it provided an opportunity to get on the good side of a few Sisters, who at times could become very angry and upset with the children. Being chosen to close the windows also broke the monotony of studying, taking tests, and staying at your desk all day. The catechism lessons, saying our morning prayers, and the afternoon knee-bruising rosaries became a bit much at times.

In short, it gave you a chance to break away from the strict daily academic and religious regimentation, and do something different. To my recollection, the girls were never asked to close the windows. I believe it was because chivalry was still alive during days gone by, and ladies were not expected to perform such a chore.

As far as I was concerned, there were a lot of the girls who would have been able to open and close the windows as well as any one of us boys. After all, if they could participate in a pump, pump, pull away game, play dodgeball, and play mumbly peg with a knife, why not hoist up a long pole and close a few windows? Mary Ellen, who was quite pretty and athletic, could run as fast as most of the boys, and she could also throw a pretty good punch into a boy's arm.

She was quite capable of handling and hoisting that pole up if she had been selected to close the windows. I had a crush on Mary Ellen, which never developed into anything serious, Oftentimes I wish it had and by chance have her father, owner of Tommy's local bar and grill restaurant, invite me in for one of the best hamburgers and cheeseburgers in town.

Carmen jumped up quickly from his desk when asked to close the windows. He went directly to the dark cloakroom and turned on the overhead lights. Inside, he would retrieve the long, varnished oak pole, with its brass blunt hook used to open and close the windows. On bright sunny days, after the brass hook had been polished to a gleaming finish, as it was being raised up, its shape seemingly took on that of a horse. This horse shape would reflect itself onto the classroom walls and blackboards, and bounce into the eyes of some of the children.

Using both hands to steady, balance, and hold the long heavy pole waving about in the air, Carmen walked up slowly toward the windows. He carefully raised the pole higher into the air as it came in contact with a window and brought its hook down to meet with a window's brass ring. He made contact and skillfully inserted the hook into the round brass ring on the top of the first window.

He continued on that day maneuvering the pole skillfully until all six of the upper and lower windows were pushed closed and locked tightly. After class was dismissed, would Sister make a check to see that they were? Once the windows were closed and at the direction of Sister, the children, except for the boys caught dropping their desktops, got up quietly.

In an orderly manner and by their respective desk rows, they walked to the rear of the classroom in pairs of two and started a long double-column line. Those children who had lunch boxes in the cloakroom would go in and retrieve them for use on Monday morning and get back in line quickly.

While the children were lined up and waiting on the classroom door to be opened, Sister was passing out instructions. The children were to do the fractions on page twelve and the multiplication tables on page eight of their arithmetic books for their homework assignment.

Sister then proceeded to hand out duplicated copies of the pages to the children, even the disorderly boys still sitting at their desks and looking very glum. Textbooks at Saint Colman's were limited, always in short supply, and rarely allowed to be taken home for use without special permission and a signature. Assignments for all subjects were always duplicated on paper.

The color of the paper was whatever was available. White, pink, blue, green—it did not matter! The freshly made copies would leave blotches of purple ink etched into some of the kids' hands as they took them. Some of the boys would try to dab it onto another child's arm or face while Sister was not looking. If one did not get any ink on their hand, they'd better check the paper, since no ink could mean the machine was running dry and some of the homework would not be visible.

Going back to class the next day and telling Sister you did not complete your homework assignment because some of the work was not there, was comparable to telling a nun of today that it had been done but the dog ate it! If you were smart, you would do what work was visible, and this would buy you some time with Sister to complete the rest of the assignment.

Even with all this knowledge and knowing what Sister's reaction would be there would always be some of us children who did not do our homework and would suffer the consequences.

This assignment caused a lot of low mumbling and groaning, which could be heard coming out of the children's mouths as they extended their arms and hands to take the homework papers. The boys as always, including me, would do some pushing, punching in the arms and backs, and shoving one another while standing in line. A quick chop or punch to the thigh was a favorite, since the boys loved it when they could make another boy ache from a swelling thigh, or "charley horse" as it was called.

On occasion, when the boys were really hyperactive, they would begin slapping the back of someone's head or neck. Some would even begin to pull the hair on the back of the girls' heads. In particular, they enjoyed pulling on Lillian's long blonde pigtail, woven into place by her Polish mother, which fell into the small of her back.

You did not want to do this too long, since Lillian would begin throwing punches back at the boys. I liked Lillian very much, not just because she was Polish like me and her last name also ended in "ski," but because she was always very nice and studious and would help me with my assignments from time to time. Some of the other girls—like Lois, who was one of the smartest girls in class, and Jean, always the most polite—would not put up with such antics.

They would start kicking the boys in the shins and swing their arms and hands about in a flurried frenzy. They were always hoping to land a punch on the disorderly boy's face. I believe they picked up their feistiness and punching techniques by studying the boys and their fighting techniques during school-yard recess throughout the years. Observing how some Sisters physically disciplined the boys with their hands from time to time was also a technique that the girls would often copy.

Finally, after the children settled down and became orderly again, the rear door of the classrooms would be opened by each responsible Sister, or some child she may have designated. The children were then directed to march out and assemble in the outside upper and lower hallways of Saint Colman's three-story building.

While standing in the hallway, each class would be reminded by their Sister to go to confession early, say evening prayers, and receive communion on Sunday. After this, each class was marched out of the school hallways in military fashion. The eight grade class on the third floor had to march down seven steps from the third-floor stairway. The steps quickly turned into a wide right angle before coming to and marching down another seven steps on the second-floor stairway, which also turned into a wide right angle. Finally, this would lead the children down to the last three steps and two large oak outside doors. These doors were the last obstacle they would have to endure before being released into the concrete school yard.

Since this was a Friday, most, if not all, of the children would be eating fish, salmon cakes, macaroni and cheese, grilled cheese sandwiches, or bowls of tomato or potato soup for supper. Of course, all of these meals would be served with a big plateful of Mom's homemade and crispy french fries. A bottle of Heinz ketchup would be placed on their kitchen table to accompany every one of these meals.

As they were released and the outside warm summer air hit their faces, screams of joy and youthful exuberance escaped from the mouths of each child. They were finally in the school yard and on their own to do as they pleased. The inside of the school became empty and quiet of children.

That is, except for a few stragglers or the boys or girls who were held back by the Sisters for various reasons. Everyone who was in the classroom that day and now playing in the school yard knew or had their suspicions as to why the boys were being held back. After emptying the waste cans and cleaning erasers by banging them together, the boys being disciplined watched the white chalk dust fill the air.

On this day, the thick cloud of chalk dust resembled that of the puff of white smoke coming from Saint Peter's in Rome to signify selection of a new pope. It became a cloud of white smoke for a while, and then disappeared as it fell to the ground outside. After wiping off the blackboards, the boys held back by Sister for being mischievous were released.

This, of course, was done only after each one told Sister they were sorry and promised they would behave. Of course, the typical reply from Sister would be "Swear to God," with the boys all answering as one, "We swear to God." On this day, the boys were very lucky since Sister could have made them wash down the long, light gray colored granite wall outside the front of the school and facing the back of the local Atlantic and Pacific Store (A&P).

The early release of the boys, including myself, was because it was Sister's day to give her twenty-five-cents-an-hour private piano lessons in the convent, and she did not want to be late. Sisters were allowed to keep any money they earned from private tutoring or lessons of any kind. Sometimes there was no monetary consideration, and the Sisters did other things in keeping with being charitable and helping thy neighbor.

In 1907 early during its start, Saint Colman's School advertised and provided typing, stenography, and bookkeeping at "no charge." The advertisement also read "The Genuine Free School."

With the smell of fresh air swiftly rushing into their nostrils and mouths, it did not take the newly discharged, energetic children very long, if they had no after-school play planned, to disappear from the school yard and find their way home or other planned destinations.

Heading to a place other than the school yard on a Friday afternoon and looking forward to the weekend, except for their homework assignments and making confession, was all the children had on their minds. Report cards were not due to be passed out for several more weeks, but the children still worried about them and their grades. They all knew the report card had to be taken to and signed by a parent. Report cards being returned without a signature of a parent were not accepted.

There were some kids who would attempt to forge their parents' signature, but that brought further punishment, both at home and school, when they were caught! I never did this, since I knew what the sting of my father's razor strap or the cat-o'-nine-tails felt like, from doing other mischievous deeds. A lot of the children would walk up a flight of five concrete steps outside the school yard leading up into the school lunchroom (which doubled as the auditorium). This is where they would retrieve their stored bicycles and ride them home or in the school yard for a while.

Getting a heavy bike up or down these steep steps was a big task. Generally, the boys, including some of the more rowdy ones, would offer to carry the girls' bikes up and down the steps for them, when they saw them struggling to do it.

When the priests were around this area, many of the boys would eagerly volunteer to help the girls with their bikes. It was not a bad idea to get on the good side of the priests, since they could help you out at times when you were in trouble with a Sister! The school allowed the few bikes that were around, since most parents could not afford to buy them for their children. The bikes could be brought in and stored during the day, but it was forbidden to ride them in the school yard during school hours and recess periods.

Many of the children had great distances to walk to their homes, since school busing for both Catholic and public school children was not available during days gone by. Unless your parents or someone else that could be trusted picked you up in a car, or you were given a few nickels to ride the public bus, you walked to and from school every day. This walking, which was a form of good exercise and activity, was required even during those harsh winter months and deep snowfalls Pennsylvania is well known for.

Today's intelligent lawyers might someday give consideration to filing a lawsuit against the federal and local governments citing lack of exercise and school busing as the cause of overweight children, not their eating hamburgers and french fries at McDonald's or Burger King and perhaps Taco Bell burritos and the Kentucky Colonel's deep-fried chicken.

Audrey, who lived close by the school on Lynn Avenue, did not have to worry about transportation and keeping up her grades. She always studied hard and received nothing but straight As. She was one of the first students released from Saint Colman's on this bright, sunny, hot, humid day. She was very jubilant about being dismissed and looking forward to her long weekend and playing with one of her best public school girlfriends named Moneane.

She had no concern about her homework assignment and would do it on Sunday evening, after finishing her dinner and helping her mother clean up the kitchen. She was now going to hurry over to the church and go to confession before heading home.

I believe I may have hopped up onto the railroad tracks this particular day and walked all the way to the copper mill without falling off. After this, I wandered off into the woods, following the stream of the nearby creek as far as I could before coming to a pond of deep water. Later on, I would catch up with my brother, Richard, and look for empty pop bottles to cash in and metal pieces to take to the junkyard.

I have memories of being taught the basics of reading, writing, spelling, and arithmetic, and at times being disciplined and punished by some of the Sisters.

Learning was especially difficult for me during the first year of school at Saint Colman's, and as a result I was made to repeat the class. Richard, my one and only older brother, also had to repeat his first year of school at Saint Colman's. I also have fond memories of my religious instruction and the catechism lessons taught by the Sisters, which I still use today when I attend Catholic Church services.

Looking back, I attempted to analyze what could have caused holding back both of us. I would like to use the excuse that we were both very sick or slow learners, as some parents would say. This was done to save their child the embarrassment of being called stupid or a dummy when having to repeat.

However, the truth was that from a socioeconomic standpoint, we just did not possess the elementary learning skills early enough that were necessary to comprehend the simplest reading, writing, and arithmetic assignments. In addition, the Catholic schools in the diocese of Pittsburgh had principles and strict educational rules they followed and enforced. If it was thought that some children were not ready to advance, they were held back.

To this day, I do not believe my parents, due to their financial situation, could have or ever paid any tuition for me, my brother, and my two sisters attending Saint Colman's. Jokingly I say today that my brother and I being held back was retribution by the church for not being paid! I must also say that most of the parents of the children going to Saint Colman's during days gone by never paid any tuition either.

Catholic teaching at this time held and dictated that Catholic parents who did not send their children to Catholic school were living in mortal sin and should not receive communion. One could interpret this as the church saying during days gone by, "If you are poor, don't worry about paying for school, and give what you can." Today this philosophy does not exist, and those Catholic schools that cannot stay open due to financial difficulties are closed quickly.

Educational books necessary to help children get started to read or do the simplest arithmetic problems early on were nonexistent in my home at an early age. Also, as I pointed out, schoolbooks at Saint Colman's were limited and not allowed to be brought home except by special permission. My parents did very little reading that I can recall, and they did not have positions requiring higher mathematical skills than simple adding and subtracting, so we did not benefit from their work experience, in my opinion.

I loved my parents dearly. I now understand their socioeconomic situation much more, and what I write is not done in a disparaging, demeaning manner, or to bring any disdain or shame upon them!

In addition, my father had a limited education and was not able to help very much with our homework assignments. Perhaps it was because my parents, like a lot of other families in Turtle Creek, simply could not afford to buy books during and after a great depression and post-World War II. A lot of parents did not receive a high school or higher education, since they were forced to quit school at a very early age and go to work.

They did this to help their parents out with the basic necessities of life, such as food, shelter, and clothing. However, even with all of these life-cycle situations, they helped one another in time of need and learned how to survive through these rough and desperate times!

I can still vividly remember a day of school at Saint Colman's, and all I can remember is the good times I had there, the wonderful Sisters and priests, and none of the bad times. As the saying goes, you're only young once! At Saint Colman's, I lived it to the fullest, by being daring and challenging.

As I look back, I now know and truly believe that most of the punishment I received, along with many of the other boys, from the Sisters was done with just cause. I plead guilty!

CHAPTER 2

GOING TO CONFESSION

As soon as I was released from my fifth-grade class in 1946, to be at confession early, I ran through the school playground area past the wooden two-story rectory and parish house. This was where Father John Shields, who joined Saint Colman's parish in 1907 as assistant pastor, and his staff of two Irish priests, Father Reilly and Father Thomas, resided. While running, I continuously turned my head from left to right and occasionally glanced behind me, to keep ahead and to see if any other kids might be following.

The faster kids could get into the church and a confessional booth, the earlier they got out to play. The only visible sign of any dirt or grass within the school's playground perimeter that I could see was a small blocked-off area next to the parish house. What little grass had been planted in this area years ago had all but disappeared, due to years of constant trampling from the girls' shoes and the boys' heavy boot-like shoes, or clodhoppers as they were referred to. The large chestnut tree roots that surfaced over the years also helped kill off the grass. I gazed over at the parish house and adjacent garage, where the priests parked their cars.

There were times when several of us boys would volunteer and help wash the cars to get on the good side of them. During recess periods, we boys would sometimes throw and watch our rubber balls inadvertently bounce off of the car doors. Of course, this was only done when the priests and nuns were not in the school-yard area, since they became very upset when it happened. However, sometimes they would appear without our seeing them. Those of us caught doing this were often punished on the spot, and after recess it could mean a trip to the cloakroom and further discipline. On occasion, the priests would even threaten to take a boy or two down into the cellar below the church and put the boxing gloves on!

The tree roots always reminded me of humped-up whale backs. The way they twisted in different directions also made them look like coiled snakes lying in wait to strike and bite someone on their ankles or legs. Every now and then, I saw Mr. Clark, our school janitor, chopping away at these roots with a large axe to prevent them from spreading, pushing upward, and breaking up more sections of the concrete school yard.

As I continued running, I began thinking about what sins I had committed and would confess to the priest. I watched as the bare dirt below me came in contact with the soles and heels of my clodhoppers. My thoughts drifted elsewhere, and my thinking about confession and what sins I might confess disappeared for a brief period. This trampled bare area was also where we boys, and sometimes the girls, would kneel or stand up to shoot and play with our multicolored large and small marbles.

It was quite enjoyable during recess, or after school, to watch experts like Marty and Eddy play the game. They were great! It was amazing to watch how they placed a marble on their thumbnail while standing upright. Then, with a quick flick outward and from a good distance, they would knock out one or several of the marbles lying inside a large circle etched in the dirt. The boys or girls who had their marbles knocked out did not think it was so great, since the marbles would be confiscated by Marty or Eddy.

That was until the next game was played, and everyone got a chance to win back some of their earlier losses. Marty, Jimmy, Eddy, and I would sometimes kneel down on both knees, lay our heads on the ground sideways, and "eye up" the best way to shoot our master marble and knock other players' marbles out of the ring. This technique could be compared to what some golfers of today might do, eyeing up the putting green in hopes of placing their golf ball in the cup.

It took great skill to place your hand firmly on the dirt-encrusted ground, which could be muddy after a good rainfall. The players had to line their master marble up in front of their thumb or other finger they were going to do their marble-shooting with. Once you were all set, you would then, with a hard flick of the thumb or any other of your remaining four fingers, begin to knock the other players' marbles out of the inner circle to the outer circle. Each player got to keep all of the other players' marbles that he could knock out of the inner circle.

If someone missed knocking out a marble, you could not shoot anymore, and your marbles stayed in the ring. The next succeeding players would begin their process of standing up, kneeling down on one or both knees or perhaps laying their head sideways on the ground, and doing their specialized line of sight technique before doing any marble-flicking. We boys often got into fistfights and wrestling matches to decide whose marbles were in or out of the round circle, boldly etched into the dirt by someone's finger or pocketknife, or a pointy stick.

At times many of us would run to the school lavatory as soon as the game was over or just before the ending recess bell was about to ring. This was done to wash off the dirt embedded in our hands and on the sides of our faces and ears. This was especially necessary after a good rainfall had soaked the ground thoroughly. The mud on some kids' clothing was insignificant since Mom would wash it out later on. Perhaps it would not be washed out for a couple of days, since a daily change of clothing was not an option for a lot of the children.

At the end of the game, everyone, including whoever won the most marbles, stuffed them into a small canvas bag, with a drawstring attached to close it tight and secure its contents. It was hard to imagine that some of the boys in this rowdy group, like Carmen and Paul, were also altar boys and assisted the priest during his saying of Mass.

We boys also played a game called mumbly peg, which allowed us to show off our skills by throwing a small pocketknife from various positions and making the pointed end of its blade stick in the ground. The throwing would start by resting a thumb or finger on the top of one's head and placing the pointed knife end on it to avoid pricking one's skull.

Once a boy was ready to begin his session, he would flip the knife over with his free hand and try to make the blade end stick upright in the dirt. If the knife blade stuck and no portion of the handle was touching the ground, you were allowed to continue on with the throwing. A one-finger rule was always used to determine if the throw was good or not. The rule was simple enough, and it said if you could not place a finger under the handle of the knife sticking in the dirt, you could not throw again.

The next boy in the game was then allowed to start his session. If you succeeded with your first throw, you were then allowed to throw it from your forehead, eyelids, nose, lips, and chin, and continue on downward from every other body joint. This process continued until you reached the top of your shoe or foot and could stick the knife blade in the dirt from this point. The first person to accomplish every throwing feat was declared the winner. Sometimes the game was not completed due to the short recess period, but it continued with each recess until eventually a winner was declared.

The winner would be the boy who proceeded to the most downward part of a body joint. We boys preferred to play this game away from school with an ice pick, since it offered better balance, stuck better in the dirt, and was much easier to handle and throw. Ice picks were forbidden to be carried or placed anywhere on school grounds. Small-time betting, such as a couple of choice marbles, baseball card, candy bar, piece of bubble gum, or some other small item of candy could be wagered on the game.

My brother, Richard, and his friend Willy were really good with the ice pick. If the dirt was soft enough, at times they could go through each maneuver without missing a "stick in the dirt" and win. Sometimes the priests would come out of the parish house and close by the trampled area where we boys played this game. It was the only plot of dirt around the school yard. They would attempt to amuse us and try playing the game and matching our skill levels. However, their lack of practice and inexperience was obvious, and they seldom were able to stick the pocketknife blade in the dirt.

This game could cause a lot of quarrelling, and some of us boys would wrestle with one another, verbally calling one another names or fist-fighting. There were several times when Father Reilly, another priest, or the Sisters would have to intercede and physically separate us from one another as they walked around policing the school-yard grounds.

It could be quite awhile before the game would be continued or another one started, since the knife being used would often be confiscated temporarily by Father or Sister as a form of punishment. Using the boys' knives, along with some instructions on how to throw them, girls like Kathleen and Joanne would attempt to play the game and got quite good at it. However, they never became quite good enough to beat any of us boys.

The knives were carried to school by a lot of the boys in their pants pockets or in a special knife sheath located on a pair of high-top boots. Not one of us boys or any student was ever injured by one of the knives during the game or at any other time.

A lot of these knives were confiscated by the Sisters and never returned, if a boy were caught defacing school property or trees, or playing with them while in class or the lunchroom.

Under the zero tolerance policy of most schools today, carrying a knife into any school area would be cause for immediate expulsion or possible prosecution by local law enforcement. Showing or pointing a knife at someone could also result in potential prosecution.

Times have really changed, and the pointing of a finger at someone and pretending it is a gun in a classroom today can result in the individual being suspended from school. Stretching it a bit, it is possible, under existing laws that they could even be charged with being a "terrorist."

The girls' games I can recall were dodgeball, jump rope, jacks, the whip, red rover, red rover, in and out the window, roller skates, monopoly, hide-and-seek, hopscotch, and catch. Other big favorites of both the boys and girls were buckety buck and pump, pump, pull away.

The presence of the Sisters and priests around the school yard was necessary to help curtail some of the boys from teasing the girls. At times they could be heard screaming out and telling some of the girls they were going to hell or "God doesn't love you anymore." Other unkind things that could be heard were about being too tall, too short, ugly, fat, skinny, dumb, and stupid.

A lot of teasing being done seemed to be about the girls' hair and clothing, and this really got a lot of them riled up and ready to start throwing punches at the boys. Of course, if they did strike a boy, they would have to tell about it during their confession, since anger is considered a sin.

Hopefully they would not divulge nor would the priest ask what the boys' names were that caused such anger. Many of the girls would turn away crying and run to the Sisters or a priest for comfort. You did not want to be one of the boys who were caught doing this dastardly teasing, since it could result in your being disciplined, immediately, by Sister's hand. It could also bring about a physical paddling or restriction of your free activity. Worst of all, it could bring about being sentenced to do time in the dark dungeon-like cloakroom.

The lesser form of punishment and most often used would be to keep you after school to empty the waste cans and clean the erasers and blackboards. Perhaps we boys were too young, but I often wonder why the Sisters and priests never used tactics such as are employed in the military and make us clean the bathrooms and latrines.

In the years to come, many of these same boys and girls who argued and teased one another would become high school and college sweethearts. They would eventually marry, and their children and grandchildren would go on to Saint Colman's and be faced with the same growing-up experiences, social interactions, and molding of their character. Eight or nine generations of boys and girls have passed through this small school and teased one another with little or no effect on them. Today these kids' life lessons, as I once and still view it, still go on to some extent but can now be called harassment.

They are not allowed to go on for very long without legal action being pursued quickly. Rather than the parents, priests, Sisters, lay teachers, and children getting together to put a stop to it, lawyers and law enforcement officials are now called in to resolve an issue that was considered insignificant years before.

Looking back upon my days of youthful exuberance while on recess at Saint Colman's, I now know why some of the boys had to be disciplined harshly. This was done after we were lined up in a military-like file by screaming Sisters running about like penguins and blowing on small silver Boy-Scout-like whistles that hung around their necks. Suddenly my thoughts quickly shifted back to thinking about what I would be telling the priest during my confession.

I also wondered how long it might take before I would be done, do my penance, and get out of the church to enjoy my weekend. I finally stopped my daydreaming and ran even faster to get to confession. I turned sharply to my left to get to the front of the church, which was now only a few feet away.

I wanted to be the first one in line in the dreary darkness of the church sanctuary to have my confession heard. Sometimes this was very hard to do, since other children planning on receiving communion during Sunday's Mass would all head to the church on Fridays at the same time to say their confession, like me.

This often resulted in a line being formed outside the four confessional booths (two each alongside the Chapels of the Sacred Heart and St. Anthony), and people kneeling in the pew next to them, waiting to have their confessions heard also. Depending on the extent of each person's confession, you could be there a long time, which I hated. There were occasions when the line was just too long, and I decided to skip confession if no Sisters were around watching for the likes of me! I wanted to get home and play with my brother and friends as soon as possible. When I got home and my mom asked if I had been to church and confession, I would sometimes tell a white lie and say yes.

As I approached the church's three separate outside entrances, each with three heavy and large double-set oak doors, I slowed down and came to a complete halt. I looked up at the church in awe, as I had done on many other occasions before entering it. I could never stop remarking what a massive, dominant, and beautiful structure it was.

Standing in front of the church, I bent forward and took in several deep breaths of air to help my palpitating heart settle down. As I straightened up my body, I looked up into the unclouded blue sky hovering over the mighty church structure. What I saw as I lay my head back and stretched my neck as far as it would go were two tall majestic-looking towers. One tower on top of the church rose to a height of 159 feet, and the other to ninety-eight feet.

Twelve crosses covered with genuine gold leaf had been erected on the towers and other pinnacles rising above the church. A peal of three bells that announced death, funeral, time for Mass, marriages, and other important matters hung in the towers. Weighing 3150, 2280, and 1790 pounds respectively, the bells could be heard ringing in many communities for miles around.

I lowered my head and walked up to the two large heavy outside doors in the center of the church. Luck was with me, as I followed closely behind a large man ahead of me who was opening the heavy doors with ease. When I entered, I dipped my right index finger into the holy water of a nearby marble fountain, made the sign of the cross, and quickly followed behind the same gentleman.

This time he was opening another set of heavy swinging double doors, each holding a large piece of leaded glass that led into the main sanctuary. I looked around, and to my amazement there was not a single person standing in line at the confessional booth I had my eyes on. Nor were there any people sitting or kneeling in the pew next to it.

Luck or my guardian angel continued to be on my side this day. The three other booths located in the church had a few people waiting in line to make their confession.

I walked up quickly to the church pew adjacent to the confessional booth with no waiting line of people. I slid into it, placed the knee rail down on the floor, knelt down, and made the sign of the cross before saying a few prayers. The sulfuric stench coming from all the burning and smoldering wax candles in the sanctuary always made me feel nauseated as it filtered up through my nose.

I could hear in the hushed silence of the main sanctuary the sound of coins being placed in the wide mouthed metal slots by people paying to light the candles and pray for the dead, sick, or living. I could also hear the final journey of each coin as it slid down a spiral metal tube to the bottom of the metal collection box area, ending with a loud clinking sound that echoed throughout the church. I can only describe it as like the sound of coins being placed into a slot machine at a Las Vegas casino.

Although there was no visible outside line, both confessional booths of the one I had chosen were occupied, and I knew that I would have to wait my turn to make my confession.

While waiting and kneeling, I stopped praying and let my eyes wander around inside the large church sanctuary to occupy my time. I looked up at the six massive Romanesque columns that helped support the arched ceilings inside the church structure. Glancing upward at the top of each column and adorning different parts of the ceiling, I could see the life-size portraits of the twelve apostles in oil on canvas.

The large oak pulpit in the very front of the church rose above the pews near the altar of the Blessed Virgin. This pulpit provided Father Shields, Father Thomas, and Father Reilly a commanding position to overlook and deliver the Gospel and their weekly sermons to the congregation. It also gave them the opportunity to look around and observe whom they saw and did not see at Mass.

This was very easy to do, since many schoolchildren and families would arrive early before Mass and seat themselves in select pews they had occupied for many years. When the church was full except for a few open seats scattered about, the occupants in the select pews would feel a sense of invasion when an usher would bring individuals forward to seat them in "their pew."

Many of these individuals took up territorial seating positions and were reluctant to slide over when someone was brought to the pew for seating by an usher. Often the individual or group of people being seated would have to climb over several people so they could get to the open space and sit down.

One of my good friends from Saint Colman's and a high school classmate, named Paul, was a great athlete. He became a dedicated usher later on in life and just shake his head in disgust when this would occur. Paul was a big, gentle, and very polite person, but you did not want to get him mad at you. He had a passion for lifting heavy weights and practicing karate. People arriving late to Mass and having to go through this seating ordeal during the Gospel or sermon would feel the stinging look coming from the priest in the pulpit for causing such a disruption.

Most people late for Mass would remain standing at the rear of the church and would refuse seating by an usher to avoid this situation. It was also very easy for some of these people to leave Mass early, after making what I will call a "guest appearance" and avoiding dropping any money in the collection basket. For some arriving late, it did not matter, since the priest saying Mass would see this large gathering of latecomers standing in the rear of the church and invite them to come forward. I call this a Catholic gotcha.

Oftentimes Father Shields, who was not a bashful priest, would interrupt whatever he was talking about and, over the microphone system, loudly request that they come forward and be seated upfront. It was quite an embarrassing position to be put in! As the people would come forward, complicating matters even more, the select families guarding their territorial pews would begin to "spread out wide," to make it look as if there were no more seating room left in their pew.

I continued to let my eyes wander around the church and looked at four of the five large chapels inside the main sanctuary. They were the chapels of the Sacred Heart, St. Anthony, St. Joseph, and the Blessed Virgin Mary; all of them were highlighted by the multitude of antique and opalescent stained-glass windows throughout the church.

The windows were highly ornamental, with figures illustrating scenes in the lives of Christ, the Blessed Virgin, and many of the saints. The faces, hands, forms, and different scenes were thoroughly painted on the glass, burned in and guaranteed not to fade. I looked over at the gated baptistery marble font and its three artistic stained-glass windows, where my mother, her sisters and brothers, and my own brother, sisters, and I were baptized.

I knew about the fifth chapel and had been in it on occasion, but like most other people sitting in the main sanctuary, I could not see it from where I was now kneeling.

During communion, if you were on the far left-hand side of the communion rail, you could see this fifth chapel. When I knelt at this rail, one could tell it was me by looking at the worn-out soles of my clodhoppers stuffed with candy-bar cardboard wrappers to fill the holes and keep my socks dry. The fifth chapel was hidden, with its own pews and communion railing, to the right side of the main altar.

This fifth chapel was built primarily for the Sisters and other visiting personnel and was constructed so that the occupants of the chapel were completely hidden from the view of the congregation, but they could see the priest saying Mass and receive communion in this area.

Suddenly I became awakened by a hinged door being swung open from the confessional booth and disrupting my survey of the inside of the church. An elderly woman, whom I did not recognize, came out of the booth and closed her confessional door behind her. I arose quickly from my church pew and lifted the knee rail up with the toe of my clodhopper to clear my way to the booth. I continued to walk over and opened the empty confessional door, entered the booth, and knelt down, knowing I would be the next to have my confession heard.

Somehow even though I had been through this ritual on many other occasions, I always felt a lot of anxiety and was scared after entering the dark, enclosed confessional booth. My body would tremble and I would shiver a little and hope that I would not stutter when the priest spoke! What was there to fear about confession? I asked myself. Did the other kids get these same feelings when they entered the confessional booth knowing they would come face-to-face with a priest? I never once told any one of them about how I felt, for fear of being made fun of and being called a "big sissy."

Inside the booth, I could hear a small door sliding open and the priest saying "yes." I started to recite my "Bless me, Father, for I have sinned" and told the priest that it had been one week since my last confession. I was unsure of this but said it anyhow. I would never say it was longer than three weeks, since I learned this would bring a lot of questions from the priest. Perhaps even more penance! By the sound of his voice, I knew the priest hearing my confession today was not Father Reilly, whom I liked very much. He never seemed to ask what other sins I might have committed, and to me the prayers he passed out for penance were what I would call "light duty."

After awhile and choosing Father Reilly as the priest I wanted to confess to, I learned that every priest knew every boy's voice and we were not fooling any of them. I even tried muffling my voice from time to time to avoid being recognized. It never worked! Perhaps they even knew the girls' voices. If this were true, perhaps this was the reason I often saw many

31

of my friends entering and leaving the confessional booth very quickly. Did they also on occasion cut their confession short? To avoid taking a chance that the priest would identify who I was, I did not confess all of my sins.

I only confessed what were considered normal sins in the life of an eleven-year-old Catholic boy, like talking back to Mom and Dad, fighting with my brother and sisters, and having impure thoughts! For sure I was never going to tell the priest about looking at a picture inside a miniature telescope attached to a key-chain holder that showed a bare-breasted woman inside it! As the years passed and we age-of-innocence children became older, I often found myself wondering how many of us would be telling the priest of looking at the glossy magazine editions of *Hustler*, *Playboy*, and *Penthouse*.

When asked if I was sorry, I always told the priest I was and promised never to commit such sins again. I also was not going to tell him about the nude photos I had found in the alley of an older neighbor girl a few days earlier. Sometimes I believe it was after looking at these photos that I knew I was not destined to become a priest; boys were often encouraged to think about this career choice while attending Catholic school.

The priest would talk to me briefly about leading a more pure life and my responsibility as one of God's children. He then provided me absolution and, for penance, instructed me to say six Our Fathers and six Hail Marys and to make a good Act of contrition. I always said the act of contrition in record time and without missing a word of it. From comments I heard while playing in the school yard or talking in class with my friends, I found out the penance for some of them would only be three Our Fathers and three Hail Marys for the same sins.

Boys who were disruptive in the classroom were also generally given a lot more prayers to say and perhaps even a rosary. I did not know what I had done so badly to be given so many prayers for penance. You really had to have done something very bad to receive a novena as penance. This might have been for stealing something from the G. C. Murphy five-and-ten, having impure thoughts about a girl, eating a meal before communion, or eating meat on Friday.

I recall a joke I heard years ago about a man repeatedly confessing to the priest on several occasions as to stealing lumber and receiving only three Our Fathers and three Hail Marys every time for penance. Finally one day after the man again confessed to stealing lumber and the priest recognized the man's voice by this time, he asked the man if he knew how to make a novena. The man replied, "No, Father, but if you can furnish the plans, I can steal the lumber."

I finished my good act of contrition, and as I got up to leave, I could hear the small wood-and-cloth-covered confessional door separating myself from the priest sliding back into place. At the same time, I could hear the opposite confessional door sliding open and a voice saying, "Bless me, Father, for I have sinned." I left the confessional booth, closed the door behind me, stepped back into the church pew, and lowered the knee rail to the floor with the toe of my clodhopper. I knelt down again, made the sign of the cross, and said my penance as fast as I could.

While placing the knee rail down, I thought about how some of us boys during the week at daily Mass or any other event that placed us all in church at the same time would let it drop down very hard. It was similar to what we did with our desktops to make and hear a loud noise. We did this quite often during Mass, during the saying of the Stations of the Cross, or while in church for confession as a group.

Sometimes this loud banging noise would bring the Sisters running to the pew where they thought the noise came from. Raising their arms and pointing with a finger to the guilty, the Sisters would signal the boys to come out of the church pew and follow them to the rear of the church. Pappy, an altar boy, would sometimes join us in doing this act described by the Sisters as very terrible and sinful.

The punishment for dropping knee rail down so hard that they could be heard echoing even to the inside of the confessional booths was swift. It meant having to stay after school to clean erasers and the blackboards and perhaps even washing down the long gray granite wall on the outside of the school. A good paddling could also be administered to the guilty person, along with having to do confined time in the dark evil cloakroom.

Oftentimes just to keep the Sisters confused, we boys would have a plan where we would split up and get in different pews and on a signal, like the wink of an eye, drop down the knee rails simultaneously or one at a time. This really made the Sisters mad. They had to run up and down the sanctuary and survey the long rows of pews to figure out where the culprits were located.

When I finished with my penance, I made the sign of the cross gently, got up from my pew, lifted up the knee rail again with the toe of my clodhopper, and stepped into the church aisle. I knelt down and made the sign of the cross again, stood up, and did a military-like about-face to leave the church.

While walking out of the church, hands clasped together neatly and firmly and fingers pointing upright, I lifted my head up. I stared at the large upper gallery in the rear of the church, where the organ and the area for the choir group which I belonged to was located. The lovely voice of Regina Figulski and her singing of the "Ave Maria" was what prompted me to want to sing in the choir.

As I continued walking out of the main sanctuary, I looked straight ahead to see those swinging doors staring at me again and no one around to open them up. "Dammit," I mumbled to myself, which was the favorite cuss word of the sixth-, seventh-, and eighth-grade boys during recess, when the Sisters and priests were not around to hear them. I looked to my left and observed the large marble Pieta of the Virgin Mary holding Christ in her arms, and bowed my head gently.

I did not bother to dip my finger into the marble holy water fountain or make the sign of the cross again before leaving the sanctuary. I proceeded to throw my whole body against the double swinging doors inside the church sanctuary, pushing them open with all the might I could muster from my tiny arms. The doors began to move very slowly until I could walk between them and free myself from the main church sanctuary.

Once beyond these doors, I had to struggle and use all the force and strength I had remaining within me in order to open up the set of two massive, four-inch-thick, fifty-year-old, arched, shaped-oak outside doors. To my right, I noticed two Italian brothers, Joseph and Charles, entering the church and assumed they were going to confession also. They were very close friends of my brother and me, but since I was in a hurry to get home, I did not call out to greet them. Instead, I hid briefly behind one of the large Romanesque columns, hoping they would not see me.

They passed by without noticing me and entered the main church sanctuary. Due to their behavior at school this week, I thought they probably would receive penance from the priest to say a couple of novenas. It was quite possible that, after their confession, they might "borrow a few of the church candles" for a club that I, Richard, Robert, Vincent, Willy, and a bunch of other boys had started.

We had built a small clubhouse in the hills behind Valley Buick and the old abandoned Kale home, from scrap lumber we collected. We would meet there and use the candles in the evening hours to see by and play cards. As long as Saint Colman's Church was around, along with Joseph and Charles, there would never be a shortage of candles anywhere we might be in the evening hours.

I started to open the large outside doors, which had huge, heavy, ornate metal handles attached to them and seemed to be bigger than me. As the doors to the outside began to swing open, rays of bright sunshine fell upon my squinting eyes, made sensitive by the dimness inside the church. The pain rippling through my eyes was so terrible it made me feel like I was going blind for a brief period. I had thoughts of being caught in the daylight and burning up, like Dracula the Vampire, as I once saw in a movie at the Frederick theater.

I continued to push on the heavy doors, stepped sideways, and slipped between them. When I was completely outside, I turned around backward, quickly, to avoid more of the sunlight stinging me in the eyes. I had become somewhat used to being affected by the sunlight after coming out of the dimly lit interior of the church, and had this routine down pat. I would do the same thing when leaving a dark movie theater and entering the outside daylight. I gently began opening and closing my eyes several times until they had adjusted and I could see again with no pain.

I looked over and saw Audrey, a classmate, removing a handkerchief she had placed on her head earlier before entering the church. At the time, a female not wearing some sort of headpiece inside the church was considered sacrilegious and a sin. She knew if any of the rowdy boys were still hanging around the school or church playground, they would tease her.

This was especially true when there were no priests or Sisters in sight. Then they would make fun of her and her cheap hat, or doilies as the boys would call them. Luck was with her today, since none of these boys except me, Joseph, and Charles, all of whom she got along with well, were around the area.

Audrey and I were buddies, and since I was sometimes forgetful about schoolwork and constantly getting into trouble with the Sisters, I treated her nicely all the time. It worked to my advantage to behave like this, since Audrey sat directly across from me in class. Even at the risk of getting into trouble, at times she would let me look at and copy from her papers.

I was done with my confession and totally free, from school and the religious regimentation that I often thought could feel no worse than being in hell. I ran over to the town's main street located close by and was looking forward to playing a game of tin-can hockey in Farmer's Alley with my brother and George, who lived close by on Wilbur Avenue, and some of the other local guys.

I said to myself without any guilt, "I am so glad there will be no more rosaries, prayers, and hard schoolwork until Monday." I did have some concern about doing my homework assignments and wondered when I might get around to completing them.

Also, I would not have to wear those shiny bright red and gold stars all day! They were licked by the Sisters' tongues and pasted on my forehead, along with some other kids, on occasion for good schoolwork. At times they resulted in my being teased and harassed by some who never received any of the stars! Perhaps they also should have found a few smart girls that would allow them to copy from their papers.

When I got to the street corner adjacent to the large A&P store, I looked both ways, as my mother had taught me. This was done to make sure no automobiles, streetcars, buses, or other vehicles were coming before crossing. As I glanced up, I saw Police Chief Bill Whalen. He was ignoring the automatic signal light and manually directing traffic with his white gloved hand.

A Saint Colman's crossing guard by the name of Marty was wearing white strapping, with a Saint Christopher badge pinned to it, and also looking out for the traffic. He was holding everyone back, especially the schoolchildren, on the sidewalk until Chief Whalen gave the signal we could cross over. While stopped at this location, I continued doing a slow stationary run in place.

When I was finally allowed to cross over to the other side of the street, and breathing somewhat heavily, I looked up to see myself standing in front of the G. C. Murphy five-and-ten store. Several people were entering and leaving the store through large, swinging, wood-framed plate glass doors.

At this point I did not want to do battle with another set of doors and did not go inside. I walked over and looked in Neill's bakery's front window at the freshly made lady fingers and lengths of twelve maple rolls molded together. They could be separated very easy into any particular quantity an individual may want. Subconsciously I divided the flat of twelve maple rolls between me, my brother and two sisters. We could each have three pieces.

I said to myself that Sister Mary David and Sister Regina would be happy to know that I was still practicing my arithmetic. I thought about looking in the bakery window some more but avoided doing it, since it was getting late and I wanted to get home to play. Besides, I knew my mother would be making fresh sticky buns today.

I also knew that she would be asking me if I had been to confession, and this time I would be telling her the truth! Richard, who did not join me on this day for confession, had better have a good story to tell Mom, I thought to myself. I also asked myself and wondered where he was, what he was doing, and if it was worth his skipping confession.

Saint Colman's Church, main sanctuary, 1950s.

Reverend John P. Shields, 1901-1980
Assistant Pastor, January 1907 - 1919
Pastor, November 1919 - October 1964.

Barrie and sister Joy, First Holy Communion, 1943.

CHAPTER 3

THE CLOAKROOM

There were times that several of the boys, including myself, would not pay attention to the Sisters, become disobedient, and have to be disciplined. On occasion, especially during recess period, we became rowdy, teased the girls, talked back to Sister, left the school yard without permission, and ignored the bell ending recess. Come summer or winter, and just to get out of the classroom, all we kids thought about was the recess period. This was the time when we forgot about catechism lessons, daily laborious schoolwork in all subjects, and other religious training for a brief period.

We could play our fun games, run around like crazy, become raving maniacs, and drive the Sisters nuts. The Sisters had their hands full separating us from fighting and breaking up arguments between boys, girls, and sometimes the boys and girls. It was very difficult for them to get us to pay attention and not do anything that could cause bodily injury. The Sisters were pretty tolerant most of the time, but you did not want to push them and cause them to lose their temper or become upset.

Because of the misdeeds of a few boys or girls or even a single individual, Sister would often assign extra homework and not release us for recess. Some kids would have preferred a paddling or being placed in the cloakroom, rather than not being allowed to go out and play during recess. Extra penmanship assignments and writing the same letters over and over, without being allowed to lift one's palm up from the desk, would cause some kids' wrists to ache.

At times the Sisters had to run around the school yard, yelling and blowing on the silver Boy Scout-looking whistles that hung around their necks to get our attention and attempt to maintain some orderly control. Getting our attention and collecting every child into a group and their respective classroom was very difficult, especially at the end of recess. Sometimes it could take only five minutes and up to ten minutes during the winter months. But during summer recess period, it could take anywhere from fifteen to twenty minutes once the whistles started blowing.

Ignoring the whistle-blowing Sisters was always done more blatantly during the warmer weather. During the harsh cold winter days, it was quite different and a relief to feel the warmth of the classrooms again. It is no wonder that some boys, many of whom were repeat offenders, had to be collected physically and restrained by a Sister.

As we boys and girls were collected, we were told not to go anywhere and were lined up in military-like files and forcibly marched into school. A lot of us knew that based on what disobedient thing we did, we could get a paddling or be made to do a stint in the cloakroom.

These disobedient deeds were generally done before school started, during the morning and afternoon recess periods, or after school. The higher grade a boy or girl was in often meant they might be even more challenging or disobedient with a Sister and sometimes a priest. It was a rarity, however, to find any girls at any grade level that were repeat offenders of being disrespectful or disobedient to a Sister.

After being told over and over to stop with the antics and misbehaving, the Sisters' patience wore thin with many of us. Enough was enough, and after a while, the really rowdy kids could be grabbed or punched lightly in the arms, back, and side. They could even be paddled right on the spot in the school yard to get their attention and have them settle down. There was never a time that I can remember where any child was slapped or struck in the face by a Sister at Saint Colman's. However, many of us boys knew what it was like to feel the knuckles of a Sister lightly tapping on the top or side of our heads. On occasion, the same knuckles protruding from the bent fist of a Sister might be used in a light punch thrown into an arm, side, back, or chest of some boys.

I can only describe the Sisters' tapping knuckles, and the echoing sound we boys would hear, as like the noise of someone knocking on a door. Once this occurred and we drew the ire of Sister, some of us would be marched into the school and to our individual classrooms to hear what further fate awaited us.

After being captured, as I call it, by a Sister and depending on the severity of the mischievous deed or infraction of the rules, we could even be sent to Mother Superior, Sister Seraphina, or as some of us called her, the "Head Penguin," for further discipline. The worst fate that could await a kid was being told that you were going to be sent over to the priest's house for a discussion with one of the priests.

If you had to go talk with a priest because of your conduct, the only thing that you could hope for was that it would not be Father Shields. He was not very nice, from a naïve small child's perspective, when it came to giving out what I will call his "fire and damnation speeches" and saying, "You will burn in hell if you do not change your ways."

He was very good at seeing to it that the guilty party sent to him over the years by any Sister would behave a lot better! I was never sent to Father Shields, but from what I have heard from some boys he talked to, he did not administer any physical punishment. By the time he got done with his speech and making you feel guilty and embarrassed, an encounter with Father Shields was never forgotten.

After returning to the classroom, a lot of boys said they would rather receive a paddling from Sister or spend additional time in one of the dreaded cloakrooms rather than face Father Shields again. I do not nor did any of the other older boys, believe it did Frank who was constantly being paddled much good. Perhaps it was medicine he needed to settle him done, but unknowingly never sought out during this time period?

During my eight years of school, I can recall being sent to and having four or five talks with Father Reilly, whom I now consider as being a "cream puff of a priest." His manner was always gentle and soft, and he never raised his voice when talking to any child. He was well liked by all of the children, and his manner during confession struck me as being the same. It would likely be said today that because of his gentle nature with his talks, I did not learn to behave quickly enough, and this is why I was directed by the Sisters on occasion to make extra visits to the priest's house.

Father Thomas was not as mild mannered and could really scold any boy or girl sent to him, but was well liked by all of us children anyway.

On occasion, Sister might even banish someone who had to talk with a priest to spend time in the clandestine cloakroom. If a kid's behavior were such that he or she were sent to Mother Superior for further discipline, it usually meant that, in the higher grades, they were going to be struck several times on their buttocks with a paddle in the nearest cloakroom.

I must say from my experience, as well as that of the rowdy boys I played with, that such discipline was rightly deserved in most cases. After receiving this punishment and depending on Mother Superior's instructions, if any further punishment or paddling was warranted, it could be carried out by Sister. This could be done in her classroom, in front of the other children, or out of sight in that dark, evil, dreary, horrible place known as the cloakroom.

Starting around the fifth grade, which is the most vivid point of remembering my school experiences at Saint Colman's, the cloakroom was not a nice place you wanted to be sent to. The purpose of the cloakroom, which was very small and dark without the lights on, was to hang clothing and store lunch boxes. It was also used to store extra school supplies and the long pole used to open and close the classroom windows.

At the age of eleven, my deep inner thoughts were that it had to be the worst place in the world to be all alone in and the "horror of all horrors." Today I often think that the cloakrooms at Saint Colman's would have fit very well into an Edgar Allan Poe story.

Perhaps I saw too many Lon Chaney, Frankenstein, and other scary and frightful movies at the Rivoli, Frederick, and Olympic theaters, but being put into a dark cloakroom took its toll on me. While being confined, I would begin to imagine that Wolf Man and Dracula were also hiding somewhere in there with me! As my thoughts ran wild and my imagination took its toll, they mysteriously and suddenly appeared before me!

Wolf Man ran toward me, with his sharp-pointed, big white teeth showing brightly. Dracula flew toward me in the form of a bat with long fanged teeth showing, emitting screeching and hissing sounds. They both landed their bodies on me violently and began to fight each other to see who would claim my blood and soul.

Screaming out loud in pain, I could feel both of them biting down hard, and I began screaming for my life as the blood was being drained from my neck and other body parts. I believe I may have said more Our Fathers, Hail Marys, and good acts of contrition while spending time in a cloakroom than while in school, confession, and church.

In addition, I often prayed for and asked my guardian angel to help get me out of the cloakroom quickly. This never happened, but when

Sister did open the cloakroom door to let me out, could it have been my guardian angel helping me?

I was terrified, and the only thing that offered any relief was when Sister opened the cloakroom door and told me I could come out. I said a few short prayers, like "thank you, God, thank you, God," and muttered "whew" a few times, giving myself a sense of relief. Perhaps I also felt, as in the movies, that the light of day was the only thing these two villains feared and that would make them disappear.

On other occasions, I saw myself being placed on a rack, with my arms and legs being stretched from a rope tied to them by an ugly, large, burned, and disfigured man, who had only one eye in the center of his forehead! If a paddling was called for, each person who committed a serious deed or something considered an infraction of school rules could be directed to go to the cloakroom.

This was a dungeon or torture chamber as far as I was concerned during my early school years. In this solitary place, one could not defend him or herself or utter a single word other than "ouch" or "that hurt, Sister" after feeling the sting of the paddle on their buttocks. In this horrible place, you could be struck once or several times by a Sister holding a long wooden paddle, measuring approximately a foot in length and about a half inch thick.

Those schoolchildren who have felt the sting and heard the sound of a paddle meeting their buttocks will never forget it. I can only describe it as the cracking sound at the beginning of an avalanche; it carries with it an echo that seems to come from all four walls of the classroom.

While hunting in Alaska years later and standing underneath a snowcapped mountain on Admiralty Island, I was witness to this horrible sound once again. The memories of Saint Colman's and its cloakrooms flashed in and out of my mind!

There were two doors that one could use to enter into the cloakroom. One was on the far left, and the other was on the far right of the classroom, as you faced Sister's desk. Preceding the punishment process, the classroom Sister would open one of the cloakroom doors and turn on the overhead lights if necessary. Then the guilty party was directed to go into the cloakroom, and Sister would follow and close the door behind her and administer the paddling.

When the paddling was completed, both cloakroom doors opened up almost simultaneously. Sister came out from behind one door huffing and puffing, and the person being disciplined appeared from behind the other door and went directly, sometimes crying and sometimes not, to his or her desk. Paddling was sometimes administered to a girl, although this was a very rare event. On occasion, girls could also be sent to the cloakroom for a period of time, with both doors closed and no overhead lighting turned on.

No paddling would be administered if only a minor infraction was committed. However, before closing the cloakroom door, Sister might say, "The devil may even come visit you, since you are so evil and bad." At times we other children, sitting at our desks in the classroom, could hear some crying and whimpering coming from the individual before the door closed completely.

Sometimes with the boys, Sister might say, "You are going to hell if you do not learn to behave." Not only did I have to deal with the Wolf Man, Dracula, and the one-eyed guy, but on occasion while in the cloakroom, I also had to hide and run away from the red-eyed, smiling devil. Subconsciously he would appear in my mind with his fork and attempt to lure me into the flaming fires of hell. At times, I wished that the cloakroom would have been more reminiscent of the "Garden of Evil" and someone like Eve would appear to offer me an apple.

All a boy or girl could do while standing inside the dark cloakroom was pace back and forth to kill time, while waiting on the door to be opened by Sister. I would sometimes open a lunch box or lunch bag during my stints in the cloakroom, to see if there were any morsels of goodies I might enjoy and see what the other kids had brought to eat.

Most Sisters did not like it when they had to discipline a child through paddling or placing them in the cloakroom. But they also recognized if they did not enforce the rules early, they could be taken advantage of. They realized things could really get out of hand, especially with repeat offenders and I was one of them.

Many of the Sisters would offer apologies at a later time or during recess to those children they had disciplined. They would always ask, "Are you sorry for misbehaving?" Sister would then go on to say, "God does not like his children acting this way, and we should ask for his forgiveness and blessing."

The punished children would always say, "Yes, Sister." For those disciplined harshly with a paddle, Sister might even add to her comment, "If you understand what I am saying to you, swear to God you will never do it again." I guarantee you, anyone who has felt the sting of a paddle from a Sister of Mercy will swear to God to never do it again!

That is, until the next infraction comes along that results in a good paddling. I thought a good Catholic education would make you smarter, but some of us boys never learned our lesson. To my knowledge, every child, including the repeat offenders, always swore to God they would never do whatever it was they did again.

If I had to pick a time frame, being put in the cloakroom at Saint Colman's probably started for most kids about third grade. We were all too innocent before then to do anything wrong, including talking back to a Sister. This loneliness of being placed in the cloakroom was for infractions of the school rules or what was considered outrageous or disrespectful at the time.

This included, but was not limited to, biting your nails, talking back to Sister, poor penmanship, talking in class, and stealing someone else's supplies or personal items! Yes, as much as I hate to admit it, some petty stealing did go on, even in a Catholic school and under the eyes of God, the Sisters, priests, and even one's personal guardian angel! Other infractions could be chewing gum, skipping the Stations of the Cross or confession, and disobeying a Sister's orders. Additional infractions were not turning in a homework assignment, copying from someone else's paper, or just bad schoolwork.

As the girls got older and approached the higher grades, a touch of noticeable lipstick or other light makeup could make Sister or the two lay teachers, Ms. Dalzell and Ms. Miller, become somewhat irritable. By this time, young ladies being sent to the cloakroom had lost its effect, and being sent to the lavatory to remove the makeup was the only discipline administered. One day my punishment for some class disruption was having Ms. Dalzell put me under her desk for about fifteen minutes. Although it was not as bad as being confined to the cloakroom, she never had to do this again with me!

As I write, I cannot remember seeing any children at Saint Colman's ever caught smoking, and my imagination makes me wonder what the punishment would have been. I believe it would have merited a trip to the parish house, and a very long talk with Father Shields! Had this scenario become a reality, how would he have been able to explain why Father Reilly or one of his other priests could smoke in front of the schoolchildren attending St. Colman's?

Another reason for boys being sent to the cloakroom was their drawing back on a rubber band and shooting it across the room at someone. Snapping a rubber band onto the neck of the person sitting in front of you would also merit a cloakroom visit. This resulted in a very loud scream of "ouch" and "stop it" coming from the person being stung. It also resulted in getting Sister's attention quickly.

The rubbing of a piece of chalk on the blackboard to create a screeching noise, or trying to trip someone as they got up to go to the blackboard and past your desk was another reason for cloakroom visitation. If you could not trip them, then a quick punch with your fist in their arm, leg, back, or side would do just as well. Of course, this was all done when one thought Sister was not looking. Naturally, due to all the commotion, Sister could not help but notice something wrong was going on.

Sometimes when a boy or girl with chalk in hand was writing on the blackboard, he or she could inadvertently cause the screeching noise I previously described. They would look astonished (not wanting to be put in the cloakroom), and their eyes would wander to Sister, pleading their innocence and saying it was a mistake! Somehow, Sister would always know if it was done deliberately or not. One's past antics could get you sent to the cloakroom again, even if you were innocent.

Another misdeed was throwing erasers at someone in the classroom or getting up from your desk without permission when you thought Sister was not looking. Other things that brought disciplinary action were pulling on someone's hair or ears and pinching the neck of the person sitting in front of you. At times whether it was a boy or girl, if Sister were close by and caught you doing this, it could mean swift punishment being carried out on the offender with the ruler she might be holding.

The guilty party or parties doing these things could also be physically yanked out of their seat by Sister and "marched" to the front of the classroom. I do not know why, but we did a lot of marching in Catholic school. It was good training for those of us boys who entered the military later on in life. Sister might send you to the evil, dark cloakroom or have you face the class and extend one or both hands. Then she would direct you to place them palm up or palm down.

With a wood ruler she had retrieved from her desk or perhaps already had in her hand, she was preparing the individual for what was going to take place. Without saying another word and with a sudden swing, like the swift strike of a coiled rattlesnake, Sister would raise the ruler up and then down quickly to come in contact with your hands. The classroom children would hear the sharp cracking sound as the ruler came in contact with the guilty party's hand or knuckles.

At times, the guilty party would cry out loud in anticipation of pain, even before the ruler struck them, and jerk their hand or hands backward to avoid being hit. Looking into the eyes of most of the children in the classroom, the child being punished could also see them flinching, moving their body parts or hands slightly, and the grimacing looks on their faces, as if they too were being punished as the ruler found its mark.

The classes at Saint Colman's were always full and held upward of forty students, if not more, for a single Sister to educate. Therefore, in defense of the Sisters, the boys and the girls breaking the rules justly deserved the punishment they received. After meeting and talking with several of my classmates from Saint Colman's over the last sixty years, every one of them has nothing but the highest respect and praise for most of the Sisters. After maturing, especially us boys, we truly came to recognize the great task the Sisters had before them.

The psychological outcome aspired to by the Sisters putting someone in the dark clandestine cloakroom, without doing any physical paddling, was to embarrass and exile you from the rest of the class. In my opinion, it was probably felt by Sister that this embarrassment would make you think about what you had done to deserve it. Perhaps you might even think about confessing the problem you caused or what you had done to receive the punishment to the priest during your next confession.

It was highly unlikely that I would tell the priest about being placed in the cloakroom, any more than I would tell him about looking at the bare-breasted women in that small telescope attached to a key chain! I always had my confession rehearsed quite well, so I could get in and out quickly. That is, unless the priest recognized my voice and began bringing up things he had seen me doing in the school yard or complaints he had from Sister.

Even though I attempted to disguise my voice using various antics like coughing and muffling it a little with a handkerchief, it very seldom worked. I knew I was caught when the priest would say, "Please speak up, Barrie."

Sitting on a stool as a dunce in a corner, with a cone-shaped hat placed on your head, which only occurred in comic books, would have worked much better in my opinion than the cloakroom trauma. At a later age and with a lot more knowledge, I came to believe that this cloakroom technique was sort of like brainwashing, but on a much smaller scale, such as that not heard of until the Korean War!

This isolation, coupled with being ridiculed by the rest of the class later on with no Sisters around, would supposedly make you do your best to adhere to the rules and avoid the cloakroom in the future. It is hard to believe that some of us boys never learned from this experience and continued breaking the rules over and over.

I now believe the girls were absolutely correct when they called me and some of the other boys "dumb and stupid." They would often say, "When will you ever learn to stay out of trouble?" When I said, "I will not do it again," all I could hear the girls say was, "Swear to God that you will never do it again." Talk about being brainwashed!

"When will you ever learn?" was the most frequently used phase coming from the mouths of young, naïve, and ever-faithful Catholic schoolgirls. They always seemed to take their religious training a lot more seriously than some of the boys. At times Lillian, my Polish friend, who sometimes gave me a piece of her kielbasa sandwich, and Jean, my Irish friend who gave me some of her soda bread, would tell me to stop my misbehaving. They would only shake their heads while staring at me coming out of the cloakroom, as if to say again, "When will you ever learn?"

From outside the cloakroom where the corporal punishment was being administered, students sitting at their desks in complete silence could hear the beat and noise of the paddle and the sniveling student as it found its mark. Depending on which Sister was swinging the paddle, the severity of the punishment could be a few light taps or very hard, rapid swings causing severe pain and swelling of the buttocks.

There were times when Sister Ruff, while in a swinging frenzy, would miss the designated buttocks area, and the paddle would land on other parts of the individual's body. Being hit on the legs, arms, and hands accidentally happened on many occasions. To be fair, I must point out that the twisting, jumping, and moving around by the person being paddled often resulted in Sister not landing her paddle on the designated buttocks.

One day Sister Ruff while paddling one of several boys accidentally caught the rosary beads and large black crucifix with a metal figure of Christ, hanging from her black leather belt, with the end of the paddle. This caused the light chain holding everything together to break and send the beads and crucifix dropping on the floor. While Sister was busy retrieving her beads from the floor, a low chuckle could be heard coming from some of the children sitting at their desks. Sister's punishment was halted on this child, and he was ordered to return back to his desk. The lucky boys or girls who had not received their punishment yet received what we called a free pass.

Once I was paddled hard by Sister Ruff on my buttocks for some minor infraction. "Where was my guardian angel on this day?" I often asked myself. My father, Thaddeus, after hearing about this and looking at the paddle marks, called the parish house and went to have a talk with Father Shields. He was quite upset about the severity of the paddling. But my brother and I, as young as we were, could not understand at the time why it was all right for him to beat us at times with a razor strap or cat-o'-nine-tails and leave a belt mark, but Sister could not beat us with a paddle.

My father and Father Shields had their meeting and a very strong discussion about the incident, and he came home and told my mother about it. Sister was ordered to place some restraint on her discipline and handling of all children in the future! Knowing what Father Shields was like with his well-known Irish temper, and my father's temper, along with the whiskey he drank beforehand, there must have been a real donnybrook that day. Why they tolerated one another I do not know, since my father very seldom attended any school or church functions, except for a wedding or funeral.

From that day on, he and Father Shields became very good friends and often could be seen talking on the street or in the school yard together. At times, Father Shields would call on my father to provide a ride for some of the Sisters up the hill to the new convent location. My father was driving a few of them up Grant Street on September 13, 1963, and stopped the car in the middle of the road, saying he was sick. He put on the emergency brake and died! While doing a good deed, his life had ended in the middle of a road at the young age of fifty.

Children could also be paddled in the classroom at the discretion of a Sister. The individual could be bent over a desk and paddled in front of the other students. The paddle could also be used with the Sister holding the child by one hand while standing up, and using her free hand to smack the child's buttocks. This was the position that resulted in Sister Ruff's string of rosary beads being accidentally broken.

A parent going to the school or the rectory to discuss discipline problems with their children did not happen often during days gone by. The assumption by most parents whose children attended Saint Colman's was that if you were disciplined at school by the Sisters or priests, you must have done something wrong and deserved what you got!

The priests, Sisters, and public schoolteachers were held in high regard by everyone. Telling your parents you were disciplined by any of them, including being put in the cloakroom, would only bring more discipline at home. This you did not want to happen, since being disciplined at school could mean another beating at home. It could also mean you were not allowed to go out in the evening or go to a show; possibly you would even be locked in your room for the weekend.

Given a choice between being locked in my room for a week or the cloakroom for a short period of time, as much as I hated it, I would have picked the dark and haunting cloakroom. Televisions were nonexistent in just about all of the homes in Turtle Creek in the early 1950s, and therefore the threat of taking this privilege away from a child was not an option for parents. Most of the children going to Saint Colman's kept their mouths shut if they were disciplined, rightly or wrongly, by a Sister or priest at school.

The description of the cloakroom is that of a small child's memory, and my description of the Sisters' disciplinary actions is not meant to be a vicious attack on them or vindication, since most of the punishments, including those on me, were well deserved. The majority of the Sisters were always very kind, patient, and loving.

However, in some cases, there were a few Sisters at the upper grade levels who could not maintain self-control when they started paddling or physically disciplining a child. The chapter titled "Ice Hockey" describes some severe punishment handed out by one Sister in the cloakroom. The action of this one Sister and my writings should never cause the other good, kind, gentle, and responsible Sisters at St. Colman's to be looked upon with disdain.

One must realize while reading this story, that some, but not all, of the Sisters who taught at Saint Colman's went into their order at a very young age and did not have a well-rounded or higher education themselves. The Sisters during my attendance at Saint Colman's also had very little formal "credentialed" teaching and training prior to entering a classroom. They were very young and naïve when they entered the convent years before.

You could call this a good job of brainwashing, at an early age, through Catholic upbringing, school teachings, and religious instruction to obtain so many Sisters at such early ages. However, I do believe there were also some Sisters who truly felt the calling of God and a desire to become a nun. Today, many Catholic schools operate very differently and employ modern teaching methods in addition to their religious doctrine teaching.

The number of nuns in all Catholic orders, as well as the number of priests in all orders, has tapered off dramatically over the years. Now there are many lay teachers with excellent classroom experience and certified teaching credentials employed by the Catholic Church. While I attended Saint Colman's, boys were encouraged to become priests and girls were encouraged to become nuns. However, I must qualify this statement and say we were not indoctrinated about it on a daily basis.

Although my brother and I considered it, only one boy from my eighth-grade graduating class, whose name was Michael, became a priest. One other boy, by the name of Ron, who was a few years ahead of me, also became a priest. Not one girl to my knowledge ever became a nun.

Lois, who went on to a Catholic high school and to my recollection was seriously contemplating becoming a nun, changed her mind. Due to her pleasant and kind ways in school, along with being very intelligent, I always thought she would have made a wonderful nun and teacher.

Today you have nuns with accredited bachelors, masters, and doctorate degrees in every major field. They are skilled at recognizing possible mental and physical disorders, child abuse, hearing and sight disorders, stuttering, dyslexia, and other motor skill deficiencies.

I have no doubt that some of us children, while attending Saint Colman's, might have suffered from some of these conditions, but they could not be recognized by the Sisters without today's special teacher training. It is also a possibility that some of these conditions were even brought about by, contributed to, or perhaps were the underlying causes for punishment in the horrible cloakroom.

Today there are a great deal of medical publications and writings regarding the causes for attention deficit disorder (ADD) or attention deficit hyperactivity disorder (ADHD) overactive children and how they should be treated or handled. In my opinion, the 320 students, if not more, attending grades one through eight at Saint Colman's on any given day would have been diagnosed with ADD or ADHD, rather than youthful exuberance.

I think this would hold true for the children attending the public school across the street also! Perhaps the use of Ritalin, which has been described as being overused to curtail hyper or unruly children, would have been prescribed also.

A child's youthful exuberance is not all that bad; it must be recognized as such and handled accordingly. Perhaps as in days gone by, a long school yard recess period with a lot of physical activity and game playing just might be the answer to eliminating the use of Ritalin in some, though not all, overactive children.

There is never a day that I think of the terrible times I spent in the cloakroom at Saint Colman's in other than a humorous, memorable, and loving way.

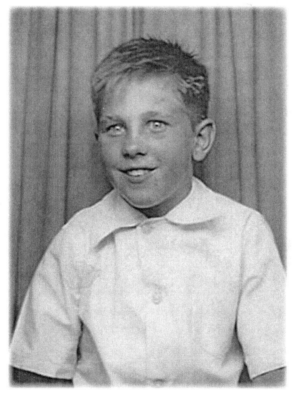

Barrie, Saint Colman's Kennywood Park Picnic, 1945.

First Sisters of Mercy arrive in Pittsburgh from Ireland, 1843.

CHAPTER 4

TOWN FLOODING

When I left my sixth-grade class and school yard at Saint Colman's to go home, like most of the kids, I ran away from the school as fast as I could. I could feel light beads of perspiration forming on my forehead, since it was a very hot and humid day, and I became quite thirsty. I continued running past the Fallers furniture store and down to the community water fountain. The fountain was located in the center of the town's military war memorial, honoring those local veterans who had served their country.

I slowed down my running, caught a few deep breaths of fresh air, and stopped quickly in the front of the fountain to get a cool drink. The water from this openly available refrigerated fountain was ice-cold. It always tasted better than the warm drinking water that came out of the faucets in the hallways of Saint Colman's. This refrigerated fountain also had better water pressure and could be dangerous! If someone was not careful in pushing on the small chrome button to release it, the water could hit you unexpectedly and quickly in the face.

There was never a problem being able to get the water into your mouth from this fountain, since the pressure caused it to arch up very high. On occasion, a lot of us kids would open our mouths as wide as we could and just let the water pressure hit and tickle our tonsils. At the same time, some of us would, like gagging, make a gargling noise that could be heard coming from the open hollow of our mouths. This act, if one were not careful, could result in some kids almost choking to death, as the water quickly slid down their throats and temporarily blocked their windpipes.

This was unlike the pressure from the water fountains at Saint Colman's, which could leave you holding your breath for a little time while placing your lips over the small spigot hole in them. Children, Sisters, priests, and any visitors had to do this to help suck out a few drops from the slow-running, trickling, and always warm water. You could hold the faucet open for a long period of time, and still no cold water would ever come out of the spigot during the summer. The only time anyone would ever get a drink of cold water from these fountains was during the colder, but not yet freezing, months of winter.

After having to suck for so long on that small hole to get a drink of warm water, many of the children would start gagging on the water. Uttering loud, short sounds of Ugh! Ugh! Ugh! they would remove their lips and mouth from the spigot and run their hands across bruised and puckered lips. As a finale to describing how bad the water tasted, some children would begin spitting away any residual water, to get rid of any germs the other kids may have left behind.

I drank heartily from the community fountain and quenched my thirst and parched throat on the ice-cold water before continuing my journey home. On the way, I ran onto the small macadamized walkway poured across the town's rusting bridge stretched over the rushing waters of the creek below it. While doing this, I was thinking about meeting up with my brother and other friends to play a game of street hockey or kick the can, as we had discussed during school recess.

This rusting, dilapidated bridge had been built a long time ago and straddled the wide banks of the creek that ran through the town. I stopped in the center of the bridge, looked down, and rested my elbows upon the weathered, peeling paint and age-old carriage-head rusting rivets! My good friend Tommy had commented many times as we crossed over the bridge together that the rivets looked like a thousand monster eyes staring up at you.

I became mesmerized as I gazed over the edge of the wide, rusty, steel plate railing of the bridge and looked at the creek's rushing water below me. Large floating logs and trees that had been uprooted and ripped from the creek banks, due to the heavy rains of the last couple of days, were swiftly passing in front of me and under the bridge. As I looked at all of the debris floating by, I knew my brother, Richard, and I would be out here on the weekend along with our dog, Boy.

We would attempt to spear the logs, just as the native Delaware Indians many years before us may have speared fish or other animals along the creek banks. We might even be joined by our good Italian brothers,

Joseph and Charles, who lived next to the creek. Freddy, another friend and also of Italian heritage, lived in a house built directly over the creek. Robert, the son of the local Jewish tailor, Mr. Berky, would also be looking for us on the bridge to play later on.

To keep occupied, we often speared the logs when the creek water was high like this, by throwing a harpoon at them. We made the harpoons out of an old broom or mop stick that we found in someone's trash. We would drill a small hole into the rounded top of the stick, pull a long piece of clothesline through it, and tie a timber hitch knot to secure it. We used this knot quite a bit, as well as several other knots we had learned as members of Boy Scout Troop 71. After this, we would take a hammer and pound a nail into the other end of the stick halfway. Then we would grind the nail's round, flat head into a sharp point like that of an ice pick.

We now had our harpoons ready to begin their airborne flight, and they would stick into whatever they came in contact with. While holding the rope in one hand, we boys would throw the harpoon into the water with our free hand at some object we would see floating by. We hoped our throwing accuracy was good enough to have the nail dig deeply into it, so we could retrieve it with a swift pull of the rope. My brother and I became quite the experts at doing this, and many of our friends would often show up for us to give them lessons.

Of course, this good deed could be recalled in the future as a means of bartering over something they could do for us or give us! Perhaps they would help us haul some items to the junkyard or give us a piece of their candy. They might even help us shovel the winter load of coal into the cellar.

Although we could spear many of them and sink the nail deep into their timber, it was always impossible to retrieve the large logs, due to their weight and the swift water pulling them loose from the nail point. On occasion the current was so swift and the nail dug in so deeply, that many of the boys, including me and my brother, had the stick yanked from our hands. I cannot tell you how many harpoons were lost—but it did not take us very long to fashion a new one.

Sometimes we boys became bored with throwing the harpoons, and while the water was still high, we would begin to shoot large sewer rats. The rats would wander out of the creek's overhead tunnels and drainage pipes and become prey for our loaded and ready Red Ryder BB guns. My brother and I, while playing after school or on the weekend, rarely went anywhere, especially into the woods, without taking them with us.

As I continued my way home, I thought about the damage the high water and flooding had brought to Turtle Creek a year earlier. I remembered the stories my mother and father had told us about several other floods over the years that played havoc on the town. All of the local businesses and homes in the lower areas were flooded, and the police and firemen went through the town in motorized boats to help remove stranded adults and children.

During the heavy rain period, I, along with the town residents and other children attending Saint Colman's and the public school across the street, could hear the local fire department and the Westinghouse Volunteer Fire Department whistles blowing constantly. These whistles were short, numerically coded, screeching bursts that were released to warn residents of a disaster or imminent disaster, such as a drowning, fire, high water, and flooding. The whistles I heard blowing during the week were warning the local residents of possible flooding.

The residents living on the upper hillsides and higher ground areas paid little attention to the whistle warnings, since they knew they were generally safe and out of harm's way. However, they all had concerns and prayed for the lower level residents, who might be affected by the flooding. Residents at the lower levels in the town rarely if ever evacuated and chose, as their parents before them had done on several occasions over the years, to stay put in their homes. I knew after listening to the whistles that, my brother and sisters and I would be helping my parents clean up after the water receded, as we had done the previous year.

In anticipation of high water and possible flooding, we had moved all the furniture and other items from our lower living levels to the upstairs rooms to save as much as possible from any flooding and water damage. Would we have to do this again? I wondered! Once the rain stopped and the flooding waters receded and disappeared, like the other families, we would have to endure.

Then the laborious task of washing away all of the mud and debris left by the rising water flowing into our cellars and lower rooms would begin. Many residents and children helping with this cleanup lived in fear of being electrocuted by bare wiring that may have come in contact with the water.

When everything was cleaned up and finally dry again, most of the residents would repaint their cellars with a coat of whitewash and begin moving the furnishings back to their lower floor locations. Neighbors helped one another, and the local fire department with their water removal pumps, along with the police force, would also pitch in and help with the cleanup. Cooking at home was almost impossible during the flooding, and everyone lived on canned soups, baloney, chipped ham, kielbasa, and cheese sandwiches.

Those mothers with children at home in the lower flooded areas could not wait for Speelman's Café to open back up for some hot meals. George's New Deal Bar and Restaurant would also open, to begin serving those great fish and hot sausage sandwiches again. The shrimp, crab cakes, and french fry orders would also be bagged and ready for someone to pick them up. There was no such thing as a pizza being delivered to your home like a Domino's of today. While waiting on an order in these establishments to be finished; the adult patrons could also partake in a quick shot of whiskey and beer chaser.

The other local communities of Braddock, Pitcairn, Wilmerding, and East Pittsburgh also suffered from flooding, and their fire and police personnel were no different than Turtle Creek in helping out their residents. A great fish, kielbasa, or hot sausage sandwich could also be obtained in any of these communities. A shot of whisky and a beer, or "hunky highball" as it was called, was also easy to come by in many of their taverns.

I took a moment while standing on the bridge to say quite a few prayers, asking God to let my mother and father, and all the other lower area residents in town, be spared and saved from any flooding and rising water. I knew that the great logs and trees being tossed about in the creek's swift, rushing waters underneath me and the bridge could cause severe damage to the town. I said one final prayer and asked God to be merciful, stop the rain, and let everyone be saved from any flooding. I knew if the rain continued and the creek were to rise any higher, the logs and trees would become jammed under the bridge. A dam would form, and the water would begin to immediately flow over the creek's old stone walls and into the town's main street.

This would cause all of the businesses and low-lying residences to flood, and those residents living on the higher level floors of their apartment buildings would become stranded and helpless to do anything about the flooding. My school friend Marty lived in one of these apartment buildings. They would be some of the luckier residents, since they would not have to do any cleanup and clearing out of the thick muddy debris left behind.

The logs, trees, and other debris that would make it through and pass under the other side of the bridge from where I stood, would float on and rush past the Westinghouse and US Steel plants. They would continue on and into the riverbanks of the next town of Braddock and eventually empty into the mighty Monongahela River.

During the night, residents from all these towns, while standing on very high locations, could still see the enormous logs, trees, and debris floating by the old US Steel Edgar Thompson Works, where cannonballs were once fabricated during the Civil War.

The mill was now making steel, to be used in the construction of tanks, battleships, and other items for the war in Europe and the Pacific. The whistles would also blow from this steel mill on a daily basis, to announce a change of shift for the workers, lunchtime, and starting and quitting times. Somehow, people growing up and living around the small low-lying towns of Turtle Creek, Braddock, Pitcairn, Wilmerding, and East Pittsburgh did not seem to need watches. They became accustomed to recognizing and letting the whistles be their time clock for just about everything.

The whistles told them when it was time to pick up the kids from school, pick up the husband, son, or father from the mill or Westinghouse, do the grocery shopping, or get ready for an appointment. Yes, they even told the local boys and girls out on a date when they had parked too long and had forgotten about the time they were to be home. When this happened, you'd better have a good story to tell, since they also told the parents when their children were late in getting home.

The floating logs and trees bobbing up and down in the swift rushing water would be lit up by the tall, sentinel-like mill smokestacks spewing out bright orange and toxic red ashy flames from the belching US Steel plant open-hearth furnaces below. After standing on the bridge during the day and watching the high water and debris, I remember my father, Richard, and me, driving to and standing on a high plateau the evening before in North Braddock.

We were looking down on the river and all the floating debris and the mill. Suddenly our father commented to us "This is a magnificent, picturesque steelworker scene that can only be described through an artist's oil painting." How, I ask myself today, could a man with such a limited education, have such feeling and vision?

From this same overlook, the tall, towering buildings located in downtown Pittsburgh could be seen rising above everything else around. This scene was also like that of an artist's finishing brushstrokes on a wonderful painting. It was highlighted, however, by the giant, bright, red-hot steel ingots and slabs moving along the banks of the river on their flatbed railroad cars. These hot ingots loaded onto a Union Railroad flatcar reminded me of lonely sentinels standing guard duty at their posts. As they moved slowly along the railroad tracks, their hot, glowing red shadows would become mirror-image reflections on the moonlit river water below them.

My wife's father, Lewis Coleman, was one of the railroad locomotive engineers who transported these hot ingots upriver to the US Steel Irvin works mill, for the rolling and fabrication of steel sheets and coils. The ingots and slabs were shaped, formed, and made into parts for bridges, automobiles, airplanes, tanks, battleships, and other products that made the city of Pittsburgh famous.

My father, Thaddeus, operated the large crane at the Edgar Thompson Works in Braddock, which lifted and moved the hot, soft, molten steel being carried in huge, deep, thick, plated steel buckets. He also placed the glowing, formed, red-hot ingots and slabs onto the Union Railroad flatcars as they were backed into the tin, sheltered steel mill loading area.

My father's brother Edward, or "Red" as he was known, operated this same crane for a period of time before enlisting in the US Marine Corps during World War II. After being discharged, Red returned to his crane operator job for a short period of time and would never return.

His being seriously wounded while fighting fanatical Japanese soldiers with the Marines on Iwo Jima, and his mental condition thereafter, would not allow him to return to his job. My book titled *The Red Schwinn Bicycle, "A Sentimental Journey,"* provides an intimate look into Red's life. His is a story of human spirit, patriotism, love of family and community, young love, and the horrors of war.

My grandfather, Janus (John), who emigrated from the small village of Nasielsk in Poland to his lifetime home in Braddock, Pennsylvania, operated this same crane for many years before both of them. The youngest brother, my uncle Robert, applied with US Steel to become a patternmaker through an apprentice program. After he was told that he should be a crane operator like his father and brothers, he refused the job and joined the merchant marines for a brief period of time.

Robert was quite upset and feels insulted to this very day that the US Steel personnel considered him incapable of becoming a patternmaker because he came from a Polish background. I know it was the 1940s, but is it possible the mentality of this human resources interviewer focused on thinking hunkies were only capable of physical labor?

Polacks, or hunkies as they were referred to, with limited educations when they first immigrated to America were often looked down upon. They were not considered as being able to do anything but hard labor jobs. The Irish went through these same difficult times when applying for many skilled jobs that did not entail digging a ditch or mixing cement. Robert went on to start his own successful trucking business several years later. He also built his own home and custom cabinetry in later years. He now spends his retirement time building custom furniture and other specialized wood items for friends, neighbors, and grandchildren.

In contrast to the beauty of the belching red flames being emitted from the tall smokestacks, the floating debris, and the hot ingots my father, Richard, and I were watching below us, something ugly and dangerous was also going on. The white or light-colored automobiles parked outside the steel mill by workers would become imbedded with the toxic red ore and ashy materials emitted by the smokestacks during the day and night. These cars would be driven home as oxen red-colored vehicles in the morning. The darker cars did not show this red ashy material as much, but white ones, such as my father's, stood out from the rest of the vehicles!

If the automobiles looked like this after only a few short hours, one can only imagine what the ash did to the lungs of steelworkers and local residents, who breathed it all in for eight hours or more a day seven days a week. There were many times when the steel mill was very busy, operating at full capacity, and the spewing ash that ran like water from the smokestacks would create a thick fog like mist in our valley.

This putrid sulphuric-smelling red ash was so thick at times, many people driving automobiles would have to turn on their headlights during daylight hours to see ahead and to avoid a possible collision with another vehicle. The worst scenario that could happen was not seeing pedestrians crossing the street and possibly hitting them!

To understand how bad the ashy mist was and how much harmful pollution was being emitted that residents were not aware of, one only has to remember what happened in Donora, Pennsylvania. Between October 26 and 31, 1948, twenty people died and over seven thousand were hospitalized as the result of severe air pollution. A heavy thick fog blanketed Donora, due in part, to yellow corrosive smoke emissions from the zinc works. Sulfur dioxide, carbon monoxide, and metal dust became trapped in the town by a layer of warm air, and resulted in the first federal clean-air act, passed in 1955.

Today Pittsburgh and its small surrounding towns like Turtle Creek have picturesque, clean, beautiful skies. The few mills that are left today no longer emit these toxic ashes, due to new laws and the filtering and environmental controls that have been put into place. Condominiums, restaurants, and other established businesses now front the riverbanks where mighty steel mills once stood. The waterfront commercial area of restaurants, movie theaters, small boutiques, and other establishments located in Homestead, Pennsylvania, is a prime example.

I now think about the debris that was being carried past and under the bridge and through this industrial valley that day. What was taking place could be compared to a life and death cycle. The rising water and flooding was uprooting trees, creek banks, and riparian vegetation and killing off other parts of the earth. The steel mills emitting their pollutants were also killing. However, at the same time, the mills were giving birth, since they were generating jobs, creating hope and prosperity for a new life!

I remembered from my geography and history lessons at school that some of this debris would eventually float into the Monongahela River and merge into the mouths of the great Allegheny and Ohio rivers. When this happened, I thought to myself, like Jonah and the whale, the debris would also be swallowed up and disappear.

The Sisters at Saint Colman's would be pleased to hear that I did learn and remember this important geography lesson about the three rivers merging together in Pennsylvania. This area is known as "the point in Pittsburgh." I realized that I could not stay on the bridge any longer, daydreaming. I took off and ran up the street a little farther, where I found some shade underneath the overhanging branches and leaves of a few mulberry and chestnut trees. I cooled down a bit and started to walk slowly past some of the town's stores.

I peeked into Taylor's, Jack's clothing, and Mandel's jewelry store along the way. I looked at some of the items that were on mannequin displays and peering out through the large pane glass windows. Price tags were hanging on some of the shoes and clothing in the window displays, and I began to mentally practice my arithmetic again, adding up the price of some of the tagged articles. A pair of shoes cost three dollars, a shirt cost three dollars, and a blouse cost three dollars.

I mentally pictured 3+3+3 = 9, a multiplication table of 3x3 = 9, and by dividing the total cost of the nine dollars by the number three, each item would again show an individual cost of $3.00. I went one step further thinking about my homework or fraction assignment and calculated that a third of the cost of each item would only be $1.00. It all balanced out, and I said to myself that the Sisters would be happy to know I was putting my arithmetic lessons to work.

I quickly forgot about school and began thinking about playing some street hockey or kick the can with my brother and friends. I knew that my mother would be looking for me to be home by now. I stopped my daydreaming again and started to walk a little faster to get home. I was hoping I did not cause her to worry too much about me. The smell of summer was in the air, and with a few beads of sweat coming from my forehead, I stopped in front of each of the small, quaint, clapboard homes on my street and looked at their starched lace curtains over the windows.

Many a day I would prick my fingers and see small dots of blood coming from them while helping my mother place freshly washed and starched curtains on the curtain holder to dry. Pricking my fingers on this wood fixture also happened when I removed the curtain, which afterward reminded me of a piece of stiff cardboard! I also looked at the various sundrops, phlox, black-eyed Susan, blue violet, and jack-in-the-pulpit flowers in some of the yards. I knelt down and gathered in the smell of fresh roses, lilies of the valley, and the deep purple lilacs in Mrs. Duffy's front yard.

The flowering lilacs were so full and heavy, they sagged and looked as if their branches were going to snap in two. As I smelled the lilacs, Mrs. Duffy came out of her house to sit on her slatted wood porch swing. She asked me if I would like some to take home to my mother. I told her, "Wow, I sure would." Mrs. Duffy grabbed a pair of pruning shears, walked down her old but sturdy wood porch steps, and began the process of snipping off some of the lilacs for me.

I knew my mother would love the lilacs since she only had roses, various stocks, and pansies planted in our yard. As the heavy load of lilacs was placed in my hands, I thanked Mrs. Duffy for them and ran home the rest of the way. Even with all of my daydreaming and stopping at the town bridge, I arrived home only ten minutes late.

The smell of my mother's baking sticky buns permeated the house when I entered. I ran into the kitchen and saw her wrapped in a white apron stitched with colored flowers that she had worked on for hours. She was just beginning to place white icing and chopped pecans on the freshly baked sticky buns. I looked up and said to her, "Here, Mother, these are for you," and handed her the lilacs.

She laid them down on the kitchen table, and with both of her arms, she pulled me close to her and gave me a big hug and several kisses. She told me how relieved she was to see me. She also told me how concerned she was about my being a little late from school, after she heard the whistles blowing to announce the high water and possible flooding. After telling me this, she placed one of her sticky buns in my hand and poured me a glass of Islay's extra-rich chocolate milk.

I carried both of them outside to sit down and eat on the front porch. I finished eating the delicious bun and drinking the savory milk quickly and walked back into the house. While walking into the house, I became aware that the screeching whistles, which had stopped for a while, had begun blowing again. They continued blowing and sending out their screeching sounds for long and short periods of time, and then suddenly the whistles stopped.

I could not believe what I was hearing—or rather, not hearing. After the whistles finally stopped blowing, I ran into the kitchen with a big smile on my face, only to be greeted by my mother rushing toward me crying heavily and saying out loud, "Thank God, thank God."

Her crying and praying did not bother me one bit since the smile on my face and the tears running down her cheeks announced that we both knew the worst was over. The latest whistles signaled that the high water was receding and there would be no flooding in our town. I thought as she was saying this that God had answered my earlier prayers, when I was standing on the bridge and asking him to save the town from flooding.

My mother then placed another one of her still warm sticky buns in my hand and went to the refrigerator to pour me a glass of Isaly's thick chocolate milk. She came back, looked at me, and said, "Here, Barrie, this will help wash it down." Then, with concern and worry reflected in her dear and loving face, she said to me, "Barrie, where are your sisters and brother? They should have been home by now." I pondered over her question and thought that my sisters might be skipping rope in the school yard. I thought Richard might be out looking for some scrap metal pieces or pop bottles to earn some money to buy a ticket for a movie show.

Main bridge crossing over Penn Avenue, 1960s.

Turtle Creek flooding, 1936.

87 Ardmore Streetcar and George's New Deal Restaurant, 1950s.

Isaly's Dairy, 1950s.

CHAPTER 5

PLAYING IN THE WOODS

I woke up very early the day after being released from Saint Colman's for the start of summer vacation. I felt relieved knowing that I was headed to the seventh grade come early September. Earlier in the week, Sister Ruff told me that I had passed and handed me my light blue-colored report card. It was marked with more Cs than anything else, but my parents signed it after giving me a stern lecture and encouraging me to do better in school.

When I returned the signed report card to Sister, she made a comment to the effect that had it been up to her, she would have failed me. Sister had a short fuse when it came to dealing with children in need of discipline, and especially the boys. At times she scolded a lot of us children verbally, but many other times, punishment came from her slapping or pushing hard on one's arms, shoulders, back, and chest or a beating with a wooden paddle.

Paddling disobedient children went on frequently at Saint Colman's, and I must say that for most of the Sisters who had to resort to it, they used light tapping on the buttocks. Frank, a boy a year ahead of me, like most of the boys, had been paddled by Sister Gruff on several occasions. However, there came a day of reckoning when he was going to be disciplined, once again, with the paddle!

He steadfastly refused to follow Sister Gruff's instruction to bend over the back rail of a desk seat. Rather than do this, Frank boldly and defiantly jumped up on the desk seat, screamed out loudly, and said to her, "Go % # # % yourself." The boys and girls in Sister's eighth-grade classroom on that day found a bold, new cuss word for their vocabulary, other than "shit" and "dammit."

My brother, Richard, who was in the classroom that day, told me Sister was so taken aback by this fierce burst of anger and filthy words that she stood in total silence for quite a while. She stopped everything she was doing, put the paddle away, and said nothing to Frank other than, "You take your seat right this minute, young man." Frank casually strolled back to his seat with a slight smile on his face!

Sister never disciplined Frank again with a paddle, no matter how disruptive he was, but continued to use the paddle on other disobedient children. Was it possible Frank was exhibiting signs of ADD/ADHD, not recognizable by anyone?

Frank, like the other eighth graders, was in his final year at Saint Colman's and would soon be moving on to the public school system. The public school system could deal with him a lot better, since many of their teachers were males and some had a known reputation for swinging a hard paddle. They could also fight very well and punch a lot harder! Frank knew about this also and was even provided with the names of those male teachers to be wary of! Because of this awareness, Frank settled down a little, caused fewer disturbances, and eventually graduated from high school.

This incident was never reported to Mother Superior or any of the priests to my knowledge, and a lot of us boys could not understand why. Perhaps it was because Sister did not want anyone to know someone had finally challenged her and won out! One has to wonder if Sister and Frank's encounter that day was the topic of conversation during dinner at the convent house that evening!

I often wonder if Frank ever confessed to the priest that he told Sister to "go % # # % herself." Saying this four-letter word was definitely a mortal sin by all Catholic teachings and would have probably merited the priest assigning several novenas to Frank as penance. My best guess, knowing Frank's personality, was that he never did confess the incident.

His distinct voice, known and recognized by everyone, would have been a dead giveaway during his confession as to who he was, and possibly would have led to more consequences with the priest! On the other hand, Frank was not bashful, and if pushed too much, he just might utter the same four-letter word to the priest and leave the confessional booth very quickly, without making a good act of contrition. I am sad to say during this writing that Frank ended his own life at a young age of 54 and for unexplained reasons.

After rubbing my eyes, yawning, and stretching my arms a little bit, I looked over and saw that Richard was lying next to me sound asleep. I sat up in bed, crawled over, straddled his body, and grabbed him on the top of his shoulders. With both my hands, I began shaking him and screaming in his ear, "Wake up, Rich, wake up, Rich." Groggily he woke up, rubbed his eyes open, looked at me, and with some fear in his voice, asked, "What's wrong?" I answered, "Nothing is wrong." Then excitedly I asked him with a pleading voice, "Do you want to go play in the woods after breakfast?"

He answered by saying, "Yes, but don't ever startle me like this again. If you do, I swear I will punch you in the face." Then he slowly started to sit up in bed alongside of me, yawn loudly, and stretch out his arms. We both stared out of the open window from our top bedroom floor and watched several groundhogs moving about slowly on the grassy green lawn at the rear of our house.

We looked at the multitude of trees dotting the woods across the road. They were so big, and with their summer leaves, they looked like one great big wall of wavy dark green carpeting. There were maple, ash, elder, larch, mulberry, black cherry, American elm, American beech, chestnut, black oak, black locust, black walnut, hickory, spruce, and pine.

As always, we could run and hide in this forest for hours, and no one could ever find us, unless we wanted them to! We could wander through the trees forever and went swimming during the summer months in pools we would dam up with water diverted from the nearby creek. Eddy, one of our classmates at Saint Colman's, had a great swimming hole in the creek nearby. It was just a short walking distance from his house and located off of Thompson Run, behind the old copper mill. In addition, Cocky Hunter's small grocery store with jars full of candy was located close by! Ted Kindler's was another candy store we could also visit.

There were deep pools of water, and the concrete walls built to hold up the railroad trestle above them made great diving platforms to stand on. The rocks around these pools of water had been cleared away long ago. The clearing was probably done years earlier by boys such as ourselves, or possibly even our Irish uncles, Brendan, Vincent, Patrick, and Warren Byrne, who lived on Larimer Avenue, which was also very close to the swimming area.

During the summer months, we would meet up with our friends Joseph, Charles, Robert, Willy, and Vincent, who lived close by us, head into the woods, and play all day. Sometimes the girls who were tomboys, as they were called during days gone by, like Marion, Tootsie, and Hope, would also join us. However, they were never allowed to stay in the woods after dusk. If they did stay, with or without us, and their parents had to come find them, they were not allowed to play again in the woods for quite a while.

Rich and I always took our dog, "Boy," and our Red Ryder BB guns with us. Each of our friends had their own Daisy or Red Ryder BB guns. Today would be no different, except the girls were not told that we would be in the woods. We ate our breakfast, consisting of some scrambled eggs, slab bacon, kielbasa, and toast with homemade grape jelly.

As we hurried to get out of the house, we grabbed the brown bag full of egg sandwiches ladled with Heinz ketchup, salt, and pepper, and wrapped in waxed paper, which our mother had prepared for us. We kissed her good-bye and headed out the front screen door, which was about to fall off, due to the years of rotted wood and unstable hinges. We whistled and called out to our dog. He came running after us, and we headed for the woods.

We walked over to the rented apartments of Willy, Vincent, and Robert and found them eagerly waiting to join us. They stood ready with BB guns in hand and their barrels fully loaded with shiny copper BBs. The front pants pocket of each boy was also laden down, with several spare corrugated paper tubes, each holding one hundred more BBs. A lot of shooting and target practice was always on the agenda when we ventured into the woods.

I remember how difficult it was to unscrew the metal cap from the barrel when I first received my BB gun. I would turn it sideways a little and start pouring in the BBs from the red-colored corrugated paper tube. This tube was about the same size as a paper coin wrapper with fifty pennies inside the holding area. As a beginner, it was difficult performing this task, and when some of the BBs would spill on the ground, the older boys would call me clumsy. This made me real mad and sometimes caused me to begin a pushing and shoving match with them.

It was no fun attempting to retrieve those expensive, shiny, small copper pellets from the dirt, and many of them would become lost forever. You had to collect a lot of empty pop bottles and redeem them at two cents each to buy another roll. After a while, I began watching how the older boys would unscrew the metal cap, open up a pack of BBs, and pour them into their mouths. They would then spit them into the metal holding area without dropping any one of them on the ground.

This is how I began loading my BBs also, and to this day have suffered no ill effects from the copper and oil preservatives applied to them. Over the years, thousands of these BBs would enter and be spit out of my mouth into the foul-tasting steel tube loading chute of the gun.

Farther up the street we went to Joseph and Charles's home, only to find out they were not around and had left earlier to go into the woods. We all assumed we would catch up with them at some of our favorite spots later on.

Before entering the woods, Richard and I would sometimes walk to the rear entrance of the Liberty Meat Market and get a big bone for our dog, Boy. There was always a multitude of leftover meaty bones being thrown away in their galvanized metal garbage cans. If there were no bones here, we could walk across the street and go to the back of the Giant Eagle to look for some.

Meat bones were given away free of charge at the main meat counter if you asked the butcher for some of them with your order. Most people in town made a variety of delicious pots of soup from them, and it helped out financially in serving a large family. As everyone knows, bones are never thrown away anymore and are very expensive; a good large one can cost you as much as a sixteen-ounce Porterhouse steak today.

We wandered into the woods from there and tacked up a white paper target on a large tree trunk. The target had several concentric black circles, and a black dot we called the bull's-eye was in the center of it. We would all take turns shooting at the target from an agreed distance away, and then determined who hit or was the closest to the bull's-eye ; that boy was declared the winner. There were many arguments that took place as to who was the closest to the bull's-eye, especially when two or more BBs split the paper in the same area.

Then we would begin to shoot at beer cans or pop bottles we collected along the way and placed on logs or hung from a tree branch. We were not concerned about the few pennies of deposit they would bring us. One always knew when they hit a can, since it would topple from the explosive force entering, exiting, and tearing up its tin. There was never a question if someone hit a bottle or not, since it exploded and shattered into small pieces immediately from the BB impact. Everyone watched as glass shards flew everywhere and fell to the ground.

Declaring winners was very easy to do when it came to a contest of shooting at cans and bottles. We all mastered this shooting, which I must say we were quite good at. Then we honed our skill by shooting at floating, bobbing bottles or cans drifting by in the swift-flowing whitecap-rippled creek water.

When we turned thirteen years old, the BB guns my brother and I had went away. In their place and after several weeks of our father teaching us about gun safety rules and practice shooting, we took our new Remington, pump-action, .22 caliber rifles with us for target practice.

On the way to the woods, if some of our local policemen were around, we would even stop long enough on the main street to chat with them. The rifles we carried were never questioned by any of them, and because of strict instructions from our father, we always kept them unloaded until we got deep into the woods. Kids doing something like this today, even with an unloaded rifle, would probably become cause to bring out the local police SWAT teams, with their military-looking uniforms and armored personnel carriers, looking for them.

No animals of any kind, except for the sewer rats, would ever be shot or harmed by Richard and me, since the consequences for doing such a bad thing would be a very severe beating from our father. The beating could come from either his razor strap or the homemade cat-o'-nine-tails. In addition to receiving a good beating, we knew the rifles would be taken away and never given back to us.

While in the woods, we would sometimes roast hot dogs and marshmallows over open fires, which we would build out of small, dry, dead tree branches. The roasting was done on the end of a metal clothes hanger, opened up and straightened into a long piece that kept you away from the fire and possibly getting burned. At other times, we would drop potatoes provided by our mothers into the fiery, bright red fire embers, until they became coal black in color and started to crack open.

On occasion, the potatoes would be rolled around in mud beforehand and then thrown into the fire. They would then bake without the skin becoming blackened and crusty on the outside and sometimes becoming unpalatable to eat, because you couldn't get all the mud off. We would play a game before eating the potatoes that consisted of seeing how long someone could juggle a hot potato from the fire back and forth between their hands without dropping it.

None of us boys at an early age had watches during days gone by, so the time would be measured by one or several of the boys calling out one, two, three, four, five, and counting upward until the potato was dropped or fell to the ground. The highest number scored by each individual tossing the potato around in his hands was written in the dirt, and the boy with the highest number in the lot was declared the winner.

There was never a special prize awarded for performing this feat other than knowing and feeling good that he held it the longest. Ties were allowed, but sometimes they had to be settled by the boys tossing another potato into the fire, pulling it out, and juggling it all over again. This was really a great game to play during the winter months, since it also warmed the hands of those of us without gloves and it helped to dry out the gloves of the boys whose families could afford them.

Once in a while, my brother and I would play hooky from church on Sunday to go play around the creek and woods or go on some other adventurous trek. One day while on the way to church, we looked upward into the sky at a small plane going by and decided to play hooky. We spent several hours looking in the woods for a small parachute that was dropped from the plane, which flew a banner advertising the parachute as having a twenty-five-dollar war bond attached to it. This was a unique and eye-catching advertising method used during World War II to sell more war bonds.

Perception is everything, and looking at a floating item coming down from the sky is very tricky. We felt that the parachute was dropped right on top of us as we looked up and saw it swinging back and forth and floating down toward us! However, it was probably several miles away from where we were looking and running to get to it. No matter how long we looked, we never could find it! Maybe someone else who saw it and was a little closer got to it before us. Whoever it was, perhaps they were playing hooky from church also!

During the war and at times as we came out of the woods, many of us boys would walk along the street curbs for several miles looking for and picking up empty cigarette packs. We would then take them back to our club or homes and strip off all the aluminum foil from inside them. After this, the foil would be rolled into golf ball-size balls, and we would sell them by their weight to the junkyard as part of helping out in the war effort. It would be reprocessed and used for containers and packaging of wartime and other materials. At the same time, it helped us buy those eleven-cent show tickets at the Olympic, Rivoli, and Frederick theaters.

As to playing hooky from church, my brother and I always managed to sneak into the back of Saint Colman's Church before going back home and just in time to hear the Gospel being said. We also paid strict attention to see what color vestments the priest was wearing. This was all we needed to know when we arrived back home, in case our parents would ask if we went to Mass. We always said yes, but just in case they asked us what color the priest's vestments were or what the Gospel was all about, we were prepared to tell them.

If we were unlucky in making it to church in time for the Gospel, we always had our Sunday missals to look at and memorize key Gospel words. However, we would have to take a guess as to the color of the priest's vestments.

Skipping church on Sundays or holy days of obligation was a mortal sin at the time, and I always told the priest during my confession when I did not attend.

When asked by the priest, I never got into much discussion as to what caused me to miss church; I generally just told him I was sick. This usually went over pretty well and did not bring about any more questions. I also would ask my friends what priests were hearing confession and the booths they were in, since I did not want to lie to a priest about missing Mass again when he might recognize my voice and the same story.

To this day, I do not know what my brother's excuse might be for playing hooky and missing Mass when I was not with him, but I am sure he came up with a very new, innovative white lie. He could not say he had ringworm, since everyone knew when a child had this. Their heads were shaved, a gentian violet or purple liquid was applied, and a silk-like stocking was stretched over the individual's head afterward! Seeing someone in a getup like this today would make one think that a Brinks armored car robbery was about to take place. Perhaps it might even bring out the local police SWAT team again!

While playing and running through the woods, we would stop and cut strips of bark from the beech trees with our knives and chew on them as if they were gum. The juices hidden under the tree bark and covered from the hot sun would cool a parched mouth when licked. This all sounded dreadful to my classmates Kathleen and Jean when I told them about it at school.

One day I came out of the woods after sneaking into them during afternoon school recess, and I brought them both a small piece of the beech bark I had just freshly cut and convinced them to taste it. Reluctantly, both popped it into their mouths and tried it. To their amazement, they liked it and told me they would get some themselves any time they went into the woods.

I wondered how they would do it, since they did not carry pocketknives like we boys did. It never lost its flavor, even during the winter months when there were no leaves on the tree. They were both glad that day I first brought them the piece of bark that none of the Sisters or priests had seen me leave the school grounds. For sure, if I were caught doing this, it would have merited another trip to the dark horrible cloakroom and, also for sure, a good paddling. Leaving the school grounds without permission was not tolerated, and everyone knew of the severe consequences it would bring!

While away from home, water was never a problem for us boys and girls, since we had several springs we dammed up and drank from while in the woods. There were also some small cascading waterfalls coming down from the steep hillsides. We placed our hands under them and formed a cup to drink the water from. You had to be quick doing this, since the water could escape between your closed fingers quickly. If worse came to worst, we could always sink our knives into just about any tree bark and lick the cool, bitter juice to quench our thirst.

When we went down to the Monongahela River and filled our canteens with its water, before drinking it, we would drop a few water purification tablets, purchased at the local Army/Navy store, into it.

All of our friends left the woods after playing with us all day to go home for their supper, but on this day my brother and I stayed much later. We still had some of our egg sandwiches left to keep us from going hungry and wanted to play some more. We did not know at this time that Marion and Hope were in the woods also and darkness would be upon us all in a short while.

Marion's mother had made sandwiches for the girls to eat for lunch. They took their sandwiches and walked over to Hope's house and sat under the cool grape arbor her father had built years before. When they finished their lunch, they asked if they could go into the woods for a while. Hope's mother told the girls that they were not to go into the woods beyond the tall wooden telephone pole. This pole looked like a giant robot, with all the electrical wires and large metal circuit breaker attached to it and the stretched steel cables holding it in place.

A final word of caution issued to the girls was that they were to be out of the woods before dark and to call out if anything happened or they needed any help. This was the nice thing about where Hope lived; she was close to the woods and within calling distance of her home. This was true, of course, only if she stayed close to the telephone pole, or giant robot as it was called by all of the neighborhood kids.

Both girls wore long-sleeved shirts and dungarees to help them avoid getting any poison ivy on their arms and legs. They both knew what it looked like and avoided it, even when a large vine of tempting big wild blackberries they both liked would be interwoven into it.

They left Hope's house, crossed the street, turned around, and waved good-bye to Hope's mother, who had placed a handled small basket in Hope's hand before she left. Hope and Marion were to use it to put their picked berries and flowers in. They both stepped into the woods and quickly disappeared behind the lush green trees.

While Marion and Hope were entering the woods, my brother and I came out of the woods and stepped on top of the steel railroad tracks to see who could walk the farthest distance without slipping off. This was not hard to do during the summer, but during the winter it was very difficult, especially with frozen ice and snow lying on the bright worn silver tracks.

We sometimes could walk the entire length of the tracks, which was about a quarter mile, with our arms stretched outward to help in our balancing act, and not fall off. Generally, there was also some kind of wager associated with who could stay on the track longer and walk the farther distance. From a distance, we could see the overhead railroad trestle and any approaching trains and would each count the number of boxcars a big black coal-operated locomotive train was pulling as it passed over the trestle.

Looking up at the engineer as the train approached overhead, we both waved our arms up and down in a pulling motion. This was a signal all of the locomotive engineers recognized, and shortly thereafter, they would blow the train whistle several times for us. If in a good mood, on occasion they would even pull the chord to let a few puffs of smoke pop up and out of the coal-fired engine smokestack.

There are no more coal locomotives operating on long distances today except for a few commercial tourist attractions, but kids still look for the engineer to blow that whistle when given the signal. The modern-day version of this request is when children make the same signal to large trucks on the highways.

Most truckers are pretty accommodating and will let out a few blasts from their air horns, except when local ordinances prohibit it or they have done it too much already. If you are a kid or still have a little kid in you, try it sometime, and you may be the lucky one to get a train whistle or trucker's horn blown for you.

Richard and I queried one another as to how many cars we counted that day and could not agree on the number; a big argument took place. I finally agreed that his number was correct, since I did not want him mad at me when I asked him later on that evening if I could read his latest *Superman* and *Batman* comic books.

As Hope and Marion wandered off into the woods, the last thing they heard Hope's mother screaming at them from a distance was for them to be home before it became dark. The small town of Turtle Creek and surrounding areas was so safe during these times that most parents set no time limits on kids. Parents generally would only impose the "before dark," "before nightfall," or "before the streetlights come on" and "behave yourself" rules, which were rarely if ever broken.

Most of the families in the local community knew one another and kept an eye on each other's children when they were playing. Even the local police and firemen knew what child belonged to what family. If they didn't, in such a small town, someone else did in case of an emergency.

Richard and I continued walking along the railroad tracks. We were heading to our favorite concrete wall, next to Cocky Hunter's candy store, situated on the corner of Larimer Avenue and Railroad Street and adjacent to the old copper mill. This concrete wall ran alongside the creek, and was twelve to fifteen feet high and a foot wide at the top. This made it very convenient to place our homemade harpoons on and collect the things we would spear when the creek water was high.

In addition, our dog could not jump up on the protruding portion of the wall from street level and possibly tumble into the water. The wall was located at a strategic point where the creek's rushing water would curve into its high side and bring with it a lot of concentrated debris.

The wall ran along both sides of the creek for fifty yards or more, and if anyone was to fall into it when there was swift running water, they would be pulled under by the swirling current and surely drown. During the time we lived and played in Turtle Creek, I never heard of a single person drowning in the creek.

One time, after throwing our harpoons and spearing pieces of wood for a long time, we became bored. I made a bet with my brother for a Clark candy bar that he could not spear a smaller floating object than me in the next hour. The candy bar would be bought at Ted Kindler's store down the road, and my brother took the bet.

We both began throwing our harpoons that particular day in a very speedy manner until they would stick into something, and then we would pull it in with the attached clothesline rope. We could tell by looking at the large railroad clock hanging on the wall inside Cocky Hunter's candy store when the hour was up. I won the bet by producing a small piece of a two-by-four wood plank lying on the top of the wide flat wall. Richard could produce nothing smaller, and to this day I remember him having to buy me that Clark candy bar, which I gladly shared with him.

We picked up our BB guns and egg sandwiches and went back into the woods, which once were the home of the Delaware Indians, who may have traveled into the valley years ago from Canada. They lived in the natural caves surrounding the valley and hills of Turtle Creek long before any pioneer settlers. The woods provided all the nuts, deer, bear, turkey, rabbit, and squirrel needed for food and clothing. In addition, the creek provided them with fresh fish and meat from the turtles they caught.

There were times we would run through the woods acting as if we were Indians and make bows from the various tree saplings. The moist saplings would bend easily into a half-moon shape, and we secured each notched end with a strong cord, piece of rope, or thin monkey ball vine. Our arrows were made from the saplings also, and sharp stone tips were fastened to the front of them. Feathers dropped by the pigeons living under the railroad trestle were slipped into notched slots at the rear of the arrow and cut open with our Barlow pocketknives.

We learned all of these techniques from seeing a great deal of cowboy and Indian movies at the Olympic, Frederick, and Rivoli theaters. Our training as Boy Scouts with local troop 71 and tests assigned by scoutmaster M. Hahn also helped us a great deal. In addition, our overnight or weekend scouting trips to Camp Twin Echo, in Ligonier, Pennsylvania, also provided us with a great deal of knowledge on how to survive in the woods.

By now, Hope and Marion had been in the woods for several hours and had collected a considerable amount of berries and flowers. It was getting late, dusk was approaching, and they started to walk back home.

As they continued walking through the woods back to Hope's house, they both heard a low whimpering coming from some faraway bushes and stopped to look around. The whimpering sounded like that of a small dog or child crying, and then it turned into a low squealing sound like that of a small dog. Placing a finger across her lips, Hope signaled Marion to be very quiet, and they slowly started to sneak up on the bushes where the sound was coming from. As they got closer to the bush, the squealing sound became louder, and soon they would be directly on top of it.

Although the sound was getting louder now, as they continued to look around, they could see nothing. Hope and Marion became frightened. Marion screamed at the next sound of loud squealing, and Hope dropped the basket she was carrying. They each then picked up a small dead tree sapling, which was common to find in these woods, to protect themselves from whatever horror they were to face. They began poking and moving the branches in front of them back and forth and up and down, to see more and isolate where the sound was coming from.

Suddenly, without warning and shaking fiercely, Marion emitted a bloodcurdling scream several times that scared Hope half to death; she began to scream and cry. Hope's screams and loud crying echoed throughout the woods. I had just found a garter snake and was walking over to show it to Richard, who was busy lying on the ground in front of a little stream he had dammed up with a homemade mud mixture. I laid down my BB gun alongside his as he was watching crayfish enter from the other small streams close by. We were looking at and admiring each other's species when we both heard a loud scream and other noises echoing in the woods.

We were quite familiar with the sound of falling pinecones, dead tree branches, rushing water, and startled deer running away; anything else was abnormal and quite distinctive. Our dog, Boy, began barking loudly after hearing the scream and would not stop until Richard told him to stop the barking. He was an obedient dog and stopped barking immediately, but continued to make a low, growling, whimpering sound as he lay back down and the screaming continued.

Richard jumped to his feet and said to me, "Hey, Barrie, did you hear that?" Just about the time I was going to answer him, there were several more ear-piercing screams and loud crying that echoed through the woods. Boy rose from his heel position and started to bark again loudly, wagging his tail; he instinctively smelled around and looked toward where the sound was coming from. However, he would not run without being told he could go.

I carefully placed the garter snake back on the ground and watched as it skittered away into a grassy area. Richard then quickly opened up his miniature mud dam to free the crayfish. Neither one of us would keep or harm any snakes, birds, or other animals that we saw or found in the woods. I said to Richard, "We should go and try to see what that screaming is all about."

We left our BB guns and remaining egg sandwiches on the ground, and like the Delaware Indians, who lived in the area years ago, ran as fast as we could, with Boy running alongside us, toward the screams and echoing sounds. We were both fascinated with Roy Rogers and Gene Autry movies and would run in these woods for hours, playing cowboys and Indian games and beating our buttocks with our hands, imagining we were riding their horses Trigger and Champion, and yelling for them to run faster. As we took off toward the screams, we both beat our buttocks, only more rapidly this particular day.

Hope became even more scared and began to cry and scream louder with every new scream coming from Marion's mouth, due to the squealing noises. This caused even more unfamiliar sounds to echo throughout the usually quiet, densely populated woods. Marion looked at Hope and said very harshly, "What is wrong with you?" Hope looked back at Marion and said sharply, "There is a big raccoon in here." She forcefully thrust her tree sapling forward and pointed it to the area as she said to Marion, "He has his front paw caught in a metal trap."

Both of them knew nothing about animal traps (raccoons and squirrels are the most rabid animals around) and were afraid of being bitten or scratched by the raccoon if they got any closer to help it. They backed away from the animal; and as they did, with her hands in the air, Hope could see her watch and noticed it was past six o'clock and dusk was approaching.

She thought out loud and said, "I am in big trouble now," realizing that her parents would be looking for her. She and Marion began calling out for help. Then she realized that while looking for the squealing sound, they both had wandered way past the robot area; they could not possibly be heard, and she did not know where they were.

Hope's mother and father started to worry when she and Marion were not home by dusk and began calling both of them by name from the back porch. When no replies came after awhile, they crossed the street and walked over to get closer to the wooded area and began calling out Hope's and Marion's names again. This time they did it even louder. The parents did not know their frightened calls of concern could not be heard since the girls were way beyond the robot.

When it became even darker outside, Hope's parents stopped their calling out to the girls. They turned around and started to run back to their house to call the local police and fire department and report the girls missing. This would mean after the call was taken that the fire department whistles would begin to blow, giving the signal that something was wrong.

It was almost completely dark in the woods by now, with only the moon shining above. But like a small flashlight, the moon still provided enough light to see a little in the slowly darkening woods. The girls were still crying and calling out for help when my brother and I began yelling out, "Who are you? Who are you?" The girls continued to scream out loud, intermittently saying, "We are Hope and Marion."

Sensing we were close but still could not make out what the voices were saying, Richard, I, and the dog changed our pattern of running and zigzagged through the trees, taking shortcuts to reach the sounds more quickly. As we ran through the woods still beating our buttocks, we could now hear and identify the voices as those of girls getting closer. We started to yell out, "We hear you, and will be there soon."

We were to learn later that the girls did not know who was doing the yelling, but it offered them some relief to know help was on the way. Huffing and puffing and gasping for air, Richard and I suddenly appeared out of nowhere and came face-to-face with Hope and Marion. These two girls, who were what I would call your typical tomboy girls of the era, were neighbors and good school friends, even though Marion attended the public school.

I stopped quickly. While still breathing heavily, I looked up and said, "What the hell is going on with you two? What are you doing in the woods this late at night? This is a very stupid thing you are doing. Both of you are going to be in big trouble when your parents get hold of you." I said this because I was very afraid that they both might get a good beating.

Hope ran up to me and said, "Dammit, do not scold me. I already know I am in big trouble, and you do not have to remind me of it." She barked out at Richard and me, "This is not our fault; you are the stupid ones," and she pointed the sapling still in her hand straight ahead of her at a bush. She said, "I will show both of you why we are still in the woods."

I backed off and asked Hope where she had learned to swear like that, and she said back to me, "In the Catholic school playground, just like you."

I looked at her in amazement and said, "I hope you are going to tell the priest about using such filthy language during confession next week." I then said, "Father will probably have you say a couple decades of the rosary when he hears your whole story."

Hope thought about all the Our Fathers and Hail Marys she might have to say, looked at me, and said, "I will if you will." I said okay, and she said, "Swear to God." More brainwashing?

With the sapling stick still clutched in her hand, Hope moved the bush aside again to show both my brother and me the trapped raccoon. Due to all the yelling, talking, scolding, and swearing going on among the four of us, we had not heard the raccoon's cry for help. Because of our knowledge of the woods, animals, and traps, my brother and I knew what to do to try and help the poor animal.

We still had a little moonlight to work with and had to do something quickly since soon it would be completely dark. Richard walked up to the front of the bush, and after getting close to the raccoon and taking a better look at it, he said to me, "This is a muskrat trap, and I will need your help to get the raccoon's paw released from it." He asked me to take off my shirt and cover the raccoon's head and mouth to keep him from possibly getting bit.

The animal seemed to be in great agony, and I could not blame him for feeling this way. I did what Richard asked without question, leaned forward, and carefully wrapped the shirt firmly around the raccoon's head. Funny how brothers sometimes cannot get along together, but this was not the case with us. Trying to impress the girls was also a factor, and we were quick to cooperate with one another.

The girls watched, and both of them suddenly said, "Don't hurt it."

Richard looked up at them, glared, and said, "Don't worry, dammit, I know what the hell I am doing! Both of you need to keep your big mouths shut." Richard reached over and grabbed the raccoon's free leg and held it gently in his right hand.

Skillfully with his left hand, he started to ease a stick into the middle of the trap jaws. He partly opened the butterfly steel bars on each side of the trap. Then he carefully opened the trap enough to stand up and get some balance. Once he was upright, he placed his heavy high-top clodhopper shoe on the dual butterfly pieces, to hold them down and free the raccoon's trapped paw.

When Richard removed his foot from the spring trap, you could hear the loud sound and clang of the metal bars snapping back together. From what he could see, the raccoon's paw was not broken or bleeding badly. He would be a little sore for a while, but he would be all right. Richard gently set the raccoon down on the ground, pulled the shirt away, and watched it limp off. Suddenly the raccoon stopped dead in its tracks, turned around, and looked back at all of us as if to say thanks. Then he quickly disappeared into the thick underbrush.

Jokingly I said, "Lucky for him that it was a muskrat trap; anything bigger, and his leg would have been broken and he would not have a leg to run on." I then said to Hope and Marion, "Come on, you two, we have to get moving while we have a little light left and get you out of here and home quickly."

Hope looked at me and said, "We are so happy to see you both, and I am sorry I swore at you."

I looked at Hope and said to her quietly, "Forget it, let's get going." Knowing where we were and with a little moonlight still remaining, we asked the girls to grab onto our hands, hold on tight, and follow us through the woods.

We all, including Boy, then started running toward where the road was, in the direction of Hope's house. As she was running, Hope looked up and could see the top of the robot and jubilantly began screaming and calling out for help. The barking coming from our dog could also be heard echoing through the woods. She smiled, knowing her parents would be looking for her.

Her parents heard the calls for help and the barking dog. With tears in their eyes, they turned away from running toward their home to call the police and fire department and ran to the edge of the woods. As they got there, they almost collided head-on with my brother, me, and our dog. We emerged from the woods with Hope and Marion close behind us.

With tears in her eyes, Hope's mother kept saying, "Thank God, thank God, you are all right." After she regained her composure, Hope's mother began to scold her and told her she was in big trouble. She asked why Hope and Marion were late and what they were doing in the woods, and with boys.

She even threatened to take Hope to see the priest on Monday to discuss the matter even more. Being taken to see the priest during days gone by was the last attempt at straightening out a boy or girl from doing wrong. If the priest could not influence you to behave or do what was right, nobody could. I myself, after having to talk with a priest on several occasions, can only describe it as "a giant verbal exorcism." It was like you were automatically condemned to hell if he could not help.

I saw children beg, plead, and even cry out loud that they would behave and listen, when this threat was presented to them by Sisters or parents while attending Catholic school. It appeared as if this were the last straw toward salvation for some of us. Hope's father said he was not pleased with her not returning home on time, and he was also mad that she was in the woods with me and my brother. Today I, as a concerned parent, would probably be asking my own daughter the same question if she had been in the woods with a couple of boys. Perhaps even more harshly!

Hope started to explain and tell her father that she had not planned on this chance meeting with me and my brother, but her father interrupted and told her to keep quiet and not say another word. Richard and I did not say another word either, for fear it would make matters worse for her. Hope's mother spoke up and said she would talk to Marion's parents and let them know what happened. Then she said it would be best if Marion and Hope did not see one another for a while except for school.

Marion took a deep breath and told Hope's parents that she was sorry for what happened. Then to herself she mumbled very low, "My parents will understand and be a lot nicer about all this. In addition, being a Protestant, I get to escape the threat of being put through the priest's scary exorcism ritual and being sent straight to hell."

Since she was already in trouble and had nothing to lose, in defiance, Hope started to cry and began talking back. She blurted out to her mother and father, "Why don't you just listen to me for one minute and let me explain what happened? You both want to start punishing me for something you know nothing about. I wish I were dead and had never come out of the woods."

These words startled and astonished both of her parents. Her mother quickly apologized and said, "It is all right, dear. Hope, please stop crying, and why don't you go ahead and tell us what you have to say."

Hope, still crying hard, wiped at her eyes with the backside of her hands to clear the tears running down her cheeks. Then she started to explain and tell her parents, especially her father, in detail what had happened. She related to them how my brother and I and our dog Boy found and helped her and Marion to safety after we saved the raccoon.

Hope's father mumbled something to himself that no one could understand, and her mother said to Hope, "Do you have anything else to say?"

Hope's father, feeling somewhat left out of the conversation going on between them, blurted out for everyone to hear, "C'mon, let's get going. I am not going to stand around here all night talking about this terrible incident."

Totally ignoring her father's harsh and non-sympathetic comment, Hope looked up at her mother and said, "Yes, Mother, I do."

"While Marion and I were looking for the whimpering and squealing noises in the woods, I became frightened. I dropped and lost the good basket you gave me."

Her mother looked at Hope and said, "Let's not worry about that now." Then she took her hand and squeezed it gently, saying, "I love you, and I am so glad you are safe and unharmed."

The parents, especially Hope's mother, then thanked my brother and me for our help and protecting them.

Hope looked over at Richard and me as we followed them, and she turned around and said to us, "Thanks again. I will see both of you in Saint Colman's school yard on Monday morning. I am going to tell Father Shields about how nice you were and how you helped get Marion and me out of the woods safe and sound."

Perhaps Hope felt that we had broken some infraction of the school rules during the early part of the week or dropped a few church rails down too hard, and this might make it go easier on us. Hope probably made a mental note to also tell the priest about her swearing today during her confession next week.

Hope's mother looked at Marion and said to her, "As soon as we get home, you both can have some ice-cold watermelon. When you are finished, I will drive you to your home and explain to your parents why you are so late."

After being gone all day, my brother and I and our dog arrived home shortly after leaving Hope's house in the pitch darkness of night.

Unconcerned, knowing she had good boys, our mother was glad to see us both back home safe and sound. She never did ask where we were for so long and what we had done all day. After taking a hot bath, eating a big kielbasa sandwich, and reading a few *Captain Marvel* and *Spider-Man* comic books, we went to our bedroom with our dog.

We both knelt down by the side of our bed, each making the sign of the cross and saying our individual prayers in silence. We then made a good act of contrition and jumped up into the bed. Resting comfortably, we discussed the things that had taken place during the day. We were both almost asleep when Richard suddenly blurted out to me loudly, "Hey, Barrie, we were just as dumb as Hope. We forgot and left our BB guns and the rest of our egg sandwiches in the woods. We will have to go get them tomorrow after we attend Mass."

I did not reply, pretending to be asleep, and with a slight giggle said to myself, "I wonder what color the priest's vestments will be and what the Gospel will be about." Then I told myself silently, "If we do not make it to church to hear it, we can bone up and read passages of it from our missal."

Richard fell fast asleep, and by this time, I guessed that both Hope and Marion were probably sound asleep also.

Hope cleaned up the kitchen for her mother before going upstairs to wash and go to bed. She said good night to her father, who did not reply and was busy listening to a Pirates baseball game. In the background, you could hear the sports announcer, Rosey Rosewell, yelling over the microphone, "Open the window, Aunt Minnie, here it comes!" This was his unique way of saying that a Pirates batter had just hit a home run.

It was apparent at this point that Hope was being ignored and was not going to get a beating tonight from her father, since all of his attention was now focused on the Pirates game. "Thank God," she said very quietly as she continued walking up the stairs to her bedroom. Entering her room, Hope knelt down by her bed and made the sign of the cross.

Then she said her evening prayers, made her good act of contrition, and jumped into bed. While lying there in silence and since she had forgotten about it, she told us later that she said one last prayer for Richard and me, for all of our help that day, and asked God to watch over us and Boy.

Hope closed her eyes and said to herself, "If I do not see or get to talk to them in class on Monday, I know for sure I will see and be able to talk to them in the school yard during recess."

Cocky Hunter's Larimer Avenue store, 1950s.

CHAPTER 6

ETHNIC FOOD FEAST/SEPARATE PLAY FACILITY

Attending school at Saint Colman's was great from an educational, religious, social, and playtime gathering standpoint. There was one drawback, however, and that was not having an enclosed facility to play in during harsh weather conditions. I often wondered why the public school had such a facility and we did not. All the major physical activities that any of us kids wanted to participate in were accomplished in the school yard. They had to be done during the harshest days of winter as well as the days it rained or snowed.

There also was no air-conditioning at the school, which would have made it bearable to stay inside during those hot and humid days. Each child made a choice to go out and brave the elements in the school yard or stay in their classrooms during recess periods. At times, depending on the severity of the weather, Mother Superior would make the call if we would be allowed to go out into the school yard or not. If we could not go outside, some of us went to the small lunchroom, and others stayed in their classroom to eat their bagged or lunch-box meal.

The other factor was that most of the children during the winter months or cold season did not have a lot of protective rain gear and winter clothing. Their parents just could not afford to buy such gear that would have allowed them to play outside. Many of the children did not have boots, heavy hats, scarves, and wool or leather gloves. Some children would wear old and heavy, worn-out socks on their hands as gloves during the winter to offer some relief from the cold. One has to remember that a lot of the children's parents were just beginning to get a new start on life after emerging from the Great Depression.

There was no cafeteria at Saint Colman's school where hot meals or even cold sandwiches could be purchased. Milk in a small glass container was provided free to those children who could not afford it. It was also available for those lucky students who could pay and buy it. You either went home for lunch if you lived close by, or you ate your lunch from a brown paper bag that your parents made up. You had to use it over and over many times before you would get a new bag.

One can only imagine that during hard times, children were scolded harshly for losing or forgetting to bring this used bag back home. Some children had the luxury of a tin lunch box, which came in all shapes, sizes, colors, and your favorite Disney or some other cartoon character boldly painted on its outside cover. The lunch boxes also contained a separate thermos for the drink of your choice. Hot chocolate was the wintertime favorite, and Kool-Aid was preferred on warmer days by many of the children.

To my knowledge and being able to observe what was being eaten by the children, tuna fish sandwiches for lunch were not very popular at Saint Colman's. This was even true on Fridays and holy days, when eating meat was forbidden and considered a mortal sin. The majority of lunches contained sandwiches wrapped in wax paper and made of peanut butter and jelly or plain apple butter. At times, sandwiches would also be made up from a mixture of baloney and crushed pickles and called "ham salad." There were also a lot of plain baloney, cheese, and egg sandwiches.

Some children during lunch break, as they do today, would share or exchange a bite of their sandwich for a bite of someone else's sandwich. This meant a sampling of other ethnic food varieties would begin. When the children did not go home for lunch, they could savor tasting Paul, Joseph, Charles, Carmen, and Pappy's Italian salami, sausage, *capacola*, provolone, and cheese sandwiches or a dessert-like waffle called a *pizzelle*. They even had tiny or small peppers at times that were marinated in olive oil and somewhat similar to the pepperoncini of today.

Joseph and Charles's mother, Rose, would also pack them cold pasta shells filled with red sauce and a white cheese and her homemade pizza for lunch. This was a time when pizza was unheard of in a restaurant; it wasn't even a well-known word. Microwaves were nonexistent to quickly warm up a slice of pizza, but this did not matter since everyone loved to get a taste of this unique, thick piece of crusty, baked, garlicky, sauce-flavored dough.

Mary Louise would generally bring either egg or peanut butter and jelly sandwiches when she ate in. Ronald, Timothy, Audrey, Bernadette, Jean, Kathleen, and Mary Ellen would share their crackers and Irish cheeses. Some children at times even brought in cold, baked or boiled potatoes with the skin still on. Other children sometimes would bring only mayonnaise; ketchup, or sugar-buttered bread and boiled or corned beef sandwiches. Lillian would share her Polish kielbasa, pickled pigs' feet, buckwheat and blood sausage, black forest ham, and dill pickles.

Richard and I would share our egg, onion and bell pepper, ham, kielbasa, and pork sandwiches, cold potato pancakes, pierogi, and homemade poppy seed and nut rolls. Buddy would have his German sandwich layered with salami or braunschweiger and various cheeses and homemade potato chips. There was not a big population of American Indian, Middle Eastern, Asian, African American, or Hispanic cultures present in the town. Because of this, we never had the opportunity to taste some of their great ethnic and cultural dishes we see being served today.

As described earlier, the school's population was made up primarily of European Irish, Slavic, Italian, and German descendants. When my brother, sisters, and I went home for lunch during each of the eight years we went to Saint Colman's, we ate nothing but maple rolls from O'Neill's bakery and drank nothing but chocolate milk from Isaly's. Think about it, eight solid years of having nothing for lunch except maple rolls and chocolate milk, and no complaints from any of us. I am sure all that sugar content did, however, make us a little hyper during and after school.

Thomas would share his Greek mixed black olive and feta cheese sandwich and small homemade sausages that looked like today's packaged Slim Jims. This ethnic food exchange sounds all well and good, but sometimes, while the day's tasting was taking place in the small auditorium, there was an awful lot of yuks, gagging, and gurgling sounds that could be heard coming from the mouths of some of the children.

This was a precursor to the children quickly showing their dislike of someone else's food by deliberately spitting it out, either at you, on the floor, or on the table you were sitting at. One had better not let the policing priests or Sisters see this display of manners, or it would be off to the cloakroom for the guilty party—and maybe Sister following close behind with paddle in hand.

The breakfasts that were eaten by many of the children at home, before going to school, consisted of cut slab bacon, eggs, home fries, oatmeal, pancakes, waffles, and even coffee soup for some. This coffee soup consisted of bread being broken into chunks and placed into a bowl. Leftover coffee and canned milk was then warmed up and poured over the bread. Heaps of sugar was then added to each child's delight to make it more tasteful and enjoyable to eat. After consuming this breakfast, one could say we were hyper wired for the day, and unknowingly, it probably caused our being disruptive at times and making it hard on Sister.

Toast came browned or lightly browned direct from the hot oven racks and was either store-bought white slices of bread or made from homemade bread or buns that Mom baked. To butter the toast, children would delight in mixing the orange and white colors of dye together. They were provided in every margarine carton to make a golden color out of their margarine spread. Some kids even preferred to eat the plain vanilla-looking margarine. When the U.S Steel Mill and Westinghouse workers went out on their strikes, which seemed like it was all the time, some children did not get three meals a day. The meals and lunches they did get were very skimpy.

If you had a note from your parents and the Sisters gave their permission, you could leave the school grounds and go to the nearby G. C. Murphy five-and-ten during lunch period. Those lucky enough to go there could buy a candy bar, a small bag of mixed candy, or a bag of popcorn. A bottle of Mission Orange or some other cool soda of one's liking could be purchased for just five cents. As a general rule, it was just the candy we children bought. Generally we kids could do our shopping very quickly, get back into the school yard, and begin playing our various games of fun and excitement.

While the girls were skipping rope even in the dead of winter or the boys were playing softball, you could always hear some of the children saying how nice it would be to play indoors. Many of us would often comment or dream about having a separate play facility or gymnasium someday at Saint Colman's. One with indoor heating, lockers, dressing rooms, and showers that would keep us away from the outside elements of rain, winter snow, summer heat, and summer's humid days.

Perhaps, maybe even a little dancing would have been allowed for us young, innocent, and naïve "children of God." But due to the ever-present "temptation of sin" and the thought of boys and girls being allowed to "wrap their arms around one another," I do not believe it would have been allowed. The mere thought of a boy's and girl's body coming in contact with one another, during this age of innocence, would have raised quite a few priests' and Sisters' eyebrows. However, the Catholic Church is much more modernized today, and attitudes have changed such that dancing with supervision is allowed in the elementary schools.

Think about it, as we often did, about having a large place where all the pushing, shoving, fighting, scuffling, screaming children and Sisters cooped up together, several hours a day, could have been avoided. How wonderful it would have been to put the children in an enclosed area for some physical activity and energy release. The Penn Avenue elementary public school had such a facility, and even allowed the older children in the upper grades to dance with one another. How wonderful it would have been to play many of our school-yard games indoor during inclement weather.

Saint Colman's had a male basketball team at the seventh—and eighth-grade levels, along with a small group of cheerleaders, but they had to do their practicing and play any games in the local Westinghouse Electric gymnasium. This provided some form of entertainment and relaxation for the players and any Saint Colman's students who could make it to the Friday after-school basketball games. Religious training was a dominant factor from the first grade, and it was the hope and wish of most of the priests and Sisters that through their religious teachings, a good percentage of the boys would go on to the seminary and become priests and the girls would enter the convent to become Sisters.

Perhaps it may have been believed by the diocese that such a facility would become the center of attraction for the children, rather than their praying, being in church, and paying more attention to God. Even though it was one of the richest parishes in the Pittsburgh diocese, it just was not meant to be; and Saint Colman's never did get around to building this much-needed separate facility for us children.

When the children at Saint Colman's got out of hand, which was almost constantly, we were told by the Sisters that we were too antsy, had too much exuberance or too much energy, were hard to settle down, or were too rambunctious. By today's psychological, psychiatric, and medically known norms, all estimated 320 children at all grade levels, and quite possibly the Sisters too, would have been classified as having attention deficit disorder (ADD) or attention deficit hyperactive disorder (ADHD). We would have been placed on Ritalin, Prozac, Zoloft, or some other medication to slow us down a bit.

This statement is my opinion only, and I acknowledge that I do not have any training, experience, working knowledge, or insight into these professions. In addition, I am positive that some good has come for some individuals from these medications and the help of the professionals mentioned above. Also, my thoughts are not meant to mock or demonize the fine work that has been accomplished by the Catholic priests and Sisters, but it is just the way it was during the period of days gone by. We were young, energetic children, full of life and enjoying ourselves to the fullest.

This same type of hyperactivity that I address today as "having a wonderful time with your friends" was also present with the public schoolchildren. I believe a statistical study of the children who graduated from both the public schools and Saint Colman's during days gone by and are still living today, would show that the majority of them are well balanced, have made a great contribution to society, and are very happy.

So, the big question one might ask, since we children at Saint Colman's never did get this separate indoor play facility, is "What did you do to release all of this pent-up youthful energy?" The answer is very simple: come hot sun, rain, or snow, we all went to the school yard for physical activity and to play games before school started, during recess, and after school.

CHAPTER 7

THE SCHOOL YARD AND GAMES

Saint Colman's school yard was surrounded by Osborne, Railroad, and Hunter Streets, with a few alleys scattered in between them, and it was a city of activity unto itself. It had its high, steel gray-colored cyclone fencing in some areas, granite walls and bricks in other areas, and concrete poured on the ground everywhere. Except for the visibility of the church towers, an outsider not familiar with what it was, might look at it as some kind of an enclosed correctional facility.

The church, school, and parish house also provided additional fencing barriers to keep the children in and the general public out. During early morning arrival at school, recesses, and even after school, there would be a group of boys and girls playing and talking or screaming out loud to one another everywhere. Another group of children would be made up of all girls, and another group would be made up of all boys.

Just like today, during days gone by, there was a clique or elite group of kids that hung out together that a lot of other children wanted to play or be closely associated with. Some of these children were even anxious to play with the kids who were the first and most likely to break the school rules. Each group of children would play their choice of games and be watched by late-arriving students, hoping someone would drop out of a game so they could replace him or her and join in the game.

No matter what physical game was being played, even if it was skip rope by the girls, it always ended with someone leaving hurt, scratched, and bleeding from falling down on nothing but the solid concrete school yard. Banging into the terra-cotta brick or Indiana and Cleveland blue stone trimmings around the church and school was no fun either. Not a blade of grass or bit of dirt existed to cushion the human body parts when someone fell down.

There was no grass or Astroturf as dominates professional sport stadiums today to save your knees and elbows from becoming scarred. In addition, there was no protective padding on each child or placed over the terra-cotta bricks or granite trimming, as you see in professional athletic stadiums today. Why, even the goalposts are padded to prevent harm to an individual who may come in contact with them accidentally. These additional measures would have helped a lot of Saint Colman's schoolchildren avoid injury when they were chasing a hard-hit fly softball or catching a pass from a paper football and fell or slammed into obstacles.

None of these protective devices were available at Saint Colman's, and everyone took their chances regarding possible and severe body injury. The bricks and granite were like the concrete in the yard, which just loved to tear your body apart, make you bleed, and provide deep scars on your body for the rest of your life. The casualties of the games, both boys and girls, being played and the ever-attacking concrete, bricks, and stone would have to go to the public school nurse to have their wounds looked at, cleaned. and bandaged as necessary. If you felt sick, had a fever, or just plain wanted to use it as an excuse to get out of a Saint Colman's classroom for a while, you went to see the public school nurse. I never could understand why children from a Catholic school were being treated at a public school!

When the injury or sickness was really bad, most of the children at Saint Colman's went to see Doctor Perry or Doctor Mennen. As I think back, I say to myself, perhaps Saint Colman's provided a dollar stipend of some sort to the public school for their costs associated with looking after us when we got injured or sick, but I doubt it.

Try sending a student from a Catholic institution to a public school today for any type of medical assistance, and you would have more lawyers filing suits and converging around the school than the losing fans of a European soccer team. We are addressing the separation of church and government here! Controversy exists even today regarding allowing parents of private and parochial schools to receive government educational vouchers!

In just about all of the games started by the boys, how they selected their teams was decided with a baseball bat. No, it is not what you are thinking; physical extortion or beating someone up with a bat was the last thing someone would do at Saint Colman's! The bat would be tossed up in the air by one boy to another boy, and the recipient could only catch it with one hand. From this point, the catcher of the bat would wrap his hand around it. Then they would alternately place their hand around it.

This process could go on several times, until one of them could no longer get at least two fingers around the top of the knobby end, as it was called. When this happened, you lost the first pick, or choice of a player to start on your team. Naturally, the winner would always pick the best runner, hitter, jumper, catcher, fielder, strongest, biggest, tallest, and so on, to ensure his chances of winning whatever the game being picked up was.

The boys' favorite game was softball, since baseball was not allowed at Saint Colman's (reading on you will find out why). The next favorite was football, and the ball was fashioned from a piece of old or used *Sun Telegraph, Post Gazette, Independent, Braddock Free Press,* or *Pittsburgh Press* newspaper. This "no-cost" football was rolled into a four—to six-inch diameter, was about eight inches long, and was tied tightly all around with Liberty Meat Market butcher string to hold it together

The number three game was called pump, pump, pullaway, and the number four game was called "buckety buck, how many fingers are up?" (I'll describe these below.)

Very few of the boys when I attended school at Saint Colman's could afford a real pigskin football, and fielding a ball while playing softball was done with your bare hands. In lieu of a bat, if one was not available, the first pickup choice could be decided with a toss of fingers being thrown out simultaneously by two boys, both yelling out odd or even.

If you threw out two fingers and yelled "even" and your opponent threw out two fingers and yelled "odd," you won first pick, or choice, of a player. At the same time, without knowing it, you were practicing your arithmetic with all of these numbers being calculated.

Yes, believe it or not, there were severe arguments that took place as to what the total fingers thrown out were and whether it resulted in an odd or even count. All even or odd number ties would result in the boy's fingers having to be thrown out again. The use of the fingers to pick teams or players was used more frequently by the girls, even though all of them were also very good at selecting team members by using the "bat" process.

Softball games had no definite innings during recess due to limited time, and whatever team had the most runs when the school bell rang to end recess won the game. Perimeters, baselines, and base locations were scribed into the concrete with a piece of white chalk. The piece of chalk was most likely carefully taken by one of the boys from a blackboard wooden ledge when Sister was not looking.

Getting caught "stealing" chalk, as Sister would call it, was not looked upon lightly and could result in having to stay after school. The wastepaper cans never ceased having to be emptied, along with the erasers needing to be dusted and cleaned, which was often a fitting punishment. There also was the option for Sister to just place the guilty parties in the cloakroom for a period of time.

The same rules and chalk-line markings were applied for a game of football, and there were no quarters like one would expect in a regular football game. The team having the most points when the school bell rang ending recess won. At times, and especially if the game were tied, the boys would just ignore the ringing bell, since one more swing of the bat or throwing of the football could result in another run being scored or a touchdown needed to win the game.

Richard, Willy, Carmen, Buddy, and Pappy were generally the first picks to be on someone's team, since they were the only ones who could hit the softball over the cyclone fence, which was a sure home run. This was because you were not allowed to open the gate and leave the school-yard grounds to retrieve the ball. On occasion and if the outfielder knew a Sister or a priest was not around and watching, he might take a chance on opening the small hinged gate. Then he would sneak out to retrieve the ball and lob it over the fence and hopefully limit the bases the batter would reach or prevent him from scoring.

If you were the pitcher during a game of softball and the batter did not like the pitches you were throwing, you better watch out, since you could find him throwing the bat at you and trying to break both of your legs. There were many terrible incidents where some of the guys, after being hit with a bat they could not dodge, thought their arms or legs were broken. Aside from a few bruises, bumps swelling up on the shins, crying or moaning, and groaning, everyone survived our Saint Colman softball games with no broken limbs.

The most seriously injured player I ever saw was Jimmy. After Richard threw his bat and hit him in both lower legs, Jimmy fell down on the concrete crying and rolling all around. He was lucky this day, survived the incident with nothing being broken, and got up and walked away limping. Richard did not like the way Jimmy was pitching the ball to him and kept telling him to keep it low. When Jimmy kept throwing the ball too high, Richard suddenly threw the bat at him and scored a direct hit on his legs.

Sometimes when a batter got a base hit and it looked like runs would score, the person catching or stopping the ball would not throw it to a baseman, shortstop, or catcher as done in a normal game. Rather, he would aim and throw the ball as hard as he could directly at the runner, hoping to hit the runner in the back or head to stop him from reaching base or scoring. If the ball did hit someone and he fell down on the concrete without reaching base and was hurt or crying, it did not matter and he was still tagged out.

At times, a well-hit ball would work its way over the school-yard cyclone fence and travel far enough to smash through one of the windows of the Knee funeral home. The funeral home was located on the corner of Larimer Avenue and Osborne Street and sat directly across from the school and church yard. When this happened, Mr. Knee or one of his employees would return the ball to the policing school-yard priest or Sister, requesting that the children be more careful.

The Knee family was Irish Catholics and received the embalming and burial business of just about all the Catholic families in town and the surrounding communities. Since they were prudent businesspeople, broken windows were tolerated to some extent.

Baseballs were much smaller and harder than softballs. They could travel faster, go farther, and cause more damage to bodies and windows even farther away than the Knee funeral home. This is why baseball was forbidden to be played anywhere in the school yard at Saint Colman's. Strange as it may seem and to my recollection, no one was ever sent to the cloakroom or paddled over a broken window. This applied even to those school windows broken by a foul tip or a poorly thrown ball. However, the ball was always confiscated by the policing Sister when this happened and ultimately returned.

Softballs were not very plentiful during this time, and again, few boys could afford to buy a new one, since most of the children at Saint Colman's came from very poor, low-income and depression era families with little formal education. However, there was some children whose parents were considered blue-collar workers and, as such, did have better educations or own a local business.

I do not recall where the balls we played with came from, since Saint Colman's provided us with nothing in the way of sporting gear. The ball could have been found somewhere by one of the boys, donated by the VFW, given to the school by another kind benefactor or civic organization, or possibly even stolen from the five-and-ten by one of the boys.

I would have to rule out Carmen, Buddy, Marty, Paul, Richard, and Pappy, who were altar boys, from ever doing something like this. Eshman's hardware and sporting goods store located on Penn Avenue was also very close to the school, and it is possible this is where some of the balls came from. This was the store several of the boys would visit on occasion to buy fishing equipment, and a ball could have been taken without paying for it then. The only person who might know if the ball were stolen would be the priest after hearing about it during confession.

I often wonder how many Our Fathers and Hail Marys someone would have had to say for penance to square things right with God over a softball. Depending on the mood of the Sisters, it could take several days for the softball that was confiscated to be returned, but not without a lecture from the Sister or priest returning the ball. When it took too long to get the ball back from a Sister, many of us boys would beg and plead with the priests to intercede and have a talk with Sister to have it returned.

At times, the priest would bargain and strike up a deal to have it returned by making the boys promise to go to confession on Friday and attend Mass on Sunday and receive communion. Even the boys who were not party to breaking the window would always agree with whatever the priest wanted us to do. Anything to get that ball back for school-yard play; that was all we cared about at the time.

The priest was always emphatic about receiving communion. Since he could see faces as the boys knelt down in front of him at the altar rail, you always had to be prepared for his knowing the truth. If you did not go to Mass or receive communion on Sunday and he asked where you had been, you could always say you went to twelve o'clock Mass or some other Mass you knew he did not say. The other agreement we made also may or may not have been kept. It seemed as if the priests had the ultimate power and authority to convince the Sisters to return the ball. After talking to the priests for a while and shortly thereafter, we got the ball back—and another lecture about being careful and not to break any more windows from the Sister returning the ball.

Now we can move on to a football game as it was played in the school yard at Saint Colman's. The game was played with a regulation eleven-squad team on each side, and the rules were simple. To avoid harm and falling on the concrete whether by running or passing the ball, any play was completed when the offensive player was "touched" by a defensive player. How quickly this short and simple word of "touch" became ignored; one has to remember that we had no such thing as a referee.

During the first couple of plays, the made-up rules were obeyed; but shortly thereafter and with no protective padding, it turned into something more like a rugby game. With each play, physical tackling around the legs, head, and upper body increased. Shirts were often torn to pieces and trousers ripped apart. Tripping someone carrying the ball with your clodhopper shoes to stop them during a long run or when they were about to score a touchdown was also very common.

Plays being called by Paul or Carmen went something like this. "Jimmy, I am going to throw you a pass, and I want you to run deep and to the right and cut over in front of the small altar boy sacristy to receive it, To distract where the ball might be thrown, I want Buddy to run to the left and alongside the chain-link fence."

The next play could involve a pass being thrown to someone in front of the large altar boy sacristy. Another pass play would have the runner going deep and cutting in front of the Sisters' chapel area. These were all dangerous plays, since they often left the runner smashing into the terra-cotta brick-and-stone facing. Other passing plays involved running straight down the middle of the concrete school yard to receive a short pass and being pummeled to the ground, whether you caught the ball or not.

Long passes could have the runner going straight ahead and deep and smashing into the cyclone fencing at the end of the school yard. You cannot imagine how much it hurt when you ran or were pushed into this steel curtain barrier. As rough and hazardous as it may seem, runners involved in these passing plays were not hurt nearly as much as someone taking a handoff and running with the ball in his arms.

A handoff to Eddy, Pappy, Jimmy, or Buddy and their sweeping to the left or right would find them with not only the defensive players on top of them, but several of the offensive players also, who were trying to pull them up to continue running.

During these days, the Statue of Liberty play was called quite often, and the runner taking the ball was pummeled to the ground very quickly. He could then wind up being punched and kicked in the body by several pairs of clodhoppers. All football plays usually ended up with a person lying on the school-yard concrete, which loved to tear your skin apart and hurt and scar you badly. Sometimes there could even be double jeopardy during a play, since after getting hurt running, you could also get hurt bouncing off of that brick-and-stone facing.

The person or persons lying on the concrete school yard, possibly with cut elbows, knees, chins, lips, foreheads, and bloody noses, would be swearing and saying things like "dammit" or "you son of a bitch, get off of me"—or even "I am going to get even and kill you when I get up." Yes, even Catholic schoolchildren promised to violate their teachings and the first commandment.

This is another saying that would not be tolerated today at most schools under the zero tolerance policy, and the child caught saying it would probably end up with a suspension or prosecution under some terrorist act. Hey, in my opinion, this might be a lot easier than a stint in the evil cloakroom and a paddling from Sister.

There were even real serious or big-time threats coming out of the mouths of crying boys, like "I'm going to tell your mother on you." Big deal, like your mother would do something about it. Yes, there was some swearing that took place even by a few of the "good" altar boys, who had a stigma attached to them as being almost as pure as the priests.

However, to this day, I cannot recall any four-letter or really foul words being uttered by any of the boys during all my years at Saint Colman's. What I have written down in this story is the extent of the swearing I ever heard. Just because I did not hear it, though, it does not mean that it did not take place when I was not around.

Okay, now that we have finished describing our clean game of "touch"-only football, we can move on and describe our game of pump, pump, pull away. Again, this was a game where the rules required you to only "touch" someone to capture them and for them to help you capture someone else. This game, with the simple word of "touch" also being ignored, however, was played even more brutally and viciously by the boys.

Running through an Indian gauntlet and being beaten and whipped, like Gary Cooper in the movies, was pale in comparison to a game of pump, pump, pull away played in the concrete school yard at Saint Colman's.

The game always resulted in more bleeding noses, heads, eyes, elbows, knees, chins, big scabs, broken or sprained bones, and chipped or loose teeth than any other game. I am positive that after banging their knees into the bricks, stone walls, steel fencing, and concrete yard, many of the boys who graduated from Saint Colman's have had a lot of orthopedic work on their limbs. If statistical records were kept by Saint Colman's, this game alone, coupled with the concrete school yard, bricks, steel fencing, and granite, would be the one causing the most casualties, visits to the public school nurse, and visits to the cloakroom.

The girls played this game also, but never suffered any serious injuries. They never played in a game with the boys that I can recall. Why, one would ask, were there no injuries with the girls when they played pump, pump, pull away? The answer was simple. The girls really obeyed the touch-only rule to catch someone to help them capture someone else.

The boys and girls would throw out the bat or do their finger calling to begin this game. The game would start with the loser having to go into the center of the school yard or softball area and stand there all alone. All the other boys participating in the game, which could number anywhere from ten to thirty, would line up alongside one another with their backs placed against the terra-cotta brick and granite facing of the school wall.

The object here was the boys would, when called upon, run from the wall to get to the other end of the school yard or cyclone fence area. The idea was to get to the other end without being touched or stopped before they got there. Anyone who was touched, or caught as it was called, was then required to help the individual in the center of the school yard catch more kids.

Now, you would have two kids in the center to touch and capture someone, and then three and then four and so on. The real brutality of the game occurred when the last boy had to run and get past the other twenty-nine boys who stood in the center of the concrete school yard at Saint Colman's waiting for their chance at getting him. Think about it! The odds were not in favor of his getting through this gauntlet with a twenty-nine to one count. Hopefully, the school bell would ring just in time to end recess and save him from being almost pummeled to death.

The game started when everyone was in position and the single individual in the center of the school yard screamed out as loud as he could, "Pump, pump, pull away." When this "war cry" was sounded and the running started, every boy went crazy and forgot about the only-touch rule to capture someone to help them.

Instead of a runner just being touched, the individual in the center of the yard would wrap his arms around your head or throw a body slam into your shoulder or perhaps even tackle you. He would then throw you to the concrete ground if he could and still hold on. At the very onset of the first run, this could result with a few fists flying and a lot of scuffling and swearing going on.

When the surviving boys reached the other end of the school yard or cyclone fence area, they would turn around and hear another, "Pump, pump, pull away" war cry being screamed out. The runners took off again, and it now looked like a football game, with runners moving around like halfbacks to avoid being tackled and thrown onto the concrete that still loved to eat and scar you up.

A quick move to the right or left by the runner could result in a knee or a head being pounded into the terra-cotta bricks. Pushing someone to the ground, holding him, and kicking at him could result in you loosing a tooth from the kick of a leg and a clodhopper shoe finding its way into your face.

The agonizing voice of the individual, such as Jimmy, Eddy, Joe, or even me, after being caught and knocked down by a horde of screaming boys echoed all around while we lay on our back on the concrete. We could be heard yelling out loud "hell," "shit," "you son of a bitch," "you bastard," or "Dammit, I'm going to get you for this." This was the strongest form of swearing I ever heard coming from any of the boys.

Joseph would always bite people whenever he could who piled up on him. Experience meant everything, and once you wrestled him to the ground, you would keep your distance from his teeth.

Those who did get bitten liked to show off the imprinted red teeth marks left on their skin later on in the day. Joseph's brother Charles must have taken lessons from him, since on occasion he would bite you also. I still have a deep scar on the top of my eyelid and right kneecap from playing this game. Eddy still has the scar showing a deep cut to his nose. Some of the boys still living probably wake up in the middle of the night dreaming about the pummeling that took place as they attempted to get through that line of maniacs when the war cry of "pump, pump, pull away" was screamed out.

Unless it has been capped, Jimmy may still be walking around today with a chip out of his upper front tooth after being severely tackled by the gang. The terra-cotta brick he was knocked into claimed another victory that day and kept a part of his tooth as a souvenir.

The game became awfully brutal toward the end, when the twenty-nine hyped-up, angry, screaming, sweating, huffing, puffing, maniacal guys would team together to catch and "touch" boy number thirty. When "pump, pump, pull away" was screamed out loud to this last remaining boy, he would often hesitate and think about what he was going to do and who he would run toward.

In most cases, he would look toward the smallest and slowest boys on their feet, in hopes of being able to break away from their grasp. Instead of beginning his run immediately and after thinking about it some more, he would sometimes plead and ask the twenty-nine screaming-out-for-death maniacs to promise not to hurt and to take it easy on him. The twenty-nine maniacs may or may not have answered him back. He would hesitate some more, and then as if making his last confession, he would scream out loud, "Will you all swear to God that you will not hurt me?"

After he heard all of us say we swore to God we wouldn't hurt him, he took off on his slow death or gauntlet run. No mercy would be shown, and he would be lucky if he was not hurt or injured. To my recollection during all my years at Saint Colman's, not a single boy ever got through this final mob of maniacs to the other side of the school yard.

The final comment made by the last runner was always, "You guys lied; you told me you would not hurt me." Catholic schoolboys were not all that smart at times and would believe anything told to them. Even your guardian angel could not help you get through these uncontrollable hyped-up maniacs.

Hopefully the bell ending recess might ring just in time and save a boy from running through this gauntlet, but again, the boys might ignore it. You just did not want to be the last person to be caught. Tempers flared, fists flew, and being kicked in the shins, back, or head by a big clodhopper was not unusual. Although you got mad at someone and did not speak for several days over the incidents or pummeling you may have received during the game, it was soon forgotten.

Why, you might ask, was this so? The answer is very simple. Because you always knew you would get another chance at the person or persons who hurt you during the next game of pump, pump, pull away. Yes, some of us carried a grudge to get even; and yes, some of the games resulted in certain boys being asked to visit the cloakroom after the game was over, bleeding or not.

Now that you have read about game number three, let me introduce you to game number four, "buckety buck", which was another favorite played in the school yard at Saint Colman's. The game of "buckety buck, how many fingers are up?" was not as brutal as the aforementioned games, but you needed a very strong back and set of rigid, strong legs to survive.

In a make-believe world, this game could be represented as a cowboy attempting to stay on top of a horse being ridden for the first time and "bucking" as hard as he could to throw the rider off. The girls at Saint Colman's played this game a lot also, but never with the boys, due to the physical punishment they would have to endure.

I am positive that their wearing of skirts during these days gone by and conducting themselves in a ladylike fashion kept many of them away from playing with the boys. In addition, it is highly unlikely that the priests and Sisters would have allowed them to participate in the game. It might also have allowed some boys the opportunity to cop a "free breast feel." Heaven forbid if one of the girls were to tumble off the horse and wind up with her undergarments showing! One can only imagine how many decades of the rosary they would have to say if the roving school-yard priest or Sister were to see this.

Had the game been played in today's times and the era of girls wearing Levis and pantsuits, I am positive that many of the girls would have participated in the game along with the boys. This would be especially true with Jean, Lillian, and Bernadette, who stood toe-to-toe with the boys and would not put up with any of their antics.

Under today's standards, the threat of a lawsuit by the girls' parents for not allowing them equal rights in participating with the boys would almost certainly allow them to start jumping on the boys' backs. In addition, I am sure the boys would also enjoy the opportunity to jump on their backs.

The teams for this game could also be selected either by the bat or finger-throwing process. The object of the game was to see how many people could place themselves on the backs of a group of others without causing the structure to collapse. This structure after several kids started the game was called the "horse."

After choosing the kids you wanted to participate in the game, which could be any number, the captains of each team would stand up straight anywhere from three to five feet apart and place their backs firmly against a section of the gray granite block that wrapped itself around the school building. This was usually done behind home plate of the softball area.

An individual would then walk up to the captain of his team and bend forward to an angle where his back was flat. Then he would place his head sideways and lay it into the belly or chest of the captain. At the same time, he would also wrap both of his arms, as tight as he could get them, around the captain's back. From this position, the game could begin.

Each captain could look straight ahead and see a long row of boys in line. They were approximately thirty feet in front of him and waiting for a signal from him. The signal would allow them to start running and jumping onto the individuals with their backs bent forward. Generally, the signal was a simple calling out of "go" from each captain.

At the signal, the first boy in line would take off running as fast as he could. He would then, like an Olympic runner out to win the gold medal, determine his speed and distance. Then, at the precise time, he would, with a hop, skip, and a jump, leap as high as he could get and land on that flat back directly ahead of him. All along, his greatest wish while doing this was that he would land hard enough on you to break your back and make the horse collapse. If the boy running landed on the horse without causing a collapse, the captain, with his back against the wall, would hold one hand up in the air and any number of fingers could be showing. He would then call out "Buckety buck, how many fingers are up?"

The individual bent over, who could not see or peek at the total amount of fingers showing, if any at all, would then have to guess what the number was. If he guessed correctly, the rider stayed on. If he guessed incorrectly, the next boy in line would start his run. When a rider failed to stay on the back of an individual after his jump or a correct number of fingers being held up were guessed, it meant he had to get off and wrap his arms around the waist of the individual bent over in front of him.

This would then extend the column of flat backs, the horse structure. This running, jumping, and finger guessing continued until one of the lines of flat backs would collapse from the sheer weight of all the individuals on top of it, and they would be declared the losers. The ringing of the bell to end recess often brought relief to those boys bent over for a considerable period of time and holding up all that weight. The weight of one or several boys on top falling onto one another during the collapse could end up in a fistfight or large scuffle and more swearing.

The school-yard concrete would also be picking your skin and bones apart and tearing up your clothing as the boys struggled to free themselves. A kick from a leg with a clodhopper shoe attached to it, just as in pump, pump, pull away, could also find its way to your ribs or face. Yes, at times, there was a lot of bleeding that occurred during this game. Joseph, again, was well-known to take a bite out of someone during this game—and it did not matter where—when he was ganged up on or someone fell too hard on him. You just did not want to have any part of your body in the vicinity of his teeth when he became mad.

At the bottom of the pile, you would hear a kid's voice screaming out, "you bastard," or "Son of a bitch, I am going to get even with you; just wait until I get up and get you."

Dodgeball was another game played in the school yard, but more so by the girls. The object of this game was to avoid being hit by a large rubber ball. Though rare, boys would play this game sometimes, when there were not enough bodies signed up to play the other four games. This game also gave you the chance to get even with the kids you knew hurt you during another game.

The idea was to throw the ball at someone "lightly" and just tap them to get them out, as it was called. To this day, just as in the understanding of the word "touch," not many boys at Saint Colman's knew or cared to know what "lightly" meant. The only part of the body Saint Colman schoolboys were interested in hitting and destroying completely was your head.

The person holding the ball would have to chase you all over the school yard for a long time, due to all the dodging and zigzagging that you might do, until the rear of your head was in his sight. Then, without pity and with all the force the thrower could muster, he threw the ball into the back of your head, hoping to knock it off or bring the runner stumbling down onto the school-yard concrete that loved to hurt you.

One might ask why the kids did not just aim for any part of the body to hit the runner much earlier to get him or her out, but the answer is simple. All the kids, including the girls, liked to hit people in the head to show their accuracy at throwing the ball. Anyone hurt during this game, which was very seldom, always got an opportunity just as in the other games to get even with you.

My recollection of a game of dodgeball is one where I thought I had knocked off Eddy's head from a severe throw and he fell to the ground moaning and groaning out loud. I was hoping none of the school-yard Sisters or possibly priests saw what I had done to hurt him. I thought to myself that day that I was in for a severe paddling, along with a stint in the cloakroom.

I ran up and knelt down by Eddy to see how badly he was hurt. As I touched him, he lurched upward quickly and scared the hell out of me while laughing at the same time. He was only pretending to be hurt, like many of us boys would often do. After all, he would have a chance to chase and throw the ball at me to get even.

Walking away from Eddy and seeing the falling leaves coming down from the two lonely maple trees by the parish house, I knew that the days of summer were drawing near.

When the school bell rang for dismissal later on that day and I entered the school yard again, I felt the fall chill descending on my body. I liked this chill, since it would not be too long before the snow and ice would come and give us boys at Saint Colman's a chance to get out on the frozen creek and play some ice hockey.

Knee funeral home, Larimer Avenue, 1940s.

CHAPTER 8

ICE HOCKEY

As long as I live, I will never forget a game of ice hockey played on a bitter cold day in February 1948 while in the sixth grade at Saint Coleman's school. I remember this incident so well because a group of us boys played the game even while under strict orders from the Sisters to stay away from the local creek and its frozen-over ice. You have to imagine this beautiful, long, wide area of white smooth frozen ice located approximately one hundred feet away from the outside perimeter of the school yard.

It also lay directly across the street from the church and convent. How tempting this frozen ice was to a bunch of young boys wanting to play a game of hockey, even with the threat of being caught and perhaps being put in the dark, evil cloakroom by Sister. I often look back and think that even with all the scapulars, crosses, and Virgin Mary and Sacred Heart of Jesus medals hanging around our Catholic necks, the devil was doing his work and telling us to ignore what Sister said about the ice! The rosary beads most of us had in our possession or carried in our pants pockets were not keeping this demonic monster away either.

The pristine, virgin ice lying on top of the creek did not help either. It looked like the well-manicured, smooth ice that the Pittsburgh Penguins play on today. The smoothness of the ice happened during the week while the creek was very low. There was no heavy rainfall to make the water rise, develop any rapids, and form their peaks into icy rough spots as the temperature dropped during the evening. Another light snowfall was lying on top of the ice the next day, making it even more inviting to walk on or play a game of ice hockey.

During the start of this particular school day, most of the boys in my class met in the school ground to play around and discuss what we would do during recess, after school, or whatever. Pappy, who was one of our resident altar boys, suggested to a few of us that we try to get together and play a game of ice hockey on the creek.

This sounded like a great idea to some of the other guys like Ronald, who was nicknamed "Lash" after a famous cowboy movie star of this period. Jimmy, Eddy, Timmy, Joe, Paul, Marty, and Carmen also said they were interested. Thus, this very smart and methodical sixth-grade planning group for the hockey game was formed.

According to the rules at Saint Colman's, a hockey game consisted of any number of boys who wanted to play, but it always had to be an equal number of players on each team. To start a game, there could be as few as two boys playing against each another, and up to eight players. It was very difficult to get a team over eight boys together except for the weekends, when you could always find additional players and friends from the nearby public school for a good, long game.

For the next several days, over the weekend and the following week of school, our thoughts and discussions, even during the other games we were playing, were about playing a hockey game on the frozen-over creek. The weather remained very cold, it did not rain, and it did not warm up. If it got warm, it would have caused the virgin layer of ice and snow that kept tempting all of us to go play on it to become uneven and lumpy.

The devil kept taunting us. The tempting ice continued to remain as pristine as ever, and another light snowfall lay on its top. Enough was enough, we all said, and like Adam being tempted in the Garden of Eden, we could not resist the temptation and decided it was time to take a bite out of the ice instead of an apple.

This was a game to be played by only the sixth graders, since the older seventh—and eighth-grade boys like Richard, Willy, Charles, and Joseph had other plans made and could not join in on our big game day. Although we tried to keep the game a secret, word began to leak out about it. Audrey, Kathleen, Lillian, Lois, and Joan, whom we often faced during our classroom spelldown contests, knew we were going to meet very soon and play a game of ice hockey on the creek.

It seemed as though everyone except the priests and Sisters knew about this big, well-planned event. Had they been informed, we certainly would not have been allowed out of the school grounds, and the Sisters would have been instructed to keep a close eye on all of us. We felt safe and secure at this point, and the big game was scheduled for Friday, to be played during the morning recess period, which would make it about a thirty-minute game.

Although everyone was forbidden to leave the school grounds without Sister's permission, we decided to take a chance and sneak off to the creek at some point. In addition to breaking the recess rule, we would also be breaking the Sisters' strict orders to each class that they were forbidden to go near the creek or to play on the ice. In retrospect, the order was being provided for our safety and concern at the time, since the priests and Sisters were fearful about the ice being too thin and breaking under our weight and someone falling in the water and drowning.

Their fears were justified, in that a few of us did break through some thin ice in the early part of winter. The water came up over our clodhoppers and legs and touched the bottom of our mackinaws. This happened on the weekend when there was no school. It was not long afterward that we rushed home and placed the wet items on top of the coal-fired floor registers to have them dry out.

No boy ever fell through the ice and became completely submerged or had to tread water. The creek was pretty shallow most times, but our mackinaw coats, when wet, became very heavy and could make it hard to pull somebody out of the water to the creek bank and dry land.

Being as young as we were at the time and without making any excuses, a lot of us boys thought the Sisters were being very mean when they told us to stay off the ice or not to do something that was against the school rules. Little did we realize at the time that these Sisters, with all their tough discipline, were providing a foundation for character building and the learning of what respect meant. Hopefully this discipline would carry us through life and help us make the correct choice between right and wrong as we grew up.

All this discipline seemed to apply while you were in school and under the supervision of the priests and Sisters. You were forbidden to play on the ice or leave the school grounds without their permission, but come the weekend or some religious holiday when we children did not go to school, the rules did not apply. Although if you were seen doing something that was forbidden, even while on your own time and away from school, the Sisters and priests would still tell you how wrong or bad it was. Some of us children would also have to worry about being disciplined again at school one way or another!

Looking back, I wonder if perhaps it was because of a possible lawsuit if we were injured while under their supervision. Being a little wiser and more educated today, I suggest this was not the case, since lawsuits and lawyers were something that very few of us naïve children and grown adults of the time knew anything about. The words *lawyer* or *suit* never appeared in any of our schoolbooks or came up during a spelldown contest either.

On Thursday the day before the big game right after school, it was agreed upon that all of the boys who were going to play would go home, get their hockey sticks, and hide them along the creek bank that evening. This way, they would be readily available in the morning during recess to access quickly and play with.

Pappy was delegated to bring an empty Carnation milk can that he was to stomp down on several times with his clodhoppers and get ready to be used as the hockey puck. Some of the boys that were about to play in the game came from very poor families, and some did not. Several would have on real gloves to play in, and the others would apply one or two pairs of old socks to their hands to play. No one ever had ice skates, and whatever footwear you had on, that was it. Generally, it was a pair of clodhoppers or some other leather-soled shoes, since during days gone by, tennis shoes were almost nonexistent in school and not very popular.

No boy had a factory-manufactured real hockey stick to play with. In addition, none of us ever touched a professional-looking hockey stick or saw a real live game. The hockey stick of the day was a piece of long, narrow wood, or a mop and broomstick handle that was used to push and smack the flattened milk-can puck around with. Meeting the next morning after hiding their hockey sticks on the creek bank the evening before, the hockey players all agreed that everything was all set to play the big game. However, to allow more time to play a full game, which would take about forty minutes, the boys decided to change and play the game during the hour-long lunch period.

Pappy, with a great big smile on his face while talking about the game, reached into his pocket and displayed an empty Carnation milk can he had smashed the night before and showed it to all of us. This was his way of telling everyone he was ready to play. The boys continued talking, and while remaining inside the school yard perimeter, they walked over to look at the creek and flat ice again. It was still very pristine looking and just waiting on someone to walk, skate, or play on it. Perhaps even the devil's disciples!

The temptation of the devil was still working and luring these boys, who had done all their methodical planning for a game of ice hockey. The bell suddenly rang out loud to start the school day with morning prayers. With the Sisters' whistles blowing, every child in the school yard was assembled into a military-type line and marched into their classrooms.

Audrey was standing beside me and whispered quietly so Sister could not hear her asking me if we were still going to play hockey today. I said yes without blinking an eye. She gave me what I came to recognize as a worried look on her face and whispered again, "I sure hope you do not get caught, because if you do, you will be taken to the cloakroom for a good paddling. Please, Barrie, don't go, since I do not want to see this happen to you again."

Audrey was always looking out for me, and I considered her to be one of the smartest individuals in the school. She often placed herself at risk of being caught by Sister when she sometimes slid her test papers to the edge of her desk for me to look at and perhaps copy from. I was lazy about doing my schoolwork from time to time since I had other, more important things to do.

On the days Sister Ruff announced we were going to have a test and I was not prepared, I would panic and look over at Audrey, who sat across from me, with a plea for help in my eyes. I could always count on her, and she often would help me get my homework assignments that I had forgotten about done in the auditorium before school started. Funny, but even with the missed homework assignments and failed tests for a lot of us boys, we all still received a good education and finally graduated from Saint Colman's.

Kathleen was also worried about us being seen and getting caught, since she, along with many other kids, knew what the consequences would be. Sister Ruff, in my eyes as a small boy, was not very friendly most of the time. However, with maturity, I am quite positive, even with her limited teacher training, during these days gone by, she had all the children's best interests at heart.

The class was done working with decimals and fractions, and we moved into percentages. A problem was placed on the blackboard by Sister that read, "In a factory, 8 percent of the machines broke down. They were replaced by new ones. How many machines are there in the shop if 144 machines were replaced?" Lillian said she knew the answer and was asked by Sister to go to the blackboard and show the class what it was and how she worked it out. Lillian wrote on the blackboard 144 divided by 8=18 x 100 = 1800. Sister said that was correct and asked if any of us needed any special help. Not a single hand was raised in response to her question, and the bell for recess finally rang.

We were all anxious to run out and play, but until we were given permission to leave, we remained seated at our desks. Sometimes, prematurely getting up from your desk without Sister's permission could mean you would be restricted to the classroom or auditorium and not allowed out to play. On this day, everyone remained seated, even the eager hockey players. Sister finally gave her permission to get up from our desks, and we went to the rear door of the classroom in single file. From here we were marched out to the school yard, where it was very cold. Most of the kids who stayed outside did a lot of physical things to keep warmed up.

Jumping rope, dodgeball, pump, pump, pull away, and buckety buck were the favorites to get you warmed up, since they required a lot of running and jumping around. On occasion, depending on the weather and especially when the sun was out, short games of softball and football were played. The boys always had the school-yard softball area tied up, and the girls never got the opportunity to use it. I sometimes wonder how we boys would have coped under today's title IX requirements or equal rights for women and men sports.

Perhaps, since federal, state, and local funding was not provided to parochial schools then or even today, we had nothing to worry about. However, I am positive that the ladies in today's parochial schools and colleges are not bashful when it comes to fighting for equal rights and speaking up against anything that carries heavily in favor of the gentlemen.

The recess bell rang, and the silver whistles hanging around the penguins' or Sister's necks started blowing to get us all lined up and marched back into class. Reluctantly, we went back to working percentage problems, and those of us who were going to play ice hockey could barely wait until the lunch bell rang. Kathleen and Audrey asked me if we were still going to do it, referring to the big hockey game, and I again said yes. "Oh, God, you better be careful and not get caught," they both said. They knew what the consequences would be, and so did I and the other boys.

It took forever, but the lunch bell finally rang, ending our anxiety. We went through our military regimentation of lining up and marching out of the classroom and into the school yard. On this day, the boys were on their best behavior and did not take a chance at punching one another's arms, backs, or heads and getting caught. This would have brought some form of punishment from Sister Ruff and prevented them from playing hockey.

We gobbled our brown-bag lunches down quickly. Looking around, we saw no priests or Sisters out in the school yard and said, "This is our chance." Then very quickly, the ten of us boys began to sneak off one by one to the creek, hoping no one would see us leaving the school yard.

Large groups attempting to sneak off the school-yard grounds were always easy targets to be seen by the patrolling priests and Sisters, and we did our best to avoid this. We all arrived at the creek bank and complimented ourselves on escaping and outsmarting the "black garb and white habit patrol."

What a wonderful job of methodical planning we had done to carry this out. We all yelled and screamed in delight while standing on the creek bank, quickly gathering up our handmade hockey sticks and putting gloves or socks on our hands. We sent select individuals (dummies) out as scouts, to tiptoe out on the ice to test how hard and safe it was.

After a minute or so, the scouts began jumping up and down on the ice. They had finally determined it was very solid all around and gave us a big high sign to come out and join them. Generally, you might send the weaker or less knowledgeable of the group or someone you did not have fond feelings for to do this dangerous mission. However, with this group, everyone was anxious to play, and everyone volunteered to do it.

Fortunately, since none of the advance scouts broke through the ice, we all felt it was very safe to go ahead and play our game of hockey. A goal line was drawn into the top, small layer of snow at opposite ends of the playing area. Another large straight line was drawn along both sides of the snow, at the outer ends of the creek banks, to represent the out-of-bounds area. We now had a big square boxed-in area that was our hockey field of play.

Some other non-players, including girls and other breakers of Sister's rule, left the school yard at Saint Colman's that day. They all lined up on the railroad tracks above and looking over the creek to watch the big game. Buddy, one of these spectators, agreed to referee the game for us, which is the only game where we ever had an official person to tell us when we were not playing by the rules. The teams assembled and lined up to protect their respective goal areas. The two selected captains of each team met and faced one another in the middle of the two goals.

With broom and mop sticks in hand and touching the ice, along with all the hype and energy they could produce, the boys waited in anticipation for the Carnation milk can puck being dropped on the ice to begin the game. They looked very intensely at each other, as if they were playing for the Stanley Cup. Buddy placed the puck in one of his hands and stood back a few feet to avoid being hit by any swinging broom and mop stick handles. He looked at Pappy and Carmen and said, "Are you ready?" When both heads of the captains gave a nod of yes, he quickly dropped the puck and backpedaled away quickly to start the game.

As they started to swing their hockey sticks, Pappy was first to make contact with the puck and sent it sailing along to Lash, who ran a little as if he were skating, and pushed it over to me. I began to imagine I was on a pair of skates and bent my knees and made motions like moving to the left and right while running, as one can imagine a downhill skier doing.

Since the ice was very slippery, I lost my balance during my showing off, and my feet slipped out from under me and I fell down. While lying on my side in the snow and ice, I got whacked across the legs by Carmen, who was on the attack defensively and doing everything to prevent a score.

I managed to push the puck over to Timmy with one of my hands before Carmen could get his broom handle on it, and he smacked it across the goal line to score the first point. A lot of yelling and screaming went on among the scoring team, and a lot of "aw shit," "Jesus Christ," and "God-dammit, why didn't you stop him?" was being hollered out by some of the defensive players. "Heaven forbid," I said to myself, "if the priests or Sisters were to hear this type of language coming from us good Catholic school kids."

After the first score, the captains came to the center of the ring and faced off with one another again. The referee dropped the puck, and the game continued along with the clashing thunder of broom and mop sticks. More screaming and swearing could now be heard coming from the crowd of gathered spectators. Kathleen was heard to say, "Heck, why didn't Eddy just trip Carmen when he did that?" Audrey was heard saying back to Kathleen, "Look at Marty. He fell on his butt—what a big dummy." Every person that was out on the main street of Turtle Creek this day had to hear all of this shouting and noise.

Another score was achieved by Eddy after about twenty minutes of play, midway through the lunch period. We had another estimated twenty minutes of playing time left, and the score was now two nothing. In the next series of plays, stick swinging, and pushing and hitting one another on various parts of the body, Jimmy pushed the puck forward to Eddy with his mop handle and fell down.

Lash moved over toward Jimmy and hit him intentionally on the side of his back with his mop stick. Jimmy yelled out, "You son of a bitch, I will get you for that." Jimmy got up quickly from the snow and ice, moved toward Lash with his mop handle, and started swinging at Lash, hoping to connect somewhere on a part of his body.

This episode stopped the game momentarily as they dueled with one another with their mop and broom handles like two skilled swordsmen with their rapiers. Buddy, the referee, stepped in between them and said, "Knock it off and get playing; there isn't much time left." They took a swing at one another with their fists, Buddy ducked out of the way, and they finally quit fighting. They moved away from one another, but both of them began to feel the welts swelling up on their arms and legs from the stings they each received off the impacting sticks, and the game went back into play.

Eddy received a beautiful pass of the puck on the next play and pushed it neatly toward Paul. Marty attempted to block this play and missed it. The puck continued to sail past Marty toward Paul, and he smacked it around with a few strikes from his mop stick and finally pushed it past Pappy and across the goal line for a point. With this score, the "shits," "god-dammits," and "Jesus Christs" were coming from the other boys, now ahead only by one point.

All of the other hollering and screaming was coming from the boys scoring the goal. Kathleen, one of the spectators, could be heard screaming out loud, "What a dummy that Pappy is." Lillian looked at her and said, "Kathleen, watch your language, or you are going to go to hell."

Over the noise of the hockey players and the crowd of spectators, Kathleen screamed back at Lillian and said, "I am not, since I am going to confession this afternoon right after school and will be forgiven by the priest." As it stood, there were going to be a lot of kids in the confessional booths this afternoon after school.

By this time the noise coming from the creek area was so loud, according to kids there, that you could hear it in the portion of the school yard close by. The game continued with the score two to one, when suddenly, the school bell rang, and the silver whistles hanging around the Sisters' necks started to blow, ending the lunch period.

This was not like a softball or football game, where you could ignore the whistles and take another swing or throw another pass, and the boys knew it. The ice may not be there tomorrow and for quite a while again! They had all taken a big chance and had better get back to school on time and without being seen outside the school yard. Every one of us boys playing hockey heard and knew what the whistles meant. During the mass confusion of kids running around in the school yard and their roundup by the Sisters, we hoped to be able to slip in with them undetected, with no one noticing we had been gone during lunch period.

We stopped our play immediately, ran off the ice, and hid our mops and broomsticks in various places along the creek bank. We then ran individually again, rather than in a group, to various areas of the school yard to sneak alongside the other kids and make it less conspicuous that we had been gone. We managed to place ourselves in line without being seen by either the patrolling priest or Sisters coming back from the creek—or so we thought!

We were quite pleased with ourselves for being able to outsmart them. We asked Joan and Jean, who were close by in line, "Did anybody see us leave or ask where we were during lunch period?" and they both said "no." We felt really great now—we had gotten away with our plan and enjoyed a good hockey game (except for the losers), and no one saw us. Therefore, no discipline or cloakroom paddling would take place.

We were soon to learn, however, about a big mistake we had made during our smart, methodical planning. In our haste to plan for and play this hockey game that the pristine ice or devil tempted us to do, we overlooked one very important detail. Stupid as it sounds now, we forgot about the fact that the Sisters' convent sat directly across from what I now call the fifty-yard line where we were playing our game of ice hockey.

Not only did this anomaly take place, but the majority of the Sisters went there this day for lunch and some relaxation. In addition to the convent being across the street and within fifty feet of the creek bank and ice, the Sisters had the advantage of being able to see and hear everything everyone said during the exciting times of the hockey game from a second-story convent window.

Their view of everything could be compared to that of an owner's private club room at a professional hockey game today. You guessed it—unknowingly we had been seen and caught red-handed playing ice hockey on the creek. The Sisters were spying on us, as we would later call it.

As we were being marched back into class after lunch and our hockey game, nothing was going on that would lead any of us boys to suspect we did not get away with our plan. Sister Ruff was not in the classroom yet, and all of the girls in the class were giggling and talking about what we had done and gotten away with. Everyone took their seats, became very quiet, and waited on the classroom doorknob to begin turning, indicating Sister would soon appear.

It was not unusual for a Sister to be late or not in her classroom right away or before the children got there. They could be with another Sister or talking with parents, the priests, or Mother Superior. Sister was about ten minutes late this day, and during this time some of the boys in class did not want to miss the opportunity to be mischievous. They created a disturbance by throwing erasers and taking head shots at one another with stretched rubber bands.

As soon as the doorknob on the rear classroom door began to turn, the disturbance stopped, the boys ran back quickly to their seats, and the classroom became very quiet and organized once again. The only thing different and obvious to one's eye that gave an indication of someone being disorderly was a few erasers and rubber bands lying on the floor and window ledges.

Again, this was pure stupidity on the part of us "good Catholic boys." We were not as smart as we thought we were, and Sister, after looking at the scene of the crime, would know we were up to no good. However, on this day, she had more important matters on her mind, and this evidence would be ignored.

Sister Ruff entered the classroom immediately after the doorknob turned without saying a word. Everyone, especially the boys, knew through their training to be quiet and settle down. No one would utter a single word until she spoke, or it was possible we would be kept in the classroom after school was let out. Sister walked down the narrow aisle past several blackboards to the front of the classroom looking straight ahead without saying a word.

She turned around and had a very serious, hard look on her face while walking over and staring directly into Lash's eyes. Her face and cheeks bulged out from behind her white habit and were beet red in color. In addition, she was nervously swinging the large cross that dangled from her rosary beads with her fingers in small circles.

To our misfortune, we boys that played hockey now found out that Sister was late because she was with Mother Superior discussing a matter concerning someone breaking school rules. Sister announced to the class that she was thinking about what form of punishment should be taken against the offenders. She then began to describe what she and several other Sisters had seen and heard by the creek during their lunch break.

How could all of us hockey players, during our detailed planning, have been so stupid and forget about the nearby convent? Not only did we forget about the convent's location and proximity to the creek, but Sister was having her lunch around the same time the hockey game started. After hearing all of the yelling and screaming and swearing for so long, several Sisters, including ours, decided to investigate where all this noise was coming from. Their journey took them upstairs to the second floor of the convent, to a window that had a clear view looking directly down on the icy creek and our hockey game.

This scene was sort of like the individual peering out of the rear window and taking everything in from an Alfred Hitchcock movie. Not only this, the Sisters also got a free pass to see a hockey game on what I call the fifty-yard line to see, hear, and absorb all the action and swearing. We boys often wondered why the Sisters did not leave the convent immediately and come get us. Many of us believe it was because they were nice and warm, in the process of eating their lunch, and did not want to stop, put on their warm wraps, and face the bitter cold outside! Sister continued with her opening remarks and advised the whole class about her instructions being disobeyed.

She continued to speak and said she would have to punish those boys who left the school yard at lunch and were seen playing hockey on the icy creek and heard swearing. None of the bystanders would receive any punishment. All of the guilty boys' hearts, including my own, began to flutter slowly, and we started to twitch nervously in our seats. We all knew what was coming next and mentally could feel the sting of a wooden paddle hitting our buttocks.

Sister then walked over to and around the backside of her desk. She retrieved a long wooden paddle that was always readily available. She did this through experience, just as we boys knew by experience the harsh punishment that would soon be applied to each guilty boy. Sister returned to the front of the classroom holding the paddle in her hand and looking very sternly with her beet-colored face. Her cheeks were still puffy and peeking out from behind her habit at all of the children, especially the guilty boys.

She began to speak rapidly as she said, "When I call out your name, I want you to come up and face the front of the class." All of the guilty boys waited nervously to see whose name would be called out first. The first name she shouted out furiously was Ronald (Lash), the next was Albert (Pappy), and she continued on to Barrie, Marty, Timothy (Timmy), Edward (Eddy), Joseph (Joe), Carmen, James (Jimmy), and finally to the last boy, Paul.

We all got up and walked nervously to the front of the classroom as instructed by Sister. We lined up with our heads lowered and could not look at the other children. Later on, we all said we were subconsciously praying the paddling we were about to receive would not hurt. Sister hollered out loud and directed that we boys raise our heads and continue looking straight ahead.

I was looking directly at Jean and Audrey, since it seemed as if their eyes were locked on me. It appeared as if they might break out crying, since they knew from past disciplinary action what punishment would be administered to each and every one of us boys.

Sister, holding the paddle in one hand, was twitching a little bit herself and still swinging her cross in the air with her other hand. She told the class in great detail about our disobedience and swearing. Without a trial or right to defend ourselves, our sentence had already been determined and was about to be carried out by Sister! Where was my guardian angel, which every Catholic has to protect them, I asked myself.

In addition, I thought we should be forgiven, like God had forgiven the sinner Mary Magdalene. We boys were condemned, and rather than being sent to a dungeon, we would be sent to the comparable and fearful cloakroom for our punishment. There would be no commuting of this sentence or pardon of any kind under any circumstances, and we all knew it. The sentence was for all of us to get a good hard paddling, or beating as Sister described it.

Sister walked over and opened the dreaded cloakroom door, located on the left side of the classroom. Speaking very loudly, she said, "I told all of you boys not to go near the ice, and after this you will learn to listen to me and behave." I kept hoping my guardian angel was going to intervene quickly, and I am sure the other boys were praying for the same thing.

Why couldn't Sister forgive us, since even Jesus forgave everyone while he was dying on the cross, including the two thieves, Dismas and Gestas. We should be worthy of salvation also! "Don't you ever disobey me again, or you will be sorry, I promise you," Sister said. I was surprised that she did not tell the lot of us that we were all going to hell. I will never forget those words as I stood in the front of the classroom that day.

Sister looked at Lash and told him to get into the cloakroom immediately. Lash walked away slowly and with his head lowered even more than the rest of us. As Lash entered the cloakroom door, Sister followed with the paddle hanging down from her hand and closed the evil cloakroom door behind her. Once inside the cloakroom, Sister switched on the overhead light and told Lash to assume the position.

This, as we all knew, meant to bend over and grab the lower part of your legs with both of your hands, in preparation to be paddled on the buttocks. Sometimes a lot of the boys, including myself, rather than do this, would just wrap our arms around our stomachs and bend forward a little. Several of the other boys standing in the lineup in the front of the classroom had been through this punishment process before. They all knew what Sister was directing Lash to do.

Suddenly, everyone heard the crack of the paddle as the first swing from Sister Ruff landed on Lash's buttocks. He yelled out very loud, "Aah! Aah! Aah!" Several more cracks came from the cloakroom, and we could all hear Lash asking and pleading with Sister to stop. The cracks continued until we saw the cloakroom door on the right side of the classroom swing open very fast and bang against the outside wall.

Lash had pushed the door forward while still on his knees crying and begging for Sister to stop the beating. Sister continued on with the beating, and the paddle landing on his back and shoulder areas. Lash was crawling, hunched over on all fours by this time like a dog.

Looking at him in this position reminded me of a horse saddled up and waiting to be ridden or perhaps someone waiting to jump on him as in the game of buckety buck. Sister was completely out of control by this time and had lost it, as we would say today. Under both the church and strengthened child abuse laws today, she would be facing criminal prosecution for this type of beating. This Sister's name, along with Sister Gruff's, have been changed for anonymity purposes.

Most of the children who passed through Saint Colman's over the years and who are still living today would probably recognize who they are. Perhaps some might even recall being paddled or handled roughly by her. There was one other Sister who stood out like this in her punishment with a paddle, but her beatings were pale in comparison to Sister Ruff, who beat Lash on that day. If records were being kept at Saint Colman's regarding parents' complaints about physical punishments carried out by Sisters, I am positive that Sisters Gruff and Ruff had several complaints registered against them over the years.

Sister finally stopped her beating of Lash. She was huffing and puffing and breathing very heavily, and told him to get up and go back to his desk. I do not remember if Lash crawled or walked back to his desk, but I do remember that he cried and sobbed very hard all the way. Even after he sat down on his hard oak seat and placed his head on the desktop, he was still sobbing.

Placing his hands underneath his stinging buttocks did not seem to offer much relief from his pain either. Sister, who had beaten him badly, was exhausted, with the paddle still hanging from her hand. She managed to regain her composure somewhat and control her labored breathing. The rest of us boys, all very nervous by now, wondered who would be told next to go into the cloakroom.

To our amazement and relief, Sister directed all of us to go sit down in our seats. Except for Lash, our guardian angels were around after all. It was very obvious to everyone in the classroom that Sister had physically and emotionally exhausted herself on Lash. She did not have the energy or strength left to beat up on nine other naïve and defenseless good Catholic boys.

This is the worst paddling (although there were memorable other ones) that I can remember seeing a Sister giving a child, and its memory will last forever in my mind. I often wonder if Sister Ruff ever told the priest, during her next confession, what she had done on this day. I ask myself, "Would God forgive her?" and then I say, "I truly believe he will and has already done so."

This was a bad thing that happened, but it was also a blessing in disguise, in that Lash prevented the rest of us guilty boys, his hockey teammates, from being put in the cloakroom and receiving our paddling. From that day on, we considered Lash our very best buddy. We thanked him every time we saw or played with him thereafter, for saving us from a terrible beating in the ghastly cloakroom.

Perhaps the devil was still doing his evil work that day and had won out, since God and our guardian angels did not intervene to stop the beating and Lash was our only savior. Like many changes that have taken place in the Catholic Church and school system over the years, paddles and the beating of children with them was stopped a long time ago.

The last time I saw Lash was in Pinky's poolroom in 1957 when he was home on leave while serving with the US Marine Corps. The first thing I said upon seeing him was, "Hello, Lash, thanks for saving me from a terrible beating." He burst out laughing and joked about that day and told me he would never forget it either. I looked at him and said, "Me too." He then asked me how I was doing.

I told him that I had just finished my tour of duty with the US Army. Then he asked if I would like to play a little nine ball. I looked at him and said, "Yes, how about five dollars a game?" We continued our discussion and reminiscing about the days gone by and the memorable and great times we had at Saint Colman's and Turtle Creek High School. He was a little better at playing pool than the Italian kid who lost to me quite often, so I paid him the five dollars he had won and left the poolroom. He was really shooting a "good stick" that day.

Some members of this great hockey team are still living in Turtle Creek, and some live in other parts of the country, thus making it difficult to get together again to finish off the game that had to stop with a two-to-one score!

The creek is still there and if we could get together, it would definitely be finished and with no repercussions by Sister! The Sisters' convent and their box seats to our ice hockey game that day were torn down many years ago.

I personally would like to play and finish this hockey game in the Pennsylvania February cold and snowy weather. How wonderful it would be, since I can now afford to buy and wear a pair of real leather or good ski gloves on my hands, instead of those old, heavy, worn-out socks.

CHAPTER 9

CHRISTMAS TURKEY RAFFLE

Every year Saint Colman's school purchased a large live turkey from the Liberty Meat Market. After we kids sold chances on it, the turkey was raffled off to a lucky winner a few days before Christmas. The turkey was always the largest one around and weighed up to twenty-five pounds. It was fed daily by the market personnel. At times the personnel would even pass out handfuls of grain to store customers and little children, so they could feed it also. The turkey was displayed daily on the sidewalk in front of the store, in a large wood and wire cage, for all the townspeople to see.

The turkey, when the time came, would be dressed out and delivered by the market to the lucky winner. The lucky winner could also choose to pick the turkey up at the store. Tickets went on sale in early November and were only sold by participating children in grades one through eight at Saint Colman's.

The child who sold the most tickets would receive praise and a prize from the school. The prize could be a small turkey, ham, box of Cargo's candy, or a gift certificate to the G. C. Murphy five-and-ten store. In addition, for every twenty tickets or one book sold, the child would receive five cents or a free ticket. If they chose the free ticket, they could enter their name or someone else's name on it for a chance at winning the "big" turkey.

Going door to door and selling tickets was not very appealing to a lot of the children, especially the younger and smaller children in the lower grades. Therefore, to help them out and protect them from the cold, snow, and rain, many of their parents would buy several tickets or a book of tickets to help them out.

The wealthier students, of which there were few, always sold more tickets, since their parents had better jobs and a little more money to buy them. This gave them a slight advantage over the other kids selling tickets and a higher chance of winning not only the prize but perhaps the turkey also.

I knew that Mary Ellen and Lois, two of my classmates in the fifth grade, whose parents were a lot better off financially, had probably, hypothetically, sold several books of tickets before they were even issued by Sister. This would make it very difficult for me to come from behind and sell as many or more to win. Pappy, Marty, Buddy, and Audrey probably had a head start on me also. I had a list of people whose doors I would be knocking on, along with the local business establishments, to ask them to buy a raffle ticket, but I knew most every other kid would be doing the same thing.

It snowed hard in early November and was still snowing the next day as I left for school with my brother and sister. We chatted and talked as we walked along hand in hand, following and stepping into other people's boot, shoe, and sled tracks. We did this to avoid getting the fresh, deep snow up over our shoes and falling inside. If this were to happen, the snow covering our socks would begin melting once we got inside the warm school building at Saint Colman's, and our feet would become very wet.

On very slushy days, where the previous fallen snow was high and melting from warmer weather, my brother and I would carry our sister Joy to school on our backs to keep her shoes and socks dry. We did not have any protective rubber galoshes or high-top boots to wear like some of the other children. We did everything possible to keep our feet dry, so as not to come down sick.

For some children, harsh as it sounds, getting their feet wet and coming down with a cold would mean they could possibly be given a beating. After all, some parents were struggling as it was to pay bills, and they could not afford the additional expense of pharmacy and doctors' bills. Along with most of the children at Saint Colman's, we did everything possible to stay healthy during bad weather conditions.

At times when the soles of our shoes wound up with holes in them, we placed the hard cardboard strip from a Clark Candy Bar or some other candy bar package inside the shoes as a temporary fix to help keep out water and snow. For some families, there was not even enough money available to have the local shoe cobbler, by the name of Frank, put new soles on them.

My brother and I often shoveled snow from the front of Frank's shop for free. He was very kind to us and let us come inside to warm our hands and bodies by his potbellied coal stove. There were many times while we were growing up that he would have us remove our clodhoppers, and he put new soles and heels on them and charged us nothing. Frank's shoe shop was wedged in between the White Tower and the Valley Buick dealership buildings, and it could not have been any bigger than a nine by twenty space or 180 square feet. Talk about a small business area!

The school bell rang and we all went to our classrooms, hung up our coats in the dreaded cloakroom, sat down in our seats, and led by Sister, started saying our morning prayers. The lesson plan for the morning seemed to go fast, except for catechism and a test afterward. Even though we were allowed a short recess mid morning I was still bored and anxious to get outside and play in the school yard a little bit with my friends. The school bell finally rang for the lunch period, and I went outside, where it was snowing very heavily. It was still snowing and very wet outside when my brother, sister, and I left the school after being dismissed, to walk home in other people's tracks again.

We were heading home for our daily lunch of Maple Rolls from O'Neil's bakery and chocolate milk from Isaly's. We ate our lunch quickly, and while my brother, Richard, and I put on our bright multicolored Sears mackinaws, Joy was putting on her dark blue Navy peacoat. These were the typical winter coats being worn at the time and kept us and a lot of other children very warm. However, when they got soaking wet from the rain or snow while playing, it felt like you had a heavy weight placed around your body.

Father was at work, and we kissed our mother good-bye after lunch and started our trek back to school. On the way back to the school, we stopped and looked through the Faller's furniture store large plate glass window. We saw several men beginning to put up the yearly Christmas display and placing train tracks on a wooden platform. There were several miniature Lionel Train locomotives, coal cars, boxcars, passenger cars, and cabooses scattered about on the floor.

By this evening many passersby would be looking at a beautifully lighted and decorated Christmas tree, mounted in the center of the platform, and the trains running around on their tracks. We could not wait for the display to be finished, and along with many others, we would be coming back tonight.

The miniature trains, just like the real ones that ran through town, would be passing over trestles and bridges and going by various crossing guards. As they continued their railroad track journey, they went up and down slight grades, passed through small tunnels, and switched over to another track line from time to time.

Slight puffs of artificial smoke could be seen coming from the black locomotive's coal stack. While standing on the sidewalk outside, many of the residents would watch this display and the caboose of each train going by. They could also hear the sound of the locomotive's steam whistles being blown. The Christmas music heard outside on speakers came from a 33 rpm record being played inside the store on an RCA Victrola. This added to the excitement and enjoyment of Christmas for everyone in town, especially for the many small children who would be coming to look at the display and visit with Santa Claus inside the store, to tell him what they wanted for Christmas and how good they had been

After recess the afternoon class and schoolwork seemed to go fast, and before I knew it, the school dismissal bell rang. As we were all trained, and to avoid any punishment, every child sat in his or her seat quietly until Sister said we could get up to leave. Sister, who was standing alongside the blackboard with her face framed by her white, heavily starched habit, was erasing several arithmetic problems when the bell rang.

Sister put the eraser she was holding down on the small narrow wood ledge of the blackboard. There was always the chance the eraser would slip off and fall to the floor. This time it did not. Sister walked to the front of the classroom and opened the top drawer of her large, oak, yellowish-looking varnished stained desk.

She retrieved several stacks of small books, each containing twenty tickets, and placed them on the desk. Then she announced out loud to the class, "Here are the chances for the turkey raffle. Who wants how many?" Every child in the classroom, including myself, started to scream out loud and all at once, "me," "me," and "me."

We all were yelling and telling her how many tickets or books of tickets we wanted, and it took awhile for Sister to bring order back to the classroom. Sister said she would call out our names in alphabetical order, and when your name was called, you could come up and get the number of books you wanted and then leave.

I was one of the lucky ones in this case, since my name began with B and there were not too many kids in the class who had a last name beginning with A. Sister recorded each child's name and number of books requested as she passed them out. I heard voices saying to Sister, "Let me have twenty, forty, sixty, and a hundred" by some of the As. When it came my turn, I said, "Please give me three hundred" very quietly, to avoid letting the other kids know what amount I had taken.

Sister looked at me strangely, counted out fifteen books, handed them to me, and said, "Barrie, this is an awful lot of tickets for you to sell. Are you sure you really want this many?" I grabbed at the tickets and said to her very politely, "Yes, Sister." My mind was racing very fast at the same time, thinking again as to whom I might be able to sell them to.

I left the classroom and walked out of the school. I waited around in the school yard for Mary Ellen, Lois, Jean, Audrey, Carmen, Pappy, Paul, Ron, Timmy, and Marty to come out. These were some of the kids whose names ended with a higher alphabet letter. I asked each of them how many tickets they had taken. After questioning them, I walked away slowly but excited and hollered out "yippee," since they had either taken an amount of tickets less than mine or none at all.

Now all I had to do was sell them, along with my brother, who I heard had taken one hundred in his upper class. I knew in my mind that he would be making a hard running dash to begin knocking on the same doors and businesses I had in mind. The same doors and businesses that often saved their empty pop bottles for us would now have to choose whom to buy a ticket or tickets from.

I did not care too much if he sold all of his tickets, since it seemed I was a sure winner if I could sell my three hundred tickets. When I asked for the three hundred tickets, I was not interested in earning the seventy-five cents if I sold all the tickets. I was more interested in obtaining the fifteen free tickets and a chance to win the turkey.

My plans were to surprise my mother with it for a Christmas present and a big turkey dinner. Winning the school prize, whatever it might be this year, for selling the most tickets was not on my mind. I had forgotten all about that and wanted only to win the turkey.

It was an early November day in 1946 when the Sisters passed out the tickets in their respective classrooms. This would leave several weeks for the children to sell as many tickets as they possibly could. The weather was bitter cold, and mounds of snow were piled up everywhere along the roads and in people's driveways. Many of the children would not be allowed to go out by themselves, and their parents would not join them in below-freezing weather. Perhaps, I thought, this might provide me with an advantage!

I did not go straight home this day but ran all the way to my first stop and a possible sale of some tickets. I opened the door into Johnny's candy store. Johnny was a good friend of my parents and liked my brother and me. I walked up to his counter and said, "Hello, Johnny." Then I asked him if he wanted to buy any tickets to win the big turkey in front of the Liberty Meat Market. Johnny, a big, boisterous, jovial Italian most of the time, looked at me and said, "Your brother was just here and hustled me to buy some of his tickets. I bought twenty from him and that's enough, since all I really need is just one to win."

I thanked him, and moaning about it a little bit, told him, "I took three hundred tickets, and it's going to be very hard selling them in this weather." Then, with a dejected look on my face, I turned away to walk out of his store. Johnny must have seen the look of rejection on my face as I turned away, and he called out to me loudly. He said, "Just a minute, you little Jabloak." He often called a lot of people this name, which was probably an Italian word that I never have understood to this day. He said, "Give me twenty of those tickets, but I better win something."

I handed him the book of tickets, and he wrote his name on the space allocated in the book. Then he tore his tickets, each with a sequential number on it, out of the book. The pieces of paper left in the book, with a ticket number to match the ticket torn off by him, would be placed in the raffle cage for the drawing. He handed me four quarters, which he took out of his National brass-plated cash register to pay for the tickets, and I put them in my mackinaw coat pocket.

I was very excited with my first sale of the day, thanked him again, and ran out of the store very happy. I was also excited, since I had at least tied my brother in selling tickets. I could never beat him at any game we played or run faster than he did, and it frustrated me at times. Perhaps, I thought, I may finally be able to beat him at selling tickets!

Outside the store and feeling very confident, I said, "This is easy. I should get rid of my tickets by tomorrow and will have to ask Sister for some more." By selling a large quantity of tickets early, it would enhance my chances of winning the turkey even more. I turned and walked home, which was only about seventy-five feet away from Johnny's candy store. It would be years later before I found out that Johnny's candy store, like most of the candy stores in town and the surrounding towns, was just a façade.

His major business was booking numbers and taking bets on the horse races. This was in addition to paying off someone who ran up a lot of points on one of the pinball machines in the store or came up with a winning number out of a punchboard. The selling of candy bars (many of which were quite often stale) and cold sodas was not all that important to the survival of his business. The stale candy bars were often used as giveaways to the local policemen patrolling the streets for overdue parking meter "red" flags.

My father was working again, and I greeted my mother and kissed her as I entered the house. She asked me if I wanted some and made me a cup of hot chocolate that I drank down in a hurry without burning my lips. Then I bundled up and got as warm as I could in my brother's hand-me-down, red and black plaid mackinaw before going out again.

I also put on a pair of old and worn gray wool hunting socks, acting as gloves to keep my hands warm, before leaving the house and setting out to sell more tickets. When I opened the door, it was still snowing lightly. The temperature was dropping fast, and the sky was becoming cloudy and turning into a swirling misty black. Nightfall was approaching fast.

My next stop would be at the Turtle Creek, auto parts store next door to my house. The owner and a few customers were standing in line inside the store when I entered it, and after talking to all of them, I only managed to sell five more tickets. If my arithmetic was correct, I still needed to sell 275 tickets.

I walked down the street and went into the White Tower, Valley Buick, Greasy Spoon, New Deal, Zafarasas's shoeshine parlor, and several other businesses close by and sold five more tickets. After entering several more businesses and talking to the owners and various patrons, none of them were interested or had already made a commitment to buy tickets from someone else.

I approached several other people as I walked up and down the main street with my hands freezing cold even though covered with the old socks, and none of them were interested either. A lot of them told me it was a bad time to be selling tickets in the cold weather. Many said the ticket was too expensive or it was just too cold to stop for. Many others said they did not want to remove their gloves to fill out their names on the ticket. I offered to take off my socks and fill the form out for them myself, but they still were not interested. "Lucky them," I said, since they had good leather or wool gloves to wear and keep their hands somewhat warm.

My hands were still freezing, even with my improvised gloves on. I walked over and stood outside the busy Giant Eagle Market and talked to a lot of people entering and leaving the store. They, too, were busy or cold and not interested in what I had to say or sell. I was becoming extremely cold by now, and in addition to my hands freezing, my feet and toes were starting to turn numb. By now it was seven o'clock in the evening, the streets were empty, and there were very few shoppers left in the stores. I decided to go home to warm up, get something to eat, and finish my arithmetic and spelling homework assignment that was due to be turned in.

Before starting the homework assignment, I laid my improvised gloves and my clodhoppers down on the floor register to dry them out so they would be ready in the morning to wear to school. I threw the socks that I had on my feet down the cellar steps for my mother to wash and would have clean, dry ones to put on in the morning. I went to bed that evening very pleased with myself and happy that I had sold some tickets already.

I did not see any other kids from school out selling tickets during the evening. This pleased me even more and made me think they were not interested and it was just too cold for them to go outside. What a bunch of sissies they all were, I mumbled to myself as I dosed off. I was asleep when Richard came home and was not able to ask him how or if he had sold anymore tickets. The next morning I asked him how many tickets he sold and he told me, "It is none of your business try and guess". This hurt me a little bit, but it was his way of agitating me at times making me become very curious.

How wrong I was about the other kids not going outside in the cold. The next day at school, several of them were already talking about how many tickets they had sold. They had sold them in the G. C. Murphy five-and-ten store, which was always a busy place, and right after school.

Like a big dummy, I had completely forgotten about going into the store in my haste to beat my brother to Johnny's store. It also was just steps away from the Giant Eagle Market, where I had stood so long and sold nothing. In addition, just as I had been afraid, Mary Ellen was telling some of the kids about the hundred tickets her father bought. This news was bad enough, but then she said she was going to ask Sister for another hundred tickets. Someone said that Bernadette in the fourth grade had sold one hundred tickets to her Irish family and friends and Audrey had sold fifty tickets to her family.

These girls did not even have to leave their houses and go out into the bitter cold, and they had already sold more tickets than me. I was the one who had walked around in the falling snow and cold weather for four hours last night. Thinking about it, I said to myself, "Selling the remaining tickets is not going to be as easy as I had thought after quickly selling twenty of them to Johnny." Today was Friday, the last day of school, and the snow had stopped falling, but it was still bitter cold outside. There would be a lot of people coming into town from all over the valley to do their weekend shopping, which should be beneficial in helping me sell more tickets.

I could not wait for school to end that day so I could get started again on selling my remaining tickets. I ran all the way home and greeted my mother, who was cleaning up her kitchen, which was permeated with the smell of rising yeast bread. With her permission, I grabbed at a group of fresh-baked homemade warm buns, tore off a couple, spread some margarine on them, and devoured them quickly. Afterward, I helped her place and tie down a small blanket and piece of oilcloth backing on our chrome and blue Formica table to protect it from damage.

Everything was covered over in our house to protect it; even the couches and chairs had plastic sheets placed over them. Most of my friends' parents did the same thing with their furnishings. The only time I can remember my parents removing these protective coverings for any period of time was for my brother's high school graduation party. After years of all these items being covered over, they looked very new and as if they had just been delivered. Both of my grandparents on the Polish and Irish side of the family also covered their furniture in the same manner.

The reality here was that people of this depression-era generation worked hard to buy the items they had acquired and assumed they might not be able to do it again. These added coverings were a way of ensuring their protection for years to come. I often laugh today and call it "hunky décor."

I started to leave the house shortly after consuming the hot buns, but my brother, Richard, came into the house.

We talked about going sledding later that evening up on the Greensburg Pike road. As we talked, he began stuffing his mouth with the homemade buns he covered with apple butter. He stopped quickly when my mother smacked the back of his hands with a large wooden spoon she was holding. Then she looked at him and said, "Mind your manners and get permission before you take something."

We set a time to meet in front of Diven's Pennzoil gas station with our sleds at six o'clock. Richard, after getting permission from Mother, consumed several more buns. He then told me, to my astonishment, that he had just sold eighty tickets for the turkey raffle. He sold them to John, the owner of the auto parts store, and several of his employees. He said he was going to keep twenty-five cents of the money rather than taking five free chances on the turkey. He also said he was going to buy us each a bowl of chili at the Greasy Spoon restaurant when we were done with our sledding that evening.

The Greasy Spoon was a small, hole-in-the-wall restaurant, run by a Greek family that catered to the locals and the hoards of people who worked at the large East Pittsburgh and Turtle Creek Westinghouse Electric plants. The Greasy Spoon gave you all the little round oyster crackers you wanted with your bowl of ordered chili. We kids often took extra handfuls of the crackers and would stuff them into our mackinaw coat pockets to eat as a snack for the next few days.

I asked Richard how many more tickets he had to sell, and he replied, "None." Then he told me he would not be asking for any more tickets to sell. I was relieved to hear him say this, since he would have visited the same territorial apartment buildings, people, and businesses I had in mind. This would have made it more difficult for me to dispose of my tickets.

My hopes of selling more tickets increased dramatically after this conversation, since one of my stiffest competitors was now quitting early. I said to him, "See you at old man Divens' gas station at six o'clock tonight; don't forget to bring your sled." I pulled on my heavy mackinaw, which had not dried out completely from the night before. I reached down to the floor register and picked up and placed the dried-out socks on my hands.

I left my house and walked over to Pullen's drugstore to attempt to sell some additional tickets. It was nice and warm inside, and some people were sitting at the soda fountain on the round, red leather, padded seats on chrome stools. Other people were sitting inside the Formica-topped booths at the rear of the store, and they all removed their coats and gloves since it was so warm. I went up to the fountain area and asked several people sitting on the stools if they wanted to buy any tickets. I placed them on the counter along with a pencil to fill in their name.

Surprisingly, I sold ten tickets right away. I wandered back to the booths in the rear of the store and sold another five tickets. I walked across the street over to Isaly's. After approaching and talking to several more people, I managed to sell ten more tickets.

Just 250 more tickets to go, I said to myself. By this time it was almost six o'clock. I remembered about meeting my brother and ran home to get my Flexible Flyer sled, leaning against the side of our rented clapboard and Insulbrick-covered house. Before leaving the house, I opened the front door and called into my mother.

When she approached, I handed her my remaining tickets and money for safekeeping and told her, "I love you," while blowing her a kiss. I did not want to take a chance on losing the money or tickets while sledding down the steep Pike and taking all those sharp turns that lay ahead. Knowing where I was going, she said, "Please be careful, and tell your brother to watch out for the trains and cars and to take care of you."

I looked at her and said, "You know he will, Mom; he always does, just like I look out for him."

I walked into the back of Farmer's Alley and pulled my sled along, with a now-frozen piece of rope behind me. I continued to pull the sled over the soft-packed snow to Divens' gas station, located at the beginning of the alley.

I found my brother waiting inside the small, but warm, gas station office talking to Irv and George, two of Mr. Divens' sons. I kicked the snow off of my clodhoppers on the side of the concrete entrance step and made them as clean as I could. I knew how much it upset Mr. Divens when people tracked a lot of snow into his office. Mr. Divens was a gruff sort of man, but all in all, he was pretty nice with my brother and me.

We were always very respectful of him, since he would let us use his compressed-air tank to blow up our bicycle tires. When there were not a lot of cars on the island or inside his stalls or work areas, he also loaned us tools and gave us free patches to fix flats on our bikes. As we became older, Mr. Divens gave us jobs of shoveling snow off his gas station grounds and putting away coal. During the summer, it was a job of changing oil and greasing and washing cars.

Mr. Divens appeared from a small room he had in the back of the office where he did his bookkeeping. He asked what I was up to. I said, "Richard and I are going to go up the Greensburgh Pike to do some sledding."

He said, "Be careful and watch out for the trains and cars." This seemed to be a common expression coming from most parents and concerned citizens worrying about us kids.

There would not be too much traffic on the road this time of night due to the icy conditions. The gas rationing, which was still in effect, would also keep many cars off the roads, but crossing or riding our sleds over the railroad tracks could be very dangerous tonight. However, there were numerous flashing red and orange colored crossing lights that would come on, and bells would start clanging to warn everyone of approaching trains.

The wooden crossing-arm guards would also drop down to stop vehicles from crossing the tracks as trains approached. At times, even with all this warning and since every boy thought his sled was faster, boys might "chance it" and go right underneath the wood crossing guards. During the great sled race that was being planned later on in the week by a lot of the boys, lookouts would be posted at this particular location to tell the sled riders to either continue on or stop.

The lookouts might wave them on to go right under the crossing, or halt them if they thought the train was getting too close for them to make it over the tracks without getting run over by the train. Other lookouts would be strung out all along the Pike from the very top down to the bottom by Divens' gas station, on the lookout for approaching cars.

Remembering about the raffle tickets, which I did not have on me at the time, I approached Mr. Divens. He seemed to be in a good mood, and I asked him if he knew about the turkey in front of the Liberty Meat Market that was going to be raffled off by Saint Colman's. He looked at me and said yes. I told him I was selling tickets but did not have them with me, and asked if he would like to buy a couple.

I proceeded to tell him that I could bring them by tomorrow sometime. He asked me, "How much are they?" I told him that they were five cents each, and he said he would buy five from me. After hearing this conversation, his two sons spoke up and said they would each buy five tickets also. I thanked all of them and said again that I would come by tomorrow with the tickets. Now I only had 235 more tickets to sell.

Richard and I left the warm office, went outside, put on our sock gloves, and headed up toward the long steep Pike. We pulled our sleds up the Pike six or seven times that evening for our long, fast, enjoyable rides down through the blizzard-like conditions. Since we had no lookouts this evening, the toes of our clodhoppers became worn down a little. This was from using them as brakes to slow down and look out for trains before we came to the dangerous railroad crossing.

Before succumbing to the cold weather, we took one last speedy ride down the steep Pike as fast as we could. At the bottom of the Penn Avenue extension, we cut through the gas station island and continued sledding to the back door of our house without falling off the sled or stopping.

This was a great feat in itself for any kid to accomplish, and the other boys around town were envious that we could do it and they could not. Of course, the right snow conditions, a little ice, great sled speed, and the skill of the driver also helped. When we reached the back of our house, we rolled off our sleds totally exhausted onto our backs and into the cold snow.

If our father were to catch us doing this, it would mean a beating from his razor strap. Clothing was expensive and not to be treated this way. We rested awhile longer on our backs and blew out rings of white cloudy air, pretending to be smoking cigarettes.

Conditions were below zero by now, but within a few months the summer heat and humidity would have both of us pleading with the owner of the icehouse on Brown Avenue to let us go inside it. At times, he would let us open the large green door, which was secured by a hasped metal handle, and go inside to be greeted by a cooling, slow-moving breeze falling upon us. When we were deep inside the icehouse, we would hop up and sit down on a fifty—or one-hundred-pound block of ice. The ice was covered over with a piece of canvas to cool it down. The canvas kept our pants dry and also helped to keep the ice from melting down too much prior to being sold to the public.

We generally got to do this when we pulled our little red wagon to the icehouse dock and ordered a couple blocks of ice to take home for our icebox. As one can guess, we did not need to get much ice during the cold winter months. My parents would nail up an old, wood-slatted, double-sided orange crate on an outside window ledge to keep perishable food, meat, milk, and butter from spoiling.

If you forgot about it, which many people did, everything would come out frozen when the outside temperature dropped below freezing. Meats were not a problem since they were thawed as needed, but frozen milk, eggs, and juices that were often needed quickly could be a problem. As tough as times were, in some cases, they would have to be thrown away.

The owner of the icehouse never expressed concern or told us how long we could stay inside. I guess he knew we would only be able to stand the cold chill for so long. It was not long after we entered that we found ourselves reaching for the hasped metal handle on the inside of the green door to let ourselves out.

The coming of spring and the hot summer heat also meant that it would be time for wallpaper cleaning, which we hated. Our old clapboard and Insulbrick house, like many of the other houses in the neighborhood, required that this task be done. The thick-layered black soot, rising through the floor registers from the potbellied coal-burning stove in the cellar below, stuck to the walls like mud. This black ashy substance, along with the town's factory-released agents, had to be carefully removed. This removal was done by using a green-colored goop, a gummy rubber material.

The material, taken out of a small metal can, had to be rolled up or shaped into the size of a small ball by each person doing the cleaning. With the ball in hand, one would begin wiping off the wallpaper with an up and down stroke. With the first stroke you took, it was like erasing the black of night and seeing the early morning light appearing behind it. By most environmental health or OSHA standards today, it would require a hazmat team to remove such material.

One thing we kids liked about the rubbery substance was that it made great throwing pieces to hit someone in the head while they were not looking. I had quite a few "goonies" on my head from when my brother really let me have it good with his throws. As I recall, he had quite a few "goonies" on his head also.

We picked ourselves up and off of the snow-covered ground and placed both sleds upright along the side of the house. On this cold night, the thin pulling ropes tied to the sleds stuck straight out. Due to the freezing temperature, they were now in a frozen state and did not fall toward the ground as the law of gravity demanded.

We cleaned the embedded snow off of our clodhoppers by scraping them across the sharp sled runners. Then we helped each other brush all of the snow off our mackinaws and pants before entering our house—and before Dad came around—to avoid a beating. Several weeks earlier, we had come home with mud and dirt all over these new mackinaws. Our father, after seeing the mackinaws, gave us both a mild beating with his homemade leather cat-o'-nine-tails.

Looking down at our clodhoppers, we both remarked about how much leather or skin we had lost from the toe end while using them as braking devices. It helped in steering the sled and slowing down when rounding a sharp curve or crossing the train tracks. We would sometimes catch hell from our father for doing this if he saw them, since he said shoes were also too expensive to be worn out so soon.

On this night we were lucky, since for sure had he seen the clodhoppers, we would have felt the sting of his razor belt or cat-o'-nine tails. In spite of the beatings, Richard and I both loved him very much and even more so as we became older.

Most kids during this time did not have a watch, and we knocked on our house door to ask our mother what time it was. She said, "Seven thirty; are you hungry?" I looked at Rich and said, "Do you still feel like a bowl of hot chili?" He said, "I sure do," and we walked over to the Greasy Spoon, less than a hundred feet away. We entered through the front wood and glass door, which was decorated with a Coca-Cola bottle decal. We sat down and twirled around a few times on the soft leather, padded chrome stools, like we were on a ride at Kennywood Park. Then we ordered two bowls of red chili from Gus the Greek.

The bowls of red chili were topped with onions if requested, and we added the free little round oyster crackers for additional filling. We gulped the chili down quickly before leaving, and Richard laid down ten cents—two buffalo and Indian head nickels—on the counter. Then we helped ourselves to some more oyster crackers and put them in our mackinaw coat pockets before we left the restaurant.

Gus saw us doing this, and when we said good night to him, he mumbled something back that we could not understand. But we could make out his last few words, which were, "I have to pay for those crackers, you know." Gus was always good to the kids in town, and even if they could not buy something on the cold winter days, he often let them step into the restaurant to warm up a little bit.

Some of these kids would help themselves to the oyster crackers on the counter when he was busy or not looking! Knowing Gus and how nice he was, we all knew that he knew we were doing this. Just as with my brother and me on occasion, Gus pretty much ignored the free oyster cracker taking, since he knew for some of them it might be their lunch or dinner.

Rich and I had exclusive rights when it came to removing snow from the sidewalk in front of the Greasy Spoon, and often we would exchange this chore for several bowls of his red chili. I should mention that we had exclusive rights on shoveling the snow off of just about every business sidewalk on both sides of the street from Turtle Creek to the beginning of East Pittsburg and Wilmerding Borough.

We would also do this Adam Smith-type of bartering for pop, candy bars, chips, comic books, and so on with some of the other local businesses. We even had the White Tower exchanging hamburgers or cheeseburgers and hot chocolate for removal of snow and ice from their sidewalk. This did not happen every time, and we were paid some money in addition to the bartering. Sometimes the snow shoveling was not an easy task, and most kids charged a higher fee than Rich and I. Often we were just paid for services rendered.

We went inside our rented house, cleaned up before going to bed, said our evening prayers, and fell asleep quickly. Although both of us had homework to do, we ignored it, since it was Friday and we still had the weekend to complete it. Waking up very late after a solid night's sleep on Saturday morning, the first thing I thought about was getting out and selling more tickets. My father had other plans, though, that would halt my ticket selling for a while.

He told Richard and me after he got up that we had to clean the heavy snow load off the top of the flat roof on the house before we did anything or could be free to play. After we finished this job, we were anxious to leave the house, but our father then decided we had to go to the slaughterhouse with him in Pitcairn to buy some kielbasa, slab bacon, and ham. The road into the slaughterhouse was never paved and very muddy most of the time, especially when snow or rain had fallen, and he said he might need us around to push the car out if he got stuck.

By the time we got back home, it was mid-afternoon, and I figured that most of the other kids probably had covered the town and local stores already and sold a lot of tickets. Because of this, I thought I would not have much luck, so I stayed home and read from a backlog of comic books I had been saving. When I got up Sunday, I figured that would be a bad day for selling tickets also, since most businesses were closed. Most people also went to church and did not like someone knocking on their door on a Sunday, a day of rest.

I decided to forget about selling any tickets and told my mother I was going to Mass. Instead, I went back to sledding on the Pike for several hours. On my last ride, I turned into the gas station at the bottom of the hill and gave Mr. Divens the fifteen tickets that he and his sons had bought. I came back home, and luckily I was never asked by my parents about the Gospel or what color the priest's vestments were. I finished my homework assignments to be turned in on Monday morning at school.

I was to learn later on what a big mistake I made by not going out on Sunday to sell more tickets. At school the next day. it was announced that Marty had sold 150 tickets in front of Saint Colman's Church on Sunday by standing outside and soliciting a lot of the parishioners who did not have any children in school. He did this before and after each Mass from 9:00 a.m. until 1:00 p.m. In addition, he also sold fifty more tickets to his family and their friends.

As far as I knew, Marty was way ahead of everyone, including Mary Ellen, by now. I was very mad at myself for what I had done and for becoming lazy. I promised myself that I would try selling tickets every day from now on up until the drawing cutoff time.

Here I was with 235 tickets still left, and Marty had sold two hundred and would probably be asking for additional tickets to sell. To add insult to injury, my good friend Audrey, who was always looking out for me and helping out with my homework, told me she had sold all of her tickets to her family. Selling tickets to your family, friends, and people on the streets seemed to be better than canvassing the local businesses and waiting on customers to appear. I tried this approach after school for several days and did not sell anything.

I was successful, though, when I visited my four Irish aunts and uncles living nearby. They were all working at the time, and they each bought twenty tickets from me. I visited my grandparents on the Irish side, and they purchased twenty tickets from me also. All the tickets I had sold to date now came to 165, which placed me close to Marty.

I had several other aunts and uncles and my grandparents on the Polish side who did not live close by. I was hoping when I did see and talk to them, they would buy some tickets also. On the way home, I stopped in John's drugstore, only to find out that Carmen had beaten me to it and sold him several tickets. Even after begging and pleading and groveling on my knees with John to buy some tickets from me, he just was not interested! I got up off my knees, thanked him, and left his store.

For the next week, the afternoons and evenings continued to be bitter cold and made me feel like my hands and feet would fall off from being frozen solid. I attempted to sell more tickets by knocking on all the local residences and apartments of people I knew and did not know, and was only able to sell another five tickets. Most of the people told me they just could not afford to buy even a single ticket and were sorry they could not help me. I still had 130 tickets to sell.

Every evening when I got home, I quickly removed my mock gloves made from the worn-out socks, clodhoppers, and socks and stood directly on top of a floor register to thaw out my feet. I would then hold my hands in the air in front of me to capture some of the register heat and fold it into my cold hands.

The weekend came again quickly, but it was just too cold outside and snowing too heavily to attempt going out. Obee's tow trucks were pulling cars out of ditches and embankments everywhere in town. Several streetcars had slid off their metal track, blocking traffic in both directions of the town's small two-lane street. At times, it was hard for even a single car to travel up the town's main road, due to the high mounds of snow. These snow mounds were created as the snowplows scraped both sides of the narrow streets and kept pushing the snow up higher and higher.

My father came in the house shortly after I arrived home and said it was a mess outside and even the bars were empty because of the heavy snowfall. You knew the weather had to be really bad outside if the bars were empty, since a good stiff shot of whiskey was what a lot of men and some women took to warm up.

Thanksgiving was approaching and made it even more difficult to sell any tickets. More people were telling me they were spending what little money they had on more important things. Some told me they were not interested in the turkey, since they had already bought a chicken or turkey from Izzy Goldstein, Duncan's, or one of the other local markets. We went to my Polish grandparents' for Thanksgiving and had chicken, rabbit, squab, ham, and kielbasa for dinner.

After the dinner, I approached my Polish grandparents, three uncles, and two aunts about the tickets I was selling, and I sold another 20 tickets. If my arithmetic was correct, I needed to sell only 110 more tickets. The next Monday at school, I turned in the money for all the tickets I had sold to date, and Sister said I was doing a good job and thanked me.

During the morning recess period, I heard that Mary Ellen, who had not gone outside in the cold even once to sell any tickets, had sold another hundred tickets to relatives. Now I had two people whom I liked very much to catch up to and sell more tickets. The closer Christmas got, the more stingy people were becoming with their money, or they had already purchased a raffle ticket on the turkey from another kid.

I kept braving the snowy days and bitter cold nights the next week after leaving school. I walked up and down countless steps in the local apartment buildings knocking on more doors and managed to sell just fifteen more tickets. Some of the people looked at me and said, "You again? Didn't I tell you the last time you were here that I was not interested? Don't bother knocking on this door again. "If you do, I will call Chief Whalen on you."

The drawing was two weeks away, and it seemed as if I would never be able to sell the ninety five tickets I had left. This would reduce my mother's chance of winning the turkey and it made me feel bad. Ninety tickets left to go, and by now I had no intention of asking Sister for any more tickets. In addition, due to taking on the task of selling the tickets, I was missing out on a lot of good sledding and playing in the snow with my friends and brother. They were all probably pulling their sleds behind them and walking up the Greensburg Pike for another great ride. Anybody who knew anything about a "super great," long, fast, and the most dangerous sled ride went up to the top of the Pike. To a good sled rider in town, the Pike was sort of like the surfer of today, wanting to catch that one big ultimate wave.

By the next week, I had exhausted all my avenues and ideas for selling more tickets. I did not want to ask my parents to buy any, since they had more important things to purchase with what little money they had for Christmas. At this juncture, I decided that I would start walking toward and visit every business on the main street that I had not taken the time to visit earlier.

I thought it might be a futile effort, since a lot of the other kids had been selling at these locations ever since the tickets were first handed out. I started at the Coney Island hot dog restaurant owned by the Cortavos family. After this, I proceeded to go into or stand outside the following businesses that lined the two sides of the main streets of Penn and Braddock Avenue. I also walked into some of the close-by side street businesses. All in all, I visited:

Carrarea's candy store

Cima's poolroom

Businessman's club

Valley Buick

Conn's Bar and Grill

The Friendly Tavern

Olympic Theatre

Mellon Bank

Myers Insurance

Axton Jewelry

A & P

Taylor's men's store

Mandell's Jewelry

Speelmans Café

Jack's Ladies' Apparel

Coleman Insurance

Terry Paint & Wall Covering

AOH Club

Little Pullen's Drug Store

Caesar's Bar & Grill

Mraz Drug Store

Ridgeway Mobile gas station

Bereyl Chevrolet

Ferri Brothers' Market

As I passed by the Ancient Order of Hibernians' Club (AOH), which is a Catholic Irish American fraternal organization, I remembered how some people referred to it differently. A lot of residents, including my Irish side of the family, would call it the "any old hunky" club. It was always said in a humorous way and often brought a good laugh from many people first hearing this saying. Especially the members of the Ancient Order of Hibernians.

I stopped after canvassing the Ferri Brothers' Market, which just about covered one side of the street. The only other businesses beyond this point were Altman's feedstore and several bars and grills, which I did not want to go into. I began counting how many more tickets I had sold on this journey and was elated to find out that I had sold another twenty and leaving only seventy five more tickets to sell.

My hands and feet were freezing badly, and my snotty nose was running terribly. The slime from my cold nostrils cascaded like a waterfall down to and over my semi-frozen lips and chin. I took the right sleeve of my mackinaw coat and quickly drew it across my nose, lips, and chin to wipe off this slimy fluid that was already beginning to freeze in place. This left hard, silver-like, shiny, crystallized formations to freeze on the coat sleeve, and they could not be brushed off.

I crossed the street to Keller's hardware and went inside, not caring if I sold another ticket at this time. All I wanted to do was get my hands and feet thawed out and my body warmed up a little. I asked Mr. Keller and several of his patrons after a while, but not one of them was interested in buying a ticket. I thanked Mr. Keller and stood next to his coal-filled potbellied stove for another ten minutes. When my hands and body were good and warm, I left the store. I proceeded to quickly canvas the following remaining businesses on this side of the street:

Mary's dairy

Bova's shoe repair

Eshman's Sporting

Tipy Walker Dry Cleaning

Milton Shoes

Murphy's 5 & 10

Caruthers Meat Market

O'Neill's bakery

Anton's soda fountain

Giant Eagle Market

Shiring Real Estate

Carlton's men's store

R&A restaurant

Loreski's Music and Hobby Store

Fine Hardware

Pinky's poolroom

Olsen's Bar & Grill

The New Deal Bar & Restaurant

The Greasy Spoon

The names and businesses I have mentioned are what one would expect to find, perhaps by a different name, in just about every small eastern town or borough during this time period. Many, if not all of them, have disappeared over the years, mainly due to the introduction of the large shopping centers. The convenience of everything being centrally located and free parking also contributed to these mom-and-pop stores going out of business.

The large box stores like Wal-Mart, Costco, Sam's Club, Target, and many others are still taking their toll even today on many small businesses. Throughout the eastern rust belt, as it is known today, one can still drive through many of these towns looking at dilapidated houses, buildings, and parcels of vacant land that once housed great factories and employed thousands of people. I managed to sell another fifteen tickets during this campaign, and afterward, I ran home as fast as I could to get warm again and something to eat.

Before entering the house, I gave my runny nose another swipe with the sleeve of my mackinaw coat, placing another layer of cold, freezing, snotty, shiny slime on it. When I entered the house, my mother commented on what was on my coat sleeve. I hung the coat up on a nail that had been pounded into the wall and told her it was rock salt the borough truck crews put on the roads to keep them from freezing over and it hit the coat while I was sledding.

She never questioned me, but told me I should know better than to leave ugly stuff like that on it and to clean it off before coming in the house. As gentle and sweet as my mother was, I now know she knew what was on the coat, and she saved me the embarrassment of a severe scolding. In addition, she was also saying something to the effect of it not being nice or mannerly to be doing such an ugly and distasteful thing!

After warming up a bit and eating a warm Polish potato pancake (*pilutski*) with some Heinz ketchup poured on the top of it, I ate another one with sour cream spread on it. I then used some more of the arithmetic lessons I had learned in school at Saint Colman's and mentally calculated in my head how many more tickets I had to sell. I went upstairs to the bathroom to clean up and into my bedroom from there. I said my evening prayers, made a good act of contrition, and jumped into bed. Richard was still out sledding. The last thing I remembered before falling fast asleep was that I only had sixty more tickets to sell.

The next day I waited on my brother, who was a year and a half older than me, after school let out. We ran home together as fast as we could to see who could get to our house first. I lost again, and to this day, he has always been faster and I never could beat him in a foot race. However, since he has had both of his knees replaced recently with orthopedic prostheses and I have not, I have been thinking about challenging him to another race! Our mother had some hot Ovaltine ready for us to drink when we arrived home, and it sure tasted good. When we finished the drink, she asked if I would walk over to the Westinghouse "I" gate and buy her the *Sun Telegraph*. This was her favorite newspaper.

I bundled up again in my mackinaw and walked over to buy the newspaper for her. When I reached the paper stand, I noticed the paperboy was selling a lot of papers to both the incoming and outgoing factory workers without doing much work. I purchased my mother's paper from him, and while walking back home, this great idea hit me. I suddenly realized that I had not stood outside of the Westinghouse "I" gate and attempted to sell any tickets to the hundreds of daytime, second-shift or nighttime workers that came from all over and different towns. This could work almost as well as what Marty had done, by standing outside the church and selling his tickets, but even more so.

The next week starting after school and without telling anyone, I went and stood in front of the "I" gate for two days and managed to sell the remaining sixty tickets with ease. It was still cold outside but a lot easier, since the paper stand was nearby and the stand's owner had a fire going in a fifty-five-gallon metal barrel. He did this to keep warm while he sold papers, and he let me use it to warm my hands. By standing close to the barrel, I was able to slide my clodhoppers under it to warm my feet up also, since it was raised up from the ground by several bricks.

Sometimes my clodhoppers got so hot, steam would begin to come off of them, and I could feel the heat coming inside them and starting to burn my feet a little. When this happened, it did not take me very long to pull my clodhoppers out from underneath the barrel. This same type of heat system was used by the Westinghouse and U.S Steelworkers labor unions to keep warm while they were out on the streets striking for better wages and benefits. If it were not for these workers and other unionized organizations like the United Mine Workers, few of us would have some of the benefits we do today.

The workers at this site buying the tickets were also able to easily write their names down for the tickets they bought by placing them on the upright and supporting newsstand. I turned in the rest of the money from the sold tickets to Sister and also filled out my fifteen earned free tickets with my mother's name on them. Sister congratulated and thanked me. I never did ask Sister for any more tickets even though there was still another week left before the drawing for the turkey. I told the other kids who still had tickets about my luck at the "I" gate, but for most of them, it was too far away from their home to walk to. The final week of the drawing had some children asking for more tickets to sell, but not in any large quantities.

Rumor had it that Mary Ellen had sold more tickets than any other kid in the school and would probably win the prize. I felt no hard feelings toward her, even knowing she did not have to work as hard as I did to sell the amount of tickets I took. It was not her fault that she had certain economic advantages I did not. I was pleased that Marty and Audrey had done so well also.

The drawing for the turkey was held on December 20 in front of the Liberty Meat Market at 4:00 p.m. The round barrel cage with all the sold tickets placed inside it, with the people's names, was also in front of the market. Its long wooden handle was sticking out, just waiting to be taken by someone's hand and whirled about feverishly to mix the tickets up.

One of the men standing in the gawking crowd, who I believe was Mr. Emil Pasquale, was tapped on his shoulder. He was asked if he would like to spin the wheel and mix up the tickets, and he said, "Yes, ah, I would a like it a very much." He wound the handle around several times, and watching the wire cage spin, every onlooker could see the tickets bouncing about inside it. The wire cage finally stopped spinning, and Mrs. Victoria was invited to reach in and pull out the winning ticket.

The small metal hinged door leading into the inside of the cage was unlocked by someone from the meat market. The door was opened up for Mrs. Victoria to put her hand inside the cage and draw out a single winning ticket. When she placed her hand in the cage, she closed her eyes, and with her tiny fingers grabbed onto a single ticket. She opened her eyes, and while holding the ticket, was asked by the individual from the market to please read out loud the name of the winner.

Mrs. Victoria looked at the printed name on the ticket closely and said out loud, for everyone to hear, "Jim Divens' Pennzoil station." After she called the name out, everyone clapped their hands, and the crowd that had formed quickly also dispersed quickly. I was disappointed that my mother had not won the turkey, but pleased after all my effort that I had sold the winning ticket. I was also happy that it was Mr. Divens, whom we kids and my family liked.

The next day at school, it was announced that all of the tickets sold by the children in grades one through eight over the last couple weeks and entered into the drawing came to 1150. This was quite a feat and made a considerable amount of money for the school, even after ticket printing and the expense of buying and feeding the turkey. It was also announced that Mary Ellen had sold the most tickets and won the prize.

To this day, I forget what the prize was. My only regret was that my mother would not be getting a turkey as I had hoped for a Christmas present. I left school that day and headed home to tell my mother about Mr. Divens winning the turkey and Mary Ellen winning the prize. She told me she was sorry and thought that I was going to win the prize for selling the most tickets, since I worked so hard at it. She walked away quietly into her kitchen and proceeded to make me a great big jumbo sandwich on white bread with a "Kraft Miracle Whip Salad Dressing" spread. After I was done eating my sandwich, I went outside to the side of the house, retrieved my sled, and headed for the Pike to catch up with my friends.

The next day, December 21, was my baby sister Judy's birthday, and there was going to be a small party for her. When I got home and entered the house, there was a lot of noise and laughing going on inside. I thought they must have started the party without me.

When I walked into the room, my mother came toward me and gave me a big hug and kiss. She then told me that Mr. Divens had told the Liberty Meat Market to dress out the turkey he won and have it delivered to our house. He told my mother and father that he watched how hard I worked at selling the tickets and with four small children in our family, we, as neighbors, could use the turkey a lot more.

I later learned that the Divens family had a turkey dinner on Thanksgiving Day and were not interested in having another one so soon. Instead, a baked ham would be placed on their dinner table Christmas Day.

I looked at my mother and said, "He only bought five tickets. Some people bought twenty and forty. How lucky can you get?" I turned, walked away, and went outside to round up some of my friends and make plans for the "Great Sled Race" we were going to have during Christmas vacation.

Father and son, James W. and James B. Divens, 1930s.

CHAPTER 10

GREAT SLED RACE

I was eight years old in 1943 and watched my older brother, Richard, wake up excitedly on Christmas Day to find a new Flexible Flyer sled under our Christmas tree. I was very envious of him, but at the same time very happy to see him receive it. He now had his own sled to go out and play with Willy, Vincent, Joseph, and Charles. Robert, our Jewish friend and the same age as me, also had a sled of his own to play with. Bobby, whom I traded comic books with, lived at the bottom of the Greensburg Pike and also had his own sled. My parents could only afford to purchase one sled this Christmas due to financial hardships, and since Richard was older, he received it. Of course, it went without saying that he was to share his sled with me.

I was given a Red Ryder BB gun this Christmas and would not have to ask him if I could use his anymore. It seemed as if I was always sharing something with him that I liked and he got before me. My sisters, Joy and Judy, never received anything like our gifts and were given dolls, small sets of dishes, and a fake tin stove to pretend cook on. I guess this was not too bad, since they never pestered me or my brother to use any of our trucks, chemistry set, erector set, and the BB gun. Likewise, we never once asked or ever wanted to play with any of their girlish gifts.

Richard and I knew by now, after questioning our parents on several occasions about the authenticity of Santa Claus, that he did not physically exist. Some of the older boys had ruined our firm belief that he did exist, telling us that he did not exist and it was parents and other people who put gifts under the tree. However, even at our young age, we knew about the spirit of Christmas and the happiness it seemed to bring for everyone during the holiday season.

Our sisters were still very strong believers in Santa Claus and all excited about receiving presents. In keeping with holiday tradition and not wanting to spoil anything, we would never tell them there was no Santa Claus. It would have to be someone else telling them in later years and watching them cry. When questioned, we would only tell them there is a Santa Claus and they better be good or Santa would not bring them anything.

All of us children shared in playing with the small replica Lionel train our father placed on a large wood platform. The platform was laden with tracks, small houses, trees, small cows and horses, a horse-drawn sleigh, railroad trestles, bridges, and tunnels. It also had various businesses, like a miniature Mellon Bank building, hay and feedstore, and ice cream parlor. A small Romanesque church with a cross rising on its tall tower and a red lightbulb inside highlighted everything.

Towering above this snowy village display was a large Christmas tree, decorated with blinking red, blue, green, and orange lights. In addition, silver strips of icicles and dangling multicolored Christmas balls and peppermint sticks were neatly placed on the tree.

Outside our house, there was a little bit of snowfall earlier in the week; however, due to a warming period, it did not last long and was melting quickly. There was a small hill behind the Westinghouse Volunteer Fire Department covered with trees, and a small patch of untouched snow lay underneath them. This was the area that Richard and I would be using to test out his new sled. The hill had a forty-five-degree slope and ran about sixty feet from top to bottom.

Without eating, we dressed quickly to go outside; it was fairly warm, and there was no need for heavy, warm clothing. Richard pulled out his pocketknife and cut off a piece of clothesline rope to run through the small, drilled, open holes on the left and right sides of the sled's flexible handle.

Once he had the rope pulled through the holes, he tied each end into a secure knot and began pulling the sled lightly across some dirt and muddy areas until we reached the bottom of the hill. At the base of the hill, Richard told me to walk behind him so as not to disturb the patch of snow that was still left. I do not know why he felt he had to tell me this since I was smart enough to figure it out on my own.

It did not take long to climb to the top of the hill, and we were not winded when we reached it. Richard picked up the sled and brushed off the mud and dirt still on the runners. He laid it down on the ground in front of him in the middle of the sloping white snow. While he was doing this, I asked him if I could take the first ride. He totally ignored me and lay down on top of the sled, getting into position to take off on his ride. He shifted his body from left to right and right to left, and then he moved forward a little bit and positioned his hands on the sled's pine steering bar.

He started to move his hands inward and outward until he had just the right grip he wanted. Instead of a nine-year-old boy, he was acting like a professional race driver and checking everything out. Everything had to be perfect for him before he would push off for his sled run. While he was doing this, all I could think about was how lucky he was and how I wished it were my sled. It would not be long before he would be pushing the soles of his clodhoppers into the dirt behind him to go forward down the steep, snow-covered hill.

Suddenly he slid off the sled, reached down, picked it up quickly, and held it to his chest. I thought he was going to run, jump forward, and slam the sled into the snow with his body on the top of it. I had seen a lot of the older boys do this from time to time, to get a good start and enhance the sled's speed. Instead, he turned around, looked at me, and pushed the sled toward me, with its sharp new runners gleaming brightly from the sun and reflecting into my eyes. Then he said, "Here, Barrie, why don't you take the first ride? I love you and will get plenty more rides with you and our friends when we get more snow."

I had been allowed to use some of my friends' sleds a couple of times prior to this morning and was not a novice at sledding. Neither was Richard. I had even ridden down the steep Penn Avenue extension and past Divens' garage all by myself. I said to him, "Gee, thanks," and without hesitating I took the sled out of his hands and quickly, but gently, laid it on the ground in the middle of the snow.

With a big grin on my face and yelling out loud with joy, I thanked him and said, "Merry Christmas. I love you." After I laid the sled down, I became hesitant about which way I would ride it. I could go down the hill sitting up or lying down on my stomach—which one would it be?

I decided to ride down the hill sitting up and placed my clodhoppers on each end of the wood steering bar. I pulled the rope up into both of my hands, to avoid having it go under the sled, hit the runners, and bring the sled to an abrupt halt. I turned around, looked at Richard, and said to him, "Please give me a push," which he did. I felt the palms of both his hands pushing firmly into my back, and away I went down the hill. The sled went slowly at first, due to the snow being fresh and not packed down, but as I picked up speed the sled rose up and seemed to float on the top of the snow.

I was going quite fast by now, and suddenly, the sled came to a grinding halt, throwing me forward and off into the snow. I had run into some lighter snow, and the sled's runners had hit dirt, causing it to stop. I got up unhurt, brushed the snow off of me, and laughed out loud. Richard came running down the hill laughing out loud also, but double-checked my body to make sure I was all right.

We both gathered up some fresh snow on the edge of the hill with our hands, and threw it onto the bare spot. After several more rides, the snow became packed down even more, and I rode down the hill on the top of Richard's back. We did this several more times before the snow became too slushy to ride on anymore.

It never did snow anymore during the two weeks we were away from Saint Colman's for this Christmas holiday. Reluctantly, my brother, I, and our friends had to return to school without getting in any great sledding. Everyone was disgusted with the whole situation, which included having to go back and kneel on those hard wooden floors to say morning prayers and afternoon rosaries. It rained off and on for the next several weeks, but the temperature never did drop low enough to bring any meaningful snowfall to town.

Some light snow fell a few times in early February, but did not stay on the ground long. During and after school, the only thing we boys talked about and prayed for was getting a whole lot of new snow. Hopefully it would allow us to get some very good sledding in and, if big enough, keep us out of school. As time passed, all the kids' sleds that were outside hanging up on or lying alongside their old clapboard houses had rusty runners on them. This was not a big thing to worry about since the rust would go away quickly after a few good runs.

We wanted some heavy snowfall to begin; boredom was setting in, and we were becoming agitated with one another. Playing our games in the school yard was not good enough, and a lot of fighting and arguments started to take place and we were not speaking much. Some of the older boys became quite disruptive in class, and instead of paying attention to Sister, they were looking out the windows and praying for snow.

When I did not see some of them during morning recess and asked my sister where they were, she told me, "Sister put them in the cloakroom for not paying attention in class." Finally, in early March, we had a heavy rain at the beginning of the week. The temperature dropped fast and went to below freezing, and snow started to fall.

This time, it stayed on the ground and hills and built up to around nine inches. That was a good sign. Even the borough trucks with their snowplows were out clearing the streets and throwing out coal cinders to help the vehicles going up the steep hills. We boys knew it was time to get our sleds out, clean up the runners a little bit, and head for the best sledding hills, streets, and roads in town. The big problem was that we all had to wait until school was out to do it.

We would take no chances and promised each other we would all be on our best behavior. None of us would risk upsetting Sister and being kept after school to clean erasers and the blackboards. If anything happened, it would not leave us a lot of time to go sledding, considering we all had homework and chores that had to be done at home.

Thank God the chores would not include any snow shoveling and putting away a couple tons of coal. Therefore, Richard and I got to go sledding for three nights. I pulled him and he pulled me on the sled along through the flat streets and partly up some of the steep roads and hills we would eventually ride down. My brother and our friends pulled their sleds up past Chick's, or Mr. Holmes's, welding shop to the top of the hill alongside Tri Boro Coal Company. This time I was not going up the hill with them. It was my turn to stand at the bottom of the hill and a sharp curve located by Divens' Pennzoil gas station as a sentry.

I would be the lookout this time and responsible to watch for approaching cars. The reason this posting was necessary is because we did not sled ride on the sidewalks when the snow was good. We did our sledding in the middle of the roads, and it could become dangerous at times. When all was clear and no cars were close by, I or whoever was posted as a sentry would scream out loud that it was all right to come down the hill. If a car suddenly approached out of nowhere, the sentries would wave off the oncoming sledders to the far left or right side of the road.

This hill was about a forty-five-degree slope and dropped down for approximately three hundred feet. If the snow was good and packed and perhaps a little icy, without stopping, riders could get an extra hundred feet or more in their ride and wind up in front of the White Tower restaurant.

This sledding would go on for several hours with my brother, Vincent, Robert, Willy, Joseph, Charles, Eddy, Billy, George, and everyone taking their turn as the lookout sentry at the bottom of the hill. Although tempting, no one was ready to try the big ride down the Greensburgh Pike. The snowplows had removed most of the snow from it. In addition, a lot of the coal cinders that had been dumped on it were still around, making it too slushy and difficult to ride on.

The boys only had to turn right when they reached the top of Penn Avenue extension and go across the railroad tracks to begin their journey up to the top of the steep notoriously hill known as the "Pike." From the top of the Pike, it was a very fast half-mile ride to the very bottom of Penn Avenue. Each rider had to be very skillful and a good handler of his sled to make it through the sharp turns and bends in the road prior to reaching the railroad track crossing. One had to make a very sharp left turn after crossing over the tracks, and if they made it this far, they would be able to continue on down the Penn Avenue extension hill.

If a rider got this far without falling off his sled and made it through the sharp curve at the bottom, it was a sign they were ready to take on the Pike. I was told by some of the older boys like Toot Kale, Eddy Cole, and George Divens, who lived close by that some other great sledding areas were on upper James and Grant Streets and Oak and Maple Avenues.

If the snow was packed and icy in spots, it was possible for a rider to start at the top of James Street and ride all the way through to the bottom of Grant or Oak, which was close to a mile-long ride. After pulling a sled the long uphill mile to the top of James Street, one ride is all that was taken by the few boys and girls who attempted to ride it out to the bottom. Of course, lookout sentries had to be posted along these street routes also.

Another great ride started from the top of Maple Avenue in the front of Tommy's Bar & Grill, then make a sharp left turn onto Grant Street (hopefully without rolling over), and wind up in front of the post office. It was also possible to go on past the post office and run into the main street of town, Penn Avenue. These sentries would be on the lookout not only for cars, but also snowplows, trucks, buses, taxicabs, police and fire vehicles, and streetcars.

My brother and I were never allowed to sled on these hills when we were very young, since they were too far away from our home. As we got older, we took many runs down them, but we were never able to reach the bottom of Oak or Grant without stopping. There were just too many long flat areas along the bottom part of James to continue at a fast enough speed to accomplish it.

These were all good places to get a thrilling sled ride, but nothing, according to the older, experienced guys, could compare to taking a run down the Pike. Once your sled run started on the Pike, it was difficult to stop. If the rider did not fall off or crash and roll his sled over on the way down, they would definitely reach the bottom without stopping.

On occasion, I would jump on my brother's back as he was going down the Penn Avenue extension hill very fast and hold onto the wooden undercarriage of the sled. Sometimes while attempting to round the sharp curve, the sled would overturn and throw us both to the ground. We took turns doing this, deliberately sometimes and at very high speeds, just for the thrill and excitement of it. There was nothing more exciting, however, than to see sparks flying out from under a sled's steel runners as they cut deep into the curve and hit raw pavement or coal cinders.

Sometimes our sledding was cut short when Chief Whalen, Riggy Driscoll, Mike Madden, or the other policemen in town thought what we were doing was too dangerous. I asked myself how they knew it was dangerous, and now I know. When they were boys, many of them had found the Pike and all the other good hills to sled ride on years before us next-generation boys.

My brother and I always pulled our sisters around on our sled or the sleds of our friends. We even watched over them as they rode down the hill by themselves or on the top of our sled as a dual rider. Joy became very good at going around the sharp curves very fast, rolling over and at times even faking she was hurt as we ran toward her. Judy was still too young to attempt this type of dangerous antic on her own.

Before the night was over, multiple sled riders would be coming down the hill side by side, with some riders even jumping off their sled onto another sled or rider's back. Two riders on a sled was very common. Like a lot of us, they saw too many cowboy movies where one horse rider would jump off his horse onto another horse to get to the bad guy, and it rubbed off. At times when a car was coming too fast around a curve and up the hill, it was too late for a sentry to notify the riders. With a vehicle's lights hitting their eyes directly, some riders had to turn quickly to the left or right of it to avoid being run over. A lot of us kids wound up on occasion smashing into a large pile of snow unexpectedly. No one ever attempted to ride under one of the cars, and not one kid in our group of friends was ever hit by any vehicle while sledding on these dangerous hills.

After the third night of hard sledding, there was no place for any of us to warm up or have our broken sled runners repaired. Mr. Holmes's welding shop, where we generally went, was not open, and we had finally worn ourselves out. The nine inches of snow that had fallen was pretty much gone also. This was after the snow disintegrated because of automobile tires, chains, coal cinders, and the big borough snowplow, and there was no new snow in the weather forecast. The weekend came shortly after this, and the snow had pretty much melted away on the roads, streets, and hillsides. The running water also moved most, but not all, of the cinders off the road.

The weekend was what we all waited on, since we would get up early to have hours and hours of daylight to sled in and see the cars or whatever else was in front of us as we came down the hill. Daylight was also the time we challenged one another to a race to see whose sled would go the fastest. There were times when my sister Joy would act as referee and get us boys all lined up in a row at the top of a short hill; then she would walk to the bottom and give a signal to begin. After she gave the signal, which could be just a simple raising of her hand or a loud scream to start, the first rider to come across the line in front of her would be declared the winner.

Once the signal was given, racers took off running as fast as they could and threw their body down on top of their sled as it hit the snow. This type of maneuver gave you a chance to get in front of anyone else and also provided a faster sled speed to get to the bottom of the hill first. If the snow were slippery in spots or someone hit any ice while running, chances were slim they would be able to finish the race. At times, many of us boys would push the boy alongside or in front of us, just to make him trip or fall over to improve our chances of winning the race. Some would call this cheating! When this happened, while lying in the snow, it was discouraging to see the winner crossing the finish line.

It was also very humiliating when the other kids, who did not slip and fall, came up to you and called you a big dummy. There were many of us who were put in this embarrassing position, but after a while we got up, laughed about it, and walked away to begin another race. Sometimes we did not worry about posting a lookout at the bottom of the hill and chanced it, if we could see no car approaching from the top of the hill. Then we would take our running start, hop on our sleds, and take a chance of getting to the bottom before a car showed up.

It did not snow heavily again for several weeks, and the little snow that did fall in between melted immediately, much to our disgust. The sleds were placed alongside our clapboard houses during this period, and we watched the runners turn to rust again. At the end of March, the weather forecast changed to rain, and heavy snow was now being predicted.

This forecast lifted all of us boys' spirits, and every one of us was very eager to hit the hillslopes again. The talk about school for the rest of the week was all about getting ready for the great sled race from the top of the Pike. In addition, a lot of discussion and guessing took place as to who the winner of the race might be.

Finally the snow began falling on a Tuesday evening, and by Wednesday morning it was so deep that traffic was jammed up all over town. Many cars were being abandoned by their owners, since the roads and streets were impassable. A lot of cars without chains became stuck in the snow; their rear wheels did nothing but spin, and the cars would not move. After a while, a few able-bodied men and some boys came around and pushed stuck cars and their drivers off the road. With this help, some drivers made it home without putting chains on, and some did not.

The borough trucks with their heavy plows kept pushing the snow up along the roadsides and main streets until nothing but tall white and grayish mounds of snow were everywhere. Obee's towing service was always very busy during these heavy snowfalls, and the local bars were filling up also.

The snow mounds offered all the boys and girls in town the opportunity to play another favorite wintertime game, called "king of the hill," when the snowplows went away for a while. This game started with an individual or a team of individuals, be it boy or girl, running up to the top of the snow mound. Then they would challenge someone else or many of us to try and come up and throw them off of the mound.

The Sisters at Saint Colman's had their hands full and were constantly telling the children to pay attention to them and not the snow. Everyone kept looking out the windows at the heavy snowflakes that were falling. Heads were turning and looking all around, and the classes were becoming disruptive as the Sisters tried to teach. We were all hoping that we would be sent home since the snow was becoming deeper and deeper, but it didn't happen.

The next day, Thursday, was different, however; because of the continuous falling of snow throughout the night, close to two feet of snow was on the ground, and the mounds of snow were even higher. The fire department whistles blew all night long, and I assumed it was because of the heavy snowfall and accidents taking place. The snowplows were late getting started the next morning and were having a hard time removing the snow or even pushing it aside.

Over three feet of snow had fallen by now, and employees at the local Westinghouse plant were being sent home for safety reasons; some workers could not get to work due to the heavy snow. The kids going to public school were told to stay home, but it was different at Saint Colman's, since school had not been cancelled, much to the disappointment of my brother and sister Joy. My younger sister, Judy, was not old enough for school during this time.

We even tried to convince our parents to let us stay home, but our pleas fell on deaf ears. So off we went trudging through the deep snow, except for Joy, who was perched on top of my shoulders for a while, before I handed her over to my brother, Richard. Thanks to Mr. Clark, the schoolroom classes were generally nice and warm when we entered them and began our studies.

A lot of moaning and groaning could be heard about why we had to be in school and the public school kids did not, but Sister just told us to be quiet and get to work. The snow kept falling, and by eleven thirty, the school yard was completely covered with over a foot of new, virgin, white snow. Mr. Clark, however, was around bright and early in the morning, shoveling at least some of it away from the school and church doorways.

When the school bell rang for lunch, we were all told by the Sisters that we were to go home and not come back until notified. The snow was just too deep and getting deeper, and they did not want us to be stranded. One can only imagine how much screaming and shouting took place from all the boys and girls in all of the classrooms when this happened.

This was one of the few times I saw Sister restrain herself and not say a word or hold anyone back from being excused. I now believe that she was elated about getting out and back to the convent, where she could relax without forty kids fidgeting and jumping about.

The first thing that I thought of after being dismissed was sledding down the mighty Pike. I stood outside the school along with my sister, waiting on my brother, in one of several pathways made by all the running children. When he arrived, I told him what was on my mind. He said he was thinking about sledding down the Pike all morning in class. He stopped talking for a moment and then said, "We should wait on Willy, Vincent, Charles, and Joseph to come out, and talk it over with them."

We all got together and decided that tonight would be a perfect time to try out a few preliminary runs on the Pike. We decided that we would all meet at six o'clock in front of the White Tower with our sleds. Richard had already said I could use his sled for a few runs. Then he said we could take a couple runs on it together later on, which made me very happy.

Joy, who had been listening to our conversation without saying a single word, just looked up at all of us boys when we finished talking. Then she asked us, "Who is going to carry me on their shoulders so I don't get my feet wet?"

The situation tonight would be ideal, except for a few scattered patches of road cinders, made visible by the snowplows and peeking up through the snow like rugged mountain peaks. We would have the flat, narrow roadways and streets that were made impassable by any cars all to ourselves. No parents need worry tonight about any of us running into or becoming injured by a car or some other vehicle. I contacted Robert, our local tailor's son, and Bobby, whom Richard and I traded comic books with and who lived at the very bottom of the Pike. After discussing what we had in mind, they both said they wanted to join in and would meet us tonight.

When Richard, Joy, and I arrived home, our mother still had our everyday lunch ready, consisting of maple rolls from Neill's bakery and chocolate milk from Isaly's. On a cold day like today, I was hoping she might surprise us and have some hot *bigos*, or Polish peasant soup, sitting on the stove. Mother was eagerly waiting on all three of us and expressed her concerns about the heavy snowfall.

While Richard and I were removing our heavy winter mackinaws and Joy was removing her heavy peacoat, Mother was surprised to hear that we were sent home early due to the heavy snow. She was also very surprised that we were not told when we had to return to school. She commented that this was an exceptional day, since she could never remember a time while she was at Saint Colman's of being sent home because of heavy snow. Things were done differently at Catholic schools during days gone by. Education, along with religious instruction, were held to be more important than the inconvenience of a little inclement weather. There were few excuses made for school to be dismissed early, let alone for a couple of days.

A lot of us children would say to one another that we wanted to go to public school, when we saw some of their kids walking past our school yard and telling us they had been dismissed due to the bad weather. Of course, we also knew that they would have to make this day up and push their scheduled June date for school closing and summer break out a bit. Too many days off like this would see the Catholic schoolchildren being released for the summer break ahead of them!

The three of us walked over to the floor register, snugly recessed on top of a weathered and scarred piece of linoleum in our kitchen. After eating our early lunch this day, we all took turns standing on it to warm our feet up. Richard and I stood there for another half hour or longer, to help dry out our wet clodhoppers. After this, we helped our mother clean up the kitchen.

We washed and dried the dishes for her and finished up by scrubbing the floor for her. Then we went up to our bedroom, played a few games on our electric pinball machine, and did our homework afterward. When the homework was done, we shouted downstairs and asked our mother if we could go out and play.

She asked what we were going to do, and we told her that we were going to go sledding on the hill in back of us. She gave us her permission to go out and told us not to go anywhere else and be home by nine thirty. By this time, it was 5:00 p.m. and starting to get dark outside, and we began changing into clothing that would help keep us warmer through a tough winter night of play.

We put on our long Polish *gutchies,* or winter underwear, and managed to get some old corduroy pants over them. It took a lot of pulling, tugging, and sliding the tight bottoms over our bulky clodhoppers until they broke free. A heavy sweater, wool cap, and our mackinaws were the only things left to put on. Once outside, we would slide a few pairs of old socks over our hands to help keep them warm.

Richard went over to the side of the house to retrieve his Flexible Flyer sled, which still looked very new. It had not been used much due to the limited amount of snow up until now. As he was doing this, our house door opened up, and Joy screamed out asking if she could come with us. We looked at her and told her to get dressed and meet us in front of the White Tower. She would make a good lookout for us tonight, just in case any cars did manage to get through the narrow roads. The top of Richard's sled, with its wooden slats still the color of light pine, heavily varnished, and the bright red metal frame, did not have a scratch on it anywhere. The Flexible Flyer name was cursively written in bright red paint on the center slat of the sled.

There was only one thing this sled was made for, and that was all-out speed and a good Polish driver. Our Italian, Irish, and Jewish friends would have a hard time keeping up with this sleek sled tonight. Richard pulled his sled along very easily with the rope in his hand and me sitting on it, through Farmer's Alley and around the bend to the front of the White Tower. We stopped in front of it and looked inside through the thick plate glass panes at the large clock with a chrome ring around it.

We could see the large and small black hands on its big white face clearly, and saw that it was 5:50 p.m. We were the first kids to arrive, but shortly thereafter, Willy showed up, whistling as he walked toward us, and we chatted with him for a while. Not long after this, Vincent, Charles, Joseph, Bobby, Robert, and Joy arrived. Several of us walked over to the metal streetlight pole and licked it lightly with our tongue. One had to be careful doing this and not let it become too frozen and stick on the pole!

We were all excited and could hardly wait to start pulling the sleds up to the top of Penn Avenue extension for a few trial runs. After this, the tough trek up the hill to the top of the Pike would be next, and then on to a few trial runs. As we started to leave the White Tower area, our little Greek friend, Tommy, showed up unexpectedly. He lived in East Pittsburgh, which was a stone's throw away from Turtle Creek, and asked if he could join us.

He had recently moved into town during the summer and introduced himself to my brother and me. Although he was several years younger than us, he became a good playmate and faithful friend. He did not go to Saint Colman's, but enjoyed playing with us boys more than his public school classmates. The other guys had met him also during the summer, liked him, and said it was all right if he joined us.

In addition, he had his own sled and was willing to share it with anyone. I thought this was great, since we could pawn Joy off on him, to watch and sled ride with during the night. In addition, I could use his sled to take part in the final race of the evening and hopefully beat my brother and some of the other guys, who always seemed to come in ahead of me.

As the ten of us started to leave, pulling sleds behind us, Joy jumped on Richard's sled and laid down on it, placing her hands on the wooden steering mechanism. As Richard pulled her along, she started to move the handle left to right and then right to left, leaving two smooth zigzag tracks in the snow behind the sled. The snow was so smooth and the sled moved along very easily, with Richard hardly noticing the added weight on top of it from Joy's body and heavy clothing.

We reached Divens' Pennzoil gas station quickly, which was always lit up very brightly. There were three tall pole lamps mounted in between the gas pumps on the concrete foundation, an island as it was called. These lights were great and we really appreciated them, since they also lit up the roadway and sharp bend at the base of the hill for us to see and navigate around. We kept off the gas station grounds and pulled the sleds on the sidewalk to the right of it and around the sharp bend in the road.

I thought this would be a good place to have Joy stand as a lookout and warn everyone of any approaching cars. She would balk and moan about this, but to appease her and keep her quiet, I would take the first lookout watch. In addition, I would ask Tommy to please let her use his sled to take the first ride down the hill. We all walked past the sharp bend that many of us would soon be steering our sleds around. We looked ahead of us at the start of a long walk, up a steeply graded sidewalk to the top of the hill. Before the night was over, we would avoid this sidewalk and be pulling our sleds up the hill in the middle of the road.

I asked Tommy again if Joy could use his sled to take a ride down the hill while I stood watch. Without hesitating, he said yes. I could see the disappointment in his eyes as to not being able to go down the hill with all the other guys on the first ride. After all, this was the big snowfall everyone was looking for to get their sleds out and take a run down the Pike.

I felt somewhat sad and sorry that it was me who would cause him to miss the first sled run opportunity. I looked at him and said, "Hey, Tommy, this is only a trial run from the top of the Penn Avenue extension hill. You will soon be joining all of us when we take our first ride down the Pike." With this, his eyes lit up like a Polish Christmas tree, and he said, "Do you really mean it?" I said to him, "Yes, I really mean it, and you sure will deserve it."

Tommy was not a Catholic at this time, and I did not have to hear him say, "Will you swear to God you're telling me the truth?" This was a standard saying many of us guys and girls going to Saint Colman's would say when it was thought someone might be lying or fibbing about something. Tommy, later on in life and with the permission of his Greek parents, would be baptized and become a Catholic.

I told Richard and everyone else that I was going to stay where I was, look for any cars, and give them the signal to start sledding down the hill. As they continued their walk up the hill, I stood by the sharp bend at the base of the hill and blew smoke rings from my mouth out into the freezing night air. Walking up the hill, they would pass Mr. Divens' house, Mr. Holmes's welding shop, and Fiola's auto repair shop, before reaching the Rainios' house and the top of the hill. They, too, would be inadvertently blowing out white smoke rings due to the huffing and puffing from the long uphill walk. The mix of warm lung air escaping from their mouths and meeting the freezing night air produced this effect!

Mr. Holmes, or Chick as he was called, was always nice to all of the kids; anytime his shop was open, he allowed us to come in and warm our hands over his flaming hearth. The warmth of the building made the rest of our bodies feel good also. On occasion, he was even good enough to weld up our broken sled runners, which would allow us to continue on with our sledding. He would also replace some of our lost bolts and nuts that held the sleds together. On this night, his shop was completely closed, and there would be no place to get warm and dry out our clothing except home.

We were all excited about starting the sledding, and everyone except Tommy lined up at the top of the hill for their first ride and my signal to begin. I carefully looked around the sharp bend toward the White Tower and up the main street of Penn Avenue all the way to Faller's furniture store. I could see no cars approaching, and there was nothing on the street, including people.

I quickly ran into the middle of the road at the base of the hill, where all the kids could see me. Then I started waving my hands up and down and screamed out to them, "It's all clear; come on down." I watched as everyone except Joy started running fast, with sled in hand, and slamming it into the snow. The sleds hit the roadway hard, the kids' bodies fell on top of them, and the race down the hill began.

Joy was still too small and had not mastered this running technique, but Richard and I would eventually teach her how to do it correctly. In the meantime, on this run, she gently placed Tommy's sled on the ground and lay on it like she had when Richard was pulling her along. From this position and with a push of the toes of her shoes, which were hanging over the rear of the sled, she began to slowly come down the steep hill.

I darted back to the safety of the sidewalk I was standing on, to avoid being run over by this gang of wild and sometimes reckless drivers. I could not make out who was in the lead at first and saw some orange colored sparks flying about in various areas, which had to be caused by the sleds' runners coming in contact with road cinders.

Bobby was the first to cross the point where I was standing and make a clean turn around the sharp bend without rolling over, and I saw him continue on down past the White Tower. Richard came next, and then in succession after him it was a slow Charles, Willy, Joseph, Robert, and Vincent. Finally Joy showed up.

No one else made it to the White Tower because they were not going fast enough and some cinders on the road slowed them down. These cinders could not be seen while walking up the sidewalk, but this would all change on the next run since everyone would be walking on the roadway and covering up any cinders that they could see.

We all found out later that night when we stopped sledding that Bobby had cheated on his first ride. Since he lived at the bottom of the Pike and directly across from the top of the hill, he saw the cinders while walking home from school. Since he knew where they were, he was able to pick a path where none were present, thus assuring he would not be slowed down.

We all gang-tackled him in a pleasant way and threw him to the snow-laden ground when he told us this story. We did not hurt him, since he had the best comic book collection around and you did not want to get on the bad side of him. Everyone put their sleds aside and began looking again where they could see cinders and covering them up.

This was done by dragging loose snow from the side of the road with your shoes to cover them, or by throwing snow on them with your hands. Once this was done, we would carefully tamp the snow down on the cinders with our shoes. The streetlights going up the hill and on both sides of the roadway provided us with enough light to see the cinders. Joy reluctantly agreed to return Tommy's sled for the next ride and stood with me at the base of the hill.

Knowing the paths where the cinders were now covered up would help the drivers figure out what course they would take in an attempt to gain maximum speed while shushing down the hill. All the riders were assembled together again at the top of the hill, and Joy and I stepped out into the middle of the road and began looking for any cars that might be coming.

Nothing was in sight, and we raised our hands up together and screamed out "It's all clear; come on down." I continued to hold her hand

and pulled her to the safety of the sidewalk and out of the way of possibly being run over by the speeding drivers coming down the hill. The cinder patch job had worked, no sparks appeared, and no one was slowed down. Everyone, including Tommy, made it around the sharp curve without rolling over and went all the way to the White Tower. Some even made it to the front of the Olympic Theater.

It was now my turn to take a ride down the hill, and Richard gave me his sled and took up a lookout position with Joy in hand. I took off running and slamming the sled down onto the snowy roadway. With my body falling on top of the sled, I was also taking my first ride. I came down the hill pretty fast, survived the sharp curve, and stopped in front of the White Tower. I was very proud of myself and took another successful run a few minutes later. The night wore on, and everyone was having a great time and making a lot of noise.

Due to the noise and seeing that we were having so much fun, Billy, Eddy, and Norma Cole and Hope Starkey, who lived on the hill, decided to get dressed and bring their sleds out also. We had a real gang of fourteen kids now, and all the sleds' metal runners and our body weight smoothed out the snow, allowing the sledders to travel at faster speeds and longer distances. Willy and Vincent made it all the way to the front of the Liberty Meat Market.

Everyone took a turn being on the lookout for cars coming up the main street and toward the Penn Avenue extension, but there were none around. It's funny, but looking back, I remember that we never had a lookout posted for any cars on the backside of this hill and running behind the Coney Island hot dog stand. Had a car managed to come up the backside of the hill, it could have run into and possibly over the riders going down. As luck would have it, none of us were ever hit by a car during all of our years of sledding in this area.

With the faster speeds being attained, many riders, including myself, were unable to round a sharp right curve successfully without being thrown off the sled and rolling onto the street. To avoid this from happening, kids tried shifting their body weight to the left side of the sled when making sharp left-hand turns. The body weight would have to shift to the right side of the sled when making sharp right-hand turns.

On one ride, Richard did the driving while Joy and I lay on top of him, and all three of us toppled off the sled as we tried to go around a very sharp curve. We all got a good laugh out of this ride. The night was going fast; it was getting much colder, and after two hours of walking up the hill and rolling around in the snow at the bottom of it, we were tired.

In addition, our clothing was wet, getting stiff, and we all decided to take three more runs and quit. The runs were good, but the cinders started to appear again and would have to be covered up tomorrow. Perhaps we would get lucky and receive some more heavy snow. On these last three runs, Richard, Joy, and I took individual rides and tried to go as fast as we could. There would be no race tonight to determine whose sled would go the fastest.

By now it was around eight thirty, according to the clock hanging inside the White Tower, and we quit our best sledding so far this year. We all decided that we would go one step further tomorrow to check out and attempt to do some riding down the Pike. There was no school, and we could even do it during the day. Everyone agreed that we would all meet around ten o'clock in front of the White Tower again.

The sledding chatter stopped among us kids, and Vincent said, "I sure am hungry." Since all of us were too small to hold any type of a paying job and most of our parents were financially strapped, none of us ever had much money to buy anything, including a candy bar.

What money we did collect came from turning in pop bottles for their deposit, shoveling snow, turning in old lard, and taking scrap iron to the junkyard. Excluding Joy and little Tommy, after rummaging through our pockets, all of us boys could only manage to come up with seventeen pennies. We knew that if we went to Gus's or the Greasy Spoon, the most we could get would be two bowls of chili at ten cents a bowl and a lot of crackers.

We decided that sharing two bowls of chili, with ten spoons digging into them, was not a good idea and we had to think of something else. Then little Tommy, whose parents owned a small restaurant nearby, held out his hand. He showed us a dime that he had and said we could have it. Tommy, being their one and only adopted child, always had a little more money since his parents gave him an allowance. He was our friend, but after this night, he would be our best friend and liked even more.

We now had twenty seven cents and a difficult time deciding what we could do with it. We decided again, that ten spoons dipping into three bowls of chili would not be good either. Vincent came up with a bright idea and said, "Why don't we all go to the New Deal down the street and get a big plate of french fries?" Vincent and his parents lived in one of the apartments above this restaurant, and this is how we found out that you could buy side orders of the french fries, starting at ten cents.

The New Deal served alcohol, and children were not allowed to sit in the bar area; however, there were a bunch of tall wooden booths at the rear of the bar, where children were allowed to sit down. George Primona, the owner, was another very nice individual and let us come in on this night. We told him we wanted to order some french fries. He told us to go sit down in the back. The ten of us or five each slid into the two separate seating areas on each side of the booth and sat down.

As I walked past the bar area, I noticed several whiskey glasses like my father had at home sitting on top of the bar. Alongside these shot glasses, as they were called, were several glasses of beer and bottles of beer. A lot of older adults were inside the place, and not a single one of the chrome bar stools, with round red leather seats, was empty. As I continued walking to the rear of the New Deal, I could smell the fresh fish, shrimp, and crab cakes being deep-fried in hot oil.

I could also smell the Italian Romano cheese that was being sprinkled on top of the hot sausage sandwiches being served. The french fries we would be ordering and putting into our cold bodies would be cooked in this same oil, which added a special and tasteful flavor to them.

Mrs. Saula, who was doing the cooking in the back kitchen and also acted as a waitress, came up to our booth and pleasantly asked us what we wanted. We all looked at her and said, "The biggest plate of french fries we could get for twenty-seven cents." Without saying another word, she turned and walked away. In about two minutes, we could hear the screeching sound of the fresh-cut watery fries being dropped into the hot boiling oil. Looking above the wire baskets that held the hot oil, we could see a light plume of moist smoke rising up from them.

Ten minutes went by, and Mrs. Saula returned with two big plates of light brown, crispy fries. She set them down on the tabletop of the booth and said, "This will cost you twenty-five cents." Willy was holding the money and placed fifteen pennies and Tommy's dime on the tabletop. Mrs. Saula did not bother to count it and walked away—and without a tip, I might add.

She handed the change to George, who never counted small change like this, and he opened up his National brass cash register and threw it into its compartmentalized coin slots. Bottles of Heinz ketchup, shakers of salt, black pepper, and hot red pepper flakes, and George's special homemade hot sauce were always available on the booth's tabletop for people to use. Shortly after the fries were placed on the table, all of us kids except Tommy removed our improvised gloves from our hands to start eating them. Tommy was the only one among us kids that evening who removed a real pair of dark brown woolen gloves his parents had bought him. We all told him how lucky he was to be able to own a pair of "real" gloves.

We all liked Heinz ketchup, and Joseph picked up a bottle and poured dabs of it all over the fries on both plates. Then we began to dig in and would devour them quickly. As we were eating, we kept count as to the amount being consumed by each individual so as to share equally. However, as much as we tried, someone always got a little greedy and was able to consume a few extra fries.

Toward the end of our eating frenzy, when there were only a few fries left on the plates, there would be a mad scramble of hands, one hundred fingers poking at the plates. On this night, Richard and I got quite a few of the remaining fries during the mad scramble and shared them with our sister.

Those of us with improvised gloves put them back on before leaving the New Deal, and while walking out, smiled and said good night to Mr. Primona. Without saying a word, he just looked and smiled back at us. On the way out, I noticed that every bar stool still had an individual sitting on it, and they were loudly conversing with one another. There were also several more glasses of whiskey and beer sitting alongside some big white plates that held large helpings of shrimp, crab cakes, big fish fillets, hot sausage sandwiches and large quantities of french fries.

We stepped outside into the cold night air, and Tommy put his gloves on. Then we all stood around and chatted with one another briefly. Everyone repeated our pledge to meet again at ten o'clock in the morning by the White Tower.

Everyone went their separate ways to go home. As my brother, sister, and I started to walk away, Tommy asked if he could come home with us for a while, and we said yes. By this time, it was only 9:15 p.m. according to the clock inside the White Tower, and we would be home in two minutes. This was fifteen minutes earlier than our mother told us to be home by. It would also give us time to play a couple of pinball machine games and perhaps a few games of war with our playing cards. It was far too late to try and melt down any pieces of lead and make a few "toy soldiers."

We knew it would be difficult to get Tommy to leave for his own home, since once he entered our house and was with Richard and me, he did not want to leave. He somehow had adopted our family, and my parents always treated him as one of their own. Fortunately on this night, when our mother told us at ten o'clock that it was time for bed, he left the house without any problem, and his parents did not have to come get him.

During the night, six more inches of fresh snow fell on the streets and roads. This was not enough to bring out the snowplows and would make it another great sledding day for us. In addition, there was not a school day or homework assignments to worry about. We got up around eight o'clock on Friday morning.

After shoveling some coal into our cellar, Richard and I ate our breakfast of oven-ready toast and skillet-fried eggs, with crispy edges that were cooked in leftover bacon grease. Joy said she wanted to go sledding some more and that she would come out later on and look for us up on the hill or around Divens' gas station. We told her that would be all right.

By this time, it was getting close to ten o'clock, and we dressed to go outside. We retrieved the sled from the side of the house and walked toward the White Tower to meet our friends. While Richard pulled his sled behind him, I sat down on it for him to pull me along. It was daylight, and we were given no particular time to be home by.

Little Tommy was waiting on us, along with Vincent and Willy. Joseph and Charles showed up shortly thereafter, and so did Robert and Bobby. In addition, a newcomer by the name of Jack, who lived close by and was several years older than all of us, showed up. Now there would be 10 of us doing some sled riding off and on.

Everyone but me had their own sled, but that was okay with me, since three extra sleds would become available after the posting of lookouts. The early lookouts for today would be standing at the major intersection of Seneca Street, the railroad crossing by Tri Boro Coal Company, and the sharp curve at the bottom of the hill by Divens' gas station. I was given permission to use Robert's Flexible Flyer, which was in excellent condition.

We all talked and decided that Charles, Robert, and Jack would take first lookout watch to warn us of any oncoming cars and other vehicles. The rest of us left the White Tower area and started walking up the middle of the Penn Avenue extension roadway to the top of the hill. While walking and pulling the sleds behind us, we all tromped down and packed the fresh snow that had fallen. This would assure us of a good snow-packed ride and also help cover up any cinders again.

Charles was posted at the sharp curve in front of Divens' gas station, and this meant he did not have to walk up the hill. We got to the top of the hill and pulled our sleds over the shiny and icy metal railroad tracks. We were now standing at the bottom of the long and steep Greensburg Pike roadway, which eventually became known as the Pike. This is where the lower part of the Pike began.

From this area, the roadway ran up, with a few minor curves at a forty-five-degree slope, approximately another 2600 feet before it flattened out. Our suicide run from the top of the Pike this morning would start at this flat spot, in front of Delaney's Morning Star Inn. It has been said that George Washington, our first president, ate, slept, and drank at this inn.

Robert assumed his position and was posted as a lookout by the railroad tracks, and we all continued pulling our sleds up the steep Pike roadway. Jack was posted as a lookout for cars and other vehicles coming out of Seneca Street and entering the Pike roadway. When all of us sled riders reached the Morning Star Inn area, we took a short break to catch our breath. The long climb and pulling the sleds up the Pike had us all huffing and puffing pretty heavily. This was it, and finally we were going to go on our first trial sled run down the magnificent Pike.

There would be no official racing competition among the riders on this run. It would only be a trial run for us to check out the snow, sleds, and road conditions. The sun was out early this morning, a little snow had melted, and water was running lightly down the Pike in some areas. This was not a good sign, and dark clouds were beginning to form in the sky above us. The temperature was dropping into the freezing range, and unknown icy spots were forming in some areas due to the running water.

The seven of us boys stood at the top of the Pike, and after catching a second breath of air, we were not huffing and puffing heavily any longer. We all stood ready to begin our perilous downhill sled ride at the given signals or screams that it was all right to start down the Pike. Charles screamed out to Robert that it was all right to come down the hill. When he heard this and after looking around, Robert screamed up to Jack that it was all right to come down; no trains were coming.

Jack could see no cars coming down Seneca Street and ran into the middle of the Pike roadway. He raised his arms and waved up to us, while screaming out loud that it was all right to come down. On this final signal, we all took off running to gain some additional speed. We slammed our sleds down hard on the snow-covered roadway. As our bodies fell on top of each sled, we all started our joyful and exuberant run down the infamous Pike.

Richard, Charles, and Joseph were in front of me, but not by much, as we went speeding down the hill. I did not have a hat on, and my ears began to wiggle back and forth as I gained speed. I came to the first curve on the Pike and handled it with no problem, as the riders in front of me had done also. Then a very long steep and straight run caused my sled to go much faster.

The turbulent air that followed fell into my face and made my lips flutter up and down and move apart. I had a hard time keeping them together, and another curve appeared before me. At the speed I was going, I maneuvered the steering handle to stabilize the sled but was not sure I would get through it without wrecking or turning over the sled.

Suddenly I saw Charles go into the curve ahead of me, and his sled began to tip over. He fell off it and rolled down the hill for several yards. I avoided his path, dug the toe of my clodhopper into the snow to slow me down a bit, and successfully negotiated the curve. I did not dare look behind me to see what was happening with the other guys or Charles. Another long steep run with a minor curve coming up would put me at the bottom of the Pike at a speed faster than I had ever gone before.

This minor curve came just before crossing over the tricky railroad tracks, but I was successful in steering through it and over the tracks safely. Now the treacherous part was coming up, and that was to make a sharp ninety-degree left turn and continue going down the Penn Avenue extension roadway without rolling over or falling off the sled like Charles did.

I saw my brother approach the ninety-degree turn without slowing down, and I could see his clodhoppers were in the air, not digging into the snow to slow him down. Then I watched as his sled lifted up on its left side off the snow and rolled over on top of him. Joseph also kept going without slowing, did not make the ninety-degree turn, and ran into a burl of snow on the shoulder of the road directly in front of him.

I decided to avoid the paths they had taken, and instead of going over the middle of the railroad tracks, I kept more to the left of them. I dug the toes of both of my clodhoppers into the snowy ground to slow me down a little as I passed by them and made the sharp left-hand ninety-degree turn. As I went into the turn, I could feel the left side of my sled and its runner lifting off the ground. However, I managed to shift most of my body weight to this side and make it through the most treacherous turn of all.

As my sled dropped back down onto its runner, I quickly pushed forward with my left hand and pulled back with my right hand on the sled's steering arm to straighten it out and continue on. Once I straightened out my sled, its speed picked up and propelled me quickly down the steep Penn Avenue extension hill. I looked to my right quickly and could see that Joseph and my brother were all right. Both of them were laughing hard and had hit icy spots I was to learn later on.

I finally came to a stop in front of the White Tower and thought that I was the only one who would make a successful run down the Pike today. It turned out that the rest of the guys behind me were taking mental notes also. They had observed me slowing down at certain spots, did the same thing, followed my course, and made it down the long run without falling off their sleds also. As I was pulling my sled back from the White Tower, lying belly down on their sleds, they all began to steer their sleds past me one by one screaming and yelling, "I made it, I made it."

This alerted everyone that they had made a successful run down the steep Pike without falling off their sled or crashing before getting to the very bottom. Little Tommy also made it successfully down the Pike, but was the last one to do it. Richard, Joseph, and his brother Charles had hopped back on their sleds after rolling over and came whizzing past Tommy and me.

We all got together and talked about the run and the fun we had. Richard, Charles, and Joseph said that if they had slowed down just before crossing over the railroad tracks, they could have made it to the bottom also without falling off. They also said that only sissies slowed a sled down when riding down the Pike.

This comment irritated the rest of us, and we all said we were just practicing but on the next run, we would not hold back or slow down. We added, "You better not get in our way." They just laughed at us and walked away pulling their sleds behind them and saying to us, "Meet you at the top of the Pike." We posted new lookouts at the three critical areas again and took several more runs that day, without anyone rolling over and becoming injured.

We all figured out during the next run by watching Jack, all you had to do after you crossed over the railroad tracks was to make a quick right turn with the sled. This put a little drag on it, reduced speed, and gave you more steering control. After this, a quick left at the ninety-degree turn would keep you going down the hill. This could not be called slowing down or cheating, since you did not dig your clodhoppers into the snow. When the great sled race started, I wondered how many of us would avoid doing this maneuver. It did slow you down a little, which could cause you to lose the race.

Joy showed up and was too afraid to take a sled ride down the Pike by herself. Richard and I also thought it was too dangerous for her. We placed her on a sled, took Richard's sled along, and began walking up the Pike together. As we walked up the steep roadway, we took turns at pulling her along until we reached the top. Once at the top, I lay down on the sled. She lay down on my back and wrapped her arms around my neck, and we took off down the Pike. Richard followed alongside talking to us, and we dug our clodhopper toes into the snow behind us to avoid going too fast and scaring Joy.

The farther we went, Joy kept screaming "go faster, go faster, please go faster, Barrie." We kept the speed of the sleds to where we negotiated all of the curves successfully, but at the same time with enough speed to get us to the White Tower without stopping. We took another run, only this time with Joy lying on Richard's back and her arms wrapped tightly around his neck, before quitting and going home for some lunch.

The first thing Joy did when she entered the house was to go screaming and tell our mother that "she had taken a successful run down the Pike, like all the boys". After lunch, Richard and I went back to taking a lot more runs on the Pike by ourselves and restricted Joy to the lower hill. She had her pick of the two extra sleds and could go by herself without much chance of getting hurt.

All of us boys, including Tommy, kept coming down the hill without slowing down, but once we hit the railroad tracks and crossed over them, we would go out of control and crash. Sleds and bodies would be all over the road, and on occasion someone could run into you and your sled while you were still lying on the snow-covered road. Seven o'clock came and it began to get dark, so we took a final run down the Pike again before everyone quit. The snow was excellent, there still were not too many cars on the road, and we talked about preparing for the great sled race.

Hopefully, it could take place tomorrow or Saturday, before the snowplows began removing snow and started dumping cinders on the roads again. In addition, Saturday was always very busy, and some cars would be attempting to make it up the Pike roadway. Some would do it with chains installed on their rear tires, and some would take a chance without any chains on their vehicles! In spite of all this, we might be able to get in a few good practice runs. Later on, if all went well, this would also be the day when someone in our gang would be known as the fastest sled rider down the mighty Pike and be named the winner of the "Great Sled Race."

After talking a few more minutes, we all agreed to spend Saturday morning looking for pop bottles and scrap metal. We needed to raise enough money for all of us to buy a bowl of chili at the Greasy Spoon after the great sled race. Joy asked if she could go too, and we told her yes but to keep her mouth shut around our parents. Richard and I would figure out some way to pay for her ten cent bowl of chili. Perhaps we might find a few pop bottle or beer bottles and get their returnable deposit. "In addition, each of us would ask our parents if they had a few pennies they could spare.

We all agreed to meet around one o'clock with our sleds in front of the White Tower, and everyone went home. That is everyone except for little Tommy, who asked Richard and me if he could spend the night sleeping at our house. When we arrived home, we kicked the snow off our clodhopper shoes. We opened up the front door, rushed inside the house, and asked our mother if Tommy could spend the night. She said yes he could if it was all right with his parents. We kept our clothes on, rushed back outside, and ran all the way to Tommy's apartment.

It was located nearby, above the Wilkins Jewelry store. His parents were happy to see him and gave him a big hug and some kisses. Tommy explained what he wanted to do, and they knew he would be in good hands at our house. They gave him permission to stay overnight with us and also stay the next day and go sledding with us. Tommy was all smiles as they handed him a large Giant Eagle paper shopping bag, stuffed full of fresh, warm clothing and sleeping pajamas.

He reached up with his outstretched arms toward his parents. Then he gave both of them a big hug and kiss and said, "Good-bye. I love you both very much." We turned around quickly, opened up his apartment door, and ran down the steps to the outside street, Braddock Avenue. We continued running without stopping until we reached our house. By now it was eight o'clock, we were very hungry, and our mother made us some scrambled eggs, home fries, and three cups of hot chocolate.

We ate heartily and gulped the chocolate down quickly and ran up to our bedroom, undressed, and took our baths. We played a few games on the pinball machine, and Richard got the highest score, 1,296, on the Coney Island Ride. Then we took out a deck of cards and played the game of war until we each had won at least once and decided it was time to get some sleep.

Waking up early the next morning, we dressed, went downstairs, and had a hearty breakfast of fried Isaly's baloney and eggs with toast. After we finished eating, Richard and I got the chores done my father had left orders for us to do. Tommy helped as much as he could, but when it came to shoveling coal into the cellar, the shovel was just too big for him to handle. After dressing warmly, we left the house and went out looking for empty pop bottles around the local garbage cans and Dumpsters. We also searched around back doorsteps and apartment rear landings, where some people would set out their empty bottles for us to pick up.

After about three hours of doing this, we had our Red Racer wagon full of empty bottles and cashed them in at Johnny's candy store. The bottle count came to sixteen, and Johnny handed Tommy four nickels. The deposit on the bottles was only one cent each at the time, but he must have felt sorry for us and gave us a little extra money.

He would more than make up the extra four cents he gave us through his numbers booking business, punchboard, billiards, and pinball machine proceeds. The selling of candy bars, cigars, cigarettes, and sodas produced an insignificant amount of money to Johnny's business. Tommy gave the deposit money to Richard to hold onto and add it to whatever additional money the other guys might have earned this morning. By this time, it was around noon; if we hurried home to eat lunch now, we would still have time to get Richard's sled and meet up with our friends.

Our mother had made a big batch of pan-fried crispy-on-the-outside-but-soft-in-the-middle Polish *pulutkies* (potato pancakes), which awaited us in the oven. She kept them on a tray that was warmed only by the oven's pilot light. We ate several of them with some sour cream and some with Heinz ketchup spread on top. They were delicious even when cold, and biting into a good chunk of fresh garlic hit the spot. The fresh garlic was part of the salt, pepper, egg, flour, grated potatoes, and minced onion batter. This combination of ingredients, along with being deep-fried in a cast-iron skillet, made them taste all the better.

We put our warm clothing back on, thanked our mother for the great meal, and told her how much we loved her. Before leaving, we asked her if she had a few spare pennies she could let us have. She said no and she was sorry, but times were tough. Joy was helping her fold clothes at the time and asked us what time she could come to go sled riding with us. We told her around five o'clock and not to be late.

She then asked if she was going to go to the Greasy Spoon and get a bowl of chili afterward with us. Richard looked at her and said, "We will have to count all the money we make first to see if we have enough for you." She looked at Richard and me and said, "You told me you would see that I got a bowl, and it will not be fair if you two do and I don't." Richard looked at her again and said, "We also told you at the time to keep your mouth shut, which you are not doing," and we left the house.

All three of us were standing in front of the White Tower at one o'clock as scheduled, and the other guys arrived shortly thereafter. We told them how much money we had made and asked them how much they made. Among the seven of them and including what few pennies they could scrounge at home, they showed us a meager forty-five cents. Willy said this would not be enough to get everyone a bowl of chili. Then he said, in a self-sacrificing voice, that he would not get a bowl of chili.

Shortly after Willy's statement, Bobby and Robert said the same thing. These were our buddies sacrificing so someone else could have a bowl of chili. After a while, we decided that if we could not each have a bowl of chili together, none of us wanted to have any chili. When we began arguing about the situation, Tommy put a closed fist in front of all of us and said, "Look here," He turned his fist over and opened his fingers up very fast. He did this to expose the palm of his hand, and in the middle of it lay two shiny new quarters. He looked at us and said, "This money is mine, and you can have it. I hope it will help and be enough to get us all a bowl of chili."

Vincent said with amazement and a big grin on his face, "Where did you get this money?" Tommy told us that he found it in the clean pants his parents had put in the shopping bag for him last night. After doing some quick arithmetic and arriving at a total amount of $1.15 Vincent said, "Not only will this be enough to get all of us, boys some chili, Joy will get hers also and there will still be five cents left over." I spoke up quickly and said, "I am happy to hear this". After I said this, Vincent looked toward Tommy and asked him, "Is this all right with you?" Tommy told him that it was all right with him. He said, "Joy is my sister, like Richard and Barrie are my brothers."

Just for being so kind, I told Tommy that after we were done sledding, I would ask his father and mother if he could spend another night with us. Selfishly, I was also thinking that he might get two more quarters stuffed in another pair of pants. If it did happen, I would be his best buddy all the next day and not tell anyone else about it! That is, except for my brother, Richard, since he and I always shared most things.

We all treated Tommy with special care the rest of the day and made sure he never was without a sled. In addition, we helped teach him some of the tricks in maneuvering through sharp turns and how to slow down using the toes of his clodhopper shoes. I showed him how to run holding his sled up in the air with both hands, slam it down on the road, and fall on top of it to get going fast.

During one of Tommy's runs that day, he told Jack and Joseph that there was no way he could win the great sled race. When they asked him why, he told them that he could not run as fast as them and the other. bigger boys. In addition, he told them that they could run faster, to get a head start and be farther ahead.

The sledding was great, even though no more snow was falling and the weather had warmed up, making some spots slushy and wet. After three runs, I challenged Robert and Jack to a race down the Pike, and lookouts were posted at the dangerous intersections and treacherous spots.

When the all-clear signal was given to us, we took off from the top of the Pike running as fast as we could. We all got off to an even start, and our sleds were side by side as we approached the first curve, traveling at a good speed. Shortly thereafter and without my knowing it, Robert suddenly hit a patch of cinders, brought up to the surface by the melting snow. His sled spit out several orange-colored sparks as its runners hit the cinders.

His sled began to sway sideways; he overcorrected his steering and turned directly into Jack's path. They collided with one another, lost control, and crashed. The sleds turned over, their bodies were thrown off, and they rolled over several times until they stopped. Jack's sled became upright again and continued running down the hill until it finally hit a sidewalk curb, jumped over it, and came to a sudden stop.

Both Robert and Jack, although shaken up a little bit, were unscathed and jumped up laughing about the whole incident. Unaware of what had happened behind me, I kept concentrating on winning this informal race. I continued down the Pike at a very good speed, as my sled runners glided easily over good, hard-packed snow. I took the next curve just before reaching the railroad tracks with ease and at a very fast speed.

Charles, who was posted by the railroad tracks as a lookout, waved me on, since no cars or trains were approaching, and I stared straight ahead planning my next move. I hit the tracks with my sled and turned it hard to the right just before clearing the last rail to slow me down a little. Suddenly, my right runner came in contact with some raised concrete roadway edging, which stopped the sled abruptly and threw me off it.

Charles ran down and over to me quickly to find out if I was all right. After looking at the sled, however, I found that I had just cracked the runner on my brother's brand-new sled. I felt so bad, cried a little bit, and was very sorry it had happened. "After all, it was just an accident," I said to myself, "and accidents do happen to everyone."

Later on, when Richard saw me pulling his sled down the hill, he asked why I was not riding it, and I told him what had happened. He became furious and tackled me hard. We fell down on the wet, snow-covered road. While we were fighting and struggling in the snow, the rest of the guys came over and separated us. I felt very bad and was crying when he told me I could never ride his sled again. Then he said, "Now I will not have my sled to take part in the great sled race tonight." Still crying, I could only look at him and tell him I was very sorry and did not mean to break it.

Jack and Robert finally showed up at the bottom of the hill and told me about the accident they had. Jack pointed down to a runner on his sled that had cracked when it hit the sidewalk curb. He told me he did not intend this to happen and it would keep him out of the race tonight also.

I got to thinking. I knew it was around four thirty, since the sky was turning into a dark gray and signaling nightfall was approaching. It also told me that Mr. Holmes's welding shop was still open; he might be able to fix both sleds. Jack and I were standing within twenty feet of his shop door, and I could see lights were still on as I looked at the small, cluttered windowpanes of glass. In addition, shadows of flashing light and hot sparks, bouncing back and forth from his weld and cutting torch, could also be seen. I looked at Richard and said to him, "Let's go see if Mr. Holmes will fix the sleds for us, especially yours."

We waited until the sparks and arcing noise that we were all familiar with stopped before we entered the building. We knew not to go in when Mr. Holmes was welding. He had told us on many occasions that looking directly at the bright welding and glare could hurt our eyes and we might even become blind.

He told us we could warm ourselves up by the fire, but to hurry since he was going to close up and go home. When I heard him say this, I quickly walked over to him and said, "Mr. Holmes, could you please do me a favor and fix my brother's sled?" He asked me, "What is wrong with it, Barrie?" When I told him, he said, while pointing his index finger toward it to leave it in the corner and he would fix it tomorrow.

Jack spoke up and showed him his broken runner also. Mr. Holmes, without speaking, pointed his index finger again toward the same corner, signaling Jack to leave his sled also. I begged Mr. Holmes to please fix it tonight if he could. He asked me, "Why is it so important that it can't wait to be fixed until tomorrow?" I explained what I had done and that Richard would not have his sled to participate in the great sled race just a few hours away.

Mr. Holmes looked at me and Richard, who was standing next to me, and said, "All right, I will fix it for you, and I will fix the other kid's sled also, but it will cost you." I told him I did not have any money to pay for it now. Mr. Holmes replied nicely and said he did not want any money. He told us if we shoveled away the large mound of snow blocking his driveway in the morning, he would trade for that. After hearing this, Richard yelled out a loud "Yippee, thank you, Mr. Holmes."

Both Jack and I agreed to do this, and Richard, so happy he was going to get his sled back, volunteered to help out also. Mr. Holmes asked all of us to leave and not bother him until he was finished. Shortly thereafter, we could hear the buzzing welding sound coming from inside his shop, and we saw the blinking of the bright lights, flashing on and off again, through the shop's small windows. This orange and white colored flashing was created when he started and stopped his welding.

We all stood outside the shop huddled around in a group to keep warm while waiting on the sleds' repairs to be finished. All of a sudden we heard someone say, "Well, am I going to get a bowl of chili with you guys tonight or not?" It was Joy, and Richard and I knew it must be five o'clock. I looked at Joy and told her, "It is a good thing your sister is so young and still in her crib at home, or we would have to put up with her bellyaching also."

Richard told her she would get her chili and also told her how his sled runner was broken and Mr. Holmes was fixing it. Then he looked over toward me and said, "Barrie, after the sled is done being repaired, you and Joy should take it out for a run and check it out." When he said this, I knew he was no longer mad at me and would be in the race tonight; I would be saying prayers for him to win it. It had not been decided yet but everyone knew that ultimately two kids would not be in the final race, due to only 9 sleds being available.

Mr. Holmes pushed one of the two large wooden doors to his shop open and told us to come in and warm up a little while he cleaned his hands up. He handed the two repaired sleds to Jack and my brother and pointed to where he had fixed them. We looked, but could not find anything that looked like it was repaired. Then Mr. Holmes took a welding rod and pointed to the repair area. The reason we could not find the broken runners or repair work was because he had also repainted the repaired runners with Red paint. His gas welding and filing down of the seam were so perfect no one would ever know they had been broken. What a kind and great individual Mr. Holmes was with us kids!

As long as he was not busy, he did this repair work for us many more times during this winter and the winter years to come. He never once asked any of us kids to pay him for the work he performed. During the summer, he would also do a little repair work on the cracked frames or other damaged areas on our bicycles and never lost his patience with us at any time. If he was busy, he would simply say, "Come back and see me later on. If I am not busy I will see what I can do."

I took my brother's sled and laid it down gently on the snow-covered sidewalk. Then I told Joy to get on it so we could take a ride. I pulled her and the sled to the top of the hill next to old man Raineo's house, where I asked her nicely to please get off Richard's sled.

I picked up the sled and walked over to the center of the Penn Avenue extension hill and laid it down gently on the snow. I was not going to take a chance on breaking it again and handled it with extreme care. I lay down on the sled, looked up, and told Joy to hop on my back. She did it with enthusiasm and threw herself hard on top of me. Once she locked her hands and small arms around my neck, I pushed hard with my hands on both sides of the sled until we began to glide down the hill.

We were going pretty fast when we passed by all the guys, who were still standing in front of the welding shop. Joy hollered out loud at them to meet us at the bottom of the hill, and they all started to run after us. As we approached the bottom of the hill and the sharp curve, I drove the sled straight ahead and dug the toes of my clodhoppers, hanging over the rear of the sled, into the snow to stop us.

I did not want to take a chance on breaking the weld if I took the curve too fast, and perhaps leave Richard with no sled to use for the great sled race tonight. There were quite a few times that some guys would continue using their sleds even with broken or cracked runners. When the snow was good, like it was now, nothing could keep you from using your sled.

It was really dark by now, and everyone walked over to the sidewalk area that was always lit up by the overhead big pole lights at the Divens' Pennzoil station. We started to talk about getting ready for the great sled race to determine who had the fastest sled and was the best driver. Whoever won would have bragging rights until the next race. Richard said he wanted to take a trial run from the top of the Pike to check out his sled. Jack joined in and said he wanted to do the same thing.

The rest of the guys said they were also ready to go to the top for a trial run. Joy, Tommy, and I agreed to be the lookouts, and walked to our locations. After this, the guys began their long walk up to the top of the Pike. When they reached the flat area in front of Delaney's Morning Star Inn, they could catch their breath and stop their huffing and puffing.

While they were doing this, they also practiced blowing out cold air, grayish smoke rings, to see who could make the biggest one. Nobody ever won at this game since the short time they were in the air was not enough to really pick a winner, Most times all everyone ever did was wind up arguing about who blew the largest ring!

Richard and Jack laid their sleds down on the ground and waited, along with the other guys, to hear the signal that it was all right to start their run down the Pike. The other guys were not concerned about their runners since they had not been damaged! They would start the downhill Pike ride by running with sleds in their hands and slamming them into the hard ground. Finally, the signal was relayed from the bottom of the hill lookout, to the railroad track lookout, to the Seneca Street lookout, and then to the eagerly awaiting sled riders.

Without hesitation, the other guys began their trial run down the hill. The runners took the early lead and were quickly on their way down the hill. Jack and my brother were lying down on their sleds. Due to them not taking a running start, their body weight held them back somewhat, and they were now furiously digging and pushing, with both hands, into the snow-covered ground to get themselves moving.

They began to pick up speed but knew they would never be able to catch the rest of the guys. This meant they would have a little race between themselves now! Jack was the older and had been sledding a few years longer than Richard, but Richard was lighter and his sled seemed to go a little faster. Richard looked over at Jack and said to him, "Race you to the bottom," and Jack said, "Okay."

They both began to maneuver their sleds into the best snow and to avoid any cinders that might not be totally covered up. Jack turned his sled to the left and right, got into a good hard pack of snow, and was ahead of my brother by about twenty feet. Richard, sensing that the snow was better on the route that Jack was taking, steered his sled toward him and began to gain on him somewhat.

A curve came up, and Jack, now going at even a faster speed, got through it with no problem. Richard followed and was also going at a faster speed when he approached the curve. He turned to the left slightly and heard a hard scraping noise come from under his sled. He knew by the sound that he had run into and over some cinders. This error slowed him down considerably, but he was not about to give up.

He looked ahead and could see Jack steering into the second curve, just ahead of the approaching railroad tracks. All of a sudden, a loud clanging of bells rang out, signaling an approaching train. The white and black diagonal guard rails started their descent downward and across the tracks on both sides of the roadway.

Tommy, who was posted at this location, saw the train and ran out to the middle of the Pike and flagged Jack down quickly. Jack could hear the train coming as its steam-operated locomotive blasted out two loud, short whoo whoos, followed by one long whoo. Every one of these blasts left a large puff of white smoke floating in the air for a period of time, along with a distinct sulfuric odor, before it disappeared. Sometimes the puffs of smoke could be nothing but coal black in color and carrying the same sulfuric odor.

Jack, being alerted that something was wrong and not wanting to take a chance on driving under the guard rails, turned his sled sharply to the right, ran it up into the driveway of Bobby's house, and came to a grinding halt. Tommy may have saved Jack's life that night, since the train came by shortly after that. The irony of it is that Jack, who later in life became an

Army paratrooper, would be killed in action during a parachute drop into enemy-held territory during the early part of the Korean War.

Richard was very lucky that the cinders slowed him down that night. When he approached the curve, he also made a sharp turn to the right and followed Jack's sled tracks, to come upon the back of his sled before stopping. The train had passed by quickly, and the guard rails began to rise up. After seeing this, Richard and Jack turned their sleds around and pushed them forward, to go down the small driveway hill they had just gone up and ride over the railroad tracks.

Richard looked at Tommy as he was sledding by and told him to hop on his back slowly and ride down the hill with him the rest of the way. Jack followed them all the way through and past the sharp curve by the gas station, until they stopped in front of the White Tower. The guys who had started out running with their sleds and went over the tracks ahead of my brother and Jack had no idea as to the potential danger and what had just happened by the railroad crossing.

It was around six o'clock by now, and we all talked about when we should start the official great sled race. Several of the guys said they wanted to take one more trial run. After this trial run, we all agreed, the next run would be the official "Great Sled Race," to determine the fastest sled and the best driver. Afterward, we would all go over to the Greasy Spoon and get our bowls of chili and all the small, round oyster crackers we could eat. In addition, several more of the crackers would be stuffed in our mackinaw coat pockets before leaving, if Gus was not watching us! Joy would have to stuff her extra crackers into her dark blue, heavy peacoat.

The same lookouts were posted, for another trial run and the riders began pulling their sleds up to the top of the Pike, wondering who would win the final race. Willy had won the great sled race the year before. Would he win again?

All of the riders knew by now that the only way they stood a chance of winning the race was never to be afraid of their speed and never try to slow down. Joy was too small and inexperienced to attempt a ride like this. Tommy who had his own sled but volunteered to be a lookout talked and wished that we could be in the race also. The riders got to the top of the Pike and lined up to begin another trial run down the steep Pike roadway.

When the lookout's signal came that it was all right to begin, most of the boys started running with sleds in their hands, slammed them down on the snow, and lay their bodies on top of them. Before leaving to go to the top of the Pike, Richard took me aside and told me, "Barrie, if I do not run and fall on the sled to test out the repair Mr. Holmes did, I will never know if it will be good enough to win the great sled race."

This same thought was running through Jack's mind. Suddenly and without notifying anyone, he started to run, catching Richard off guard. He threw his sled onto the ground and started to go down the hill. Richard did not hesitate. Quickly he followed Jack and was soon on his way down the hill as part of the group of eight riders. Sleds were everywhere.

Some were side by side and some right behind one another. Passing anyone ahead of you was difficult, and if you attempted to do it, the rider in front of you would quickly turn to the left or right to cut you off. When this happened, the rider behind, afraid that he might crash into the sled ahead of him, without thinking would automatically dig his clodhopper toes into the snow, which caused him to slow down.

Willy did this while behind Joseph, and Robert did it by following Charles too close, and Vincent did it after his sled collided slightly with Bobby's sled. When this happened, it slowed everyone down and gave my brother and Jack the opportunity to catch up a little. Both Jack's and my brother's sled runners were holding up well, even after taking the severe punishment of being thrown to the ground with a heavy body on it. Although this was supposed to be just another trial run, everyone was driving and acting like it was the official great sled race.

Joseph, Charles, and Bobby were in the lead and heading into the first curve; they turned to the left a little without slowing down. This was the same area where the cinders had caught my brother by surprise, and suddenly their sleds slowed down while belching out orange sparks in the night air. As they turned to avoid the cinders and get into some hard-packed snow, Joseph and Charles collided, and their sleds tipped over.

Bobby kept going and made it through both curves and over the railroad tracks before hitting a sheet of ice, losing control of his sled, and sliding sideways into a big pile of snow. Willy, Vincent, Robert, Jack, and Richard were still coming down the hill and picking up speed, separated from one another. Richard avoided the cinder area, but Willy and Jack were not able to and found their sleds coming to a screeching halt, with orange-colored sparks flying everywhere.

Robert and Vincent were also able to avoid the cinder area and kept going not far behind my brother. As the riders all picked up speed and were within a few feet of each other, they entered the first curve area, and without slowing down managed to steer through it. Now all they had to do was get through the second sharp curve, over the railroad tracks, and the ninety-degree turn to the left, and they had it made.

With the speed they were now traveling, the second sharp curve came upon them quickly, and they headed over the railroad tracks at an even greater speed. Richard did not slow down and forgot to make a slight turn to the right to slow down a little before attempting the ninety-degree turn. Suddenly, he overturned, and this mistake sent him and his sled tumbling over and over. He recovered quickly and stood up laughing out loud, saying, "Wow, what a ride!"

When Robert and Vincent saw what had happened to Richard, they immediately dug their clodhopper toes into the snow at the rear of their sleds to slow them down. They both successfully negotiated the treacherous ninety-degree turn and continued their ride to the bottom of the hill. They knew they could not do this slowing-down maneuver in the official race if they were to stand a chance of winning.

Joseph, Charles, Bobby, Willy, Jack, and Richard, all of whom had crashed, got back on their sleds and continued to ride them to the bottom of the hill. Everyone glided to a stop by the lit sidewalk curve and talked over their mistakes with one another. They discussed what they had had failed to do to get from the top of the Pike to the bottom of the hill and the White Tower without crashing or stopping.

Robert and Vincent never did mention their slowing down by digging both of their clodhopper shoes into the snow behind them. This allowed them to negotiate the ninety-degree turn without being called sissies the rest of the night. Richard and Jack talked about how well their repaired sled runners had held up.

This last trial run and the long walk up the Pike and all the mishaps had taken close to an hour. It was approaching seven o'clock when Joy blurted out to everyone that she was tired of standing lookout and was getting hungry. So were the rest of the guys, including me, and The "Great Sled Race" was ready to take place. Afterward, a hot bowl of chili would soon follow. Tommy said he wished he could be in the final race, but agreed to again to be a lookout at the railroad tracks. Joy said she would be a lookout at the bottom of the hill by the lit sidewalk and sharp curve.

I spoke up and voiced my unhappiness also about not being able to participate in the race, but volunteered to be the lookout at the Seneca

Street and Pike main roadway. My brother must have felt bad about me not being in the race and abruptly announced to everyone, "This is not being fair to Tommy and Barrie. They were lookouts most of the night and did not get a chance to join in any of the fun everyone was having."

Joy opened her big mouth again and said, "What about me? Don't I count? I was a lookout also." Richard said, "Joy, you are too small and it is too dangerous for you to attempt coming down the Pike by yourself, so please stay quiet or go home." Joy's lips started to quiver when she said, "Tommy got to ride on your back tonight, and I didn't." Then she dropped her head and was about to start crying, when Richard told her he was sorry for what he said to her.

The next thing Richard said amazed everyone and especially me. To this day I will never forget them. He said "he was going to give me his sled to ride in the official great sled race and he would take my place as a lookout". I started to argue with him, but he said "his decision was final and he wanted me in the race and that's all there was to it". Again to everyone's amazement, Willy spoke up and said "that he did not care about tonight's race since he had won it last year". He then said "he was going to let Tommy use his sled; he would stand guard at Tommy's lookout position". To everyone's further amazement, Jack suddenly spoke up and told everyone "that he would be glad to take Joy down the Pike for the last ride on his back". He also said "he would be careful with her and see to it she would not be hurt".

We all knew that this meant he would be digging the toes of both of his clodhopper shoes into the snow behind him to slow down from time to time. He would not take any chance on going too fast and avoid any possibility of becoming out of control, wrecking, or overturning. Of course, it also meant he would have no chance of winning the race. No one objected to Richard or Willy dropping out of the race, and we other boys were all secretly pleased with what they had done. This gave everyone a better chance of winning the race. Richard, with his new sled and repaired runner, would have been a favorite to win, along with Willy. Joseph and Vincent were very good riders and could also win the race.

Joy blurted out, "Oh goody, oh goody, I am going to get to ride down the Pike with all you big guys in the Great Sled Race." But then as quickly as she had spoken up when she heard what Jack had to say, she screamed out again, "But who will stand at my lookout position for me?" By this time, every one of the other guys with their sleds in hand, who knew they had a spot in the race, said they would drop out and take her lookout position.

We all started talking about who the lookout would be, when all of a sudden, big flakes of new snow started to fall on us and the ground. This was totally unexpected, and it meant we would still have Saturday and Sunday to do some more sledding. That is, if the vehicle traffic was not too heavy and the roads did not become impassable. Sometimes this happened when the snowplows were late getting out on the streets.

The snow was coming down even heavier by now, and no traffic was in sight looking down the main street. Charles spoke up and said, "Since no vehicles came up the hill during the past two nights, we should just forget about a lookout at the bottom of the hill. If any cars do manage to come up the hill, we would see their headlights and be able to avoid them." Also, this sharp curve at the bottom of the hill was always lit up by the Divens' Pennzoil gas station lights.

I took my brother's sled rope out of his hands and Willy handed his sled rope to Tommy. Tommy reached out and grabbed the rope quickly, saying, "Thanks, Willy, you are being very nice to me." Then he said, "It would be nice if I could win the race for you and your sled, but us smaller boys do not stand a chance of winning."

Willy asked Tommy what he meant by his comment, and Tommy just said, "Never mind; I wish I had never said anything." Richard, Vincent, and Robert also heard Tommy's comment and walked over to join Willy and find out what Tommy meant. After persistently being asked by all of us what he meant by his statement, Tommy said, "Since the bigger boys can run faster, there's no way Barrie, Bobby, or I can catch up with them." Jack, who was the oldest and wisest of the guys next to Robert, said, "Tommy's right; we have to figure out a different way to begin the race and make it fair for everyone."

While all this talk was going on, the snow continued falling heavily, and the roads were painted white again, with no cinders showing where we stood. Visibility was becoming poor, it was becoming foggy, and I spoke up and said that we better decide on something quick since it was getting late. With the long walk up the Pike, none of us might be able to see anything coming down, and there would be no more sledding tonight.

Joseph spoke up and said, "We could all just line up alongside one another with our sleds by Delaney's and lie down on them. From this position and with someone yelling out to start, we can all just push off with our hands to get going." Someone yelled out, "Let Joy give us the signal," and everyone agreed on this. Even though the bigger boys were stronger, this seemed fair, and the new snow would make the sleds move along easily for everyone pushing off with their hands. Without arguing, we all said this was all right and started pulling our sleds up the hill.

Richard and Willy moved along much faster than all of us and even ran partway up the hill to their lookout positions. The only thing that was behind any of us, as we walked up the long hill to the top of the Pike were two lines of fresh sled tracks, clodhopper shoe prints, and one small left and right imprint of Joy's rubber galoshes. By now it was around seven thirty, and at least a half inch of fresh snow covered the ground. As everyone continued walking up the hill, we all stomped down hard on the fresh snow with our feet and packed it down to make our sleds go faster.

As I walked past Richard, he looked at me and said, "Good luck, Barrie, and don't worry about my sled and the runner. Let it run, go as fast as you can, and turn the runners hard to the left once you get over the railroad tracks. After this, you must shift your body weight quickly to the left-hand side of the sled to keep it from overturning." He also told me to stay away from the icy area and the cinders that caused him to crash earlier.

Everyone, including Bobby who hit the ice and Jack who hit the cinders while riding alongside Willy, would be thinking the same thing. I had to do something besides just going fast to win this race, and I thought about it as I continued walking up the steep hill to the top of the Pike. Joseph, Charles, or Vincent, who were a year older and a little more experienced, could win this race if I did not think of something clever or unexpected. Suddenly a bright thought came to me as I continued walking, and I wondered if it would work!

I was not concerned about anyone else, especially Jack, who was handicapped with Joy on the top of his back. His steering would be hampered by this and meant he would be going at a slow pace to control his speed. We all reached the top of the Pike and were huffing and puffing very heavily. We stopped and pretended we were smoking again, and exhaled warm breaths of air that turned into small circular smoke rings as they hit the cold air.

The only individual who was not huffing and puffing was Joy, who had hitched a ride on the back of Jack's sled and was pulled up the hill. Due to the heavy snow, not one car or bus passed us as we walked up the hill. This was a good sign there would be no vehicle traffic to interfere with our run. However, we still had to be careful about any approaching trains and the railroad crossing below us.

When we were all rested, Joseph said, "Let's get started," and he drew a large line as straight as he could in the fresh snow with the side of his clodhopper across the middle of the Pike roadway. After doing this, he looked at everyone and said, "Remember, the first one to reach the front of the White Tower, even if you crash and get going again, will be declared the winner."

Everyone took their sleds and laid them down on the snow behind the start line. Lying on top of the sleds, we all kept them back behind the line with our hands and the toes of our clodhoppers. At Joy's signal, we would all be off and gliding down the Pike for the Great Sled Race. Joy yelled out as she lay on top of Jack's back, "Is everyone ready?" When we all screamed out yes, she screamed out, "Start!" and the race was on.

The snow was still falling heavily and visibility was limited when sixteen hands started to dig away frantically in the snow to get their sleds moving downhill. Joseph, Charles, and I were the first to move forward and were side by side, when Vincent and Robert shouted out, "We are catching up with you." When they shouted this out, we dug our hands harder and deeper into the snow again.

Every one of us was hoping each push would provide more speed to lead this wild and happy suicidal pack down the Pike. New snow was not always the best to sled on, and it had to become packed down hard to make the runners track smoothly. However, my sled was tracking great and going pretty fast by now down the steep Pike. I even felt comfortable enough to stop pushing anymore and bring both of my hands up to the wooden steering bar, grasp it, and hold on tight for my life.

The falling snow was hitting me on my face and eyes as I sped along, making it difficult to see. I kept steering in a straight line and was gaining additional speed, without losing control. I took my left hand off the steering bar briefly and wiped my eyes free of the snow as best I could. This was only a temporary fix, however, since due to my speed the snow kept getting in my eyes. Looking over, I could see that the two brothers

Joseph and Charles were still beside me, and I could hear the rest of the boys screaming behind me.

I continued to gain even more speed and pointed my sled straight down the Pike, without making any turns to slow down. The first curve, which was not too difficult to maneuver through, was coming up quickly, and I wiped my eyes again to see it better. I squeezed the steering bar tightly with both hands, went speeding into the curve, and negotiated it magnificently. Joseph and Charles were still alongside me, and their sleds went ahead of me slightly as we got around the curve.

I could hear no one behind me now and assumed that we were way ahead of everyone else. I also felt that one of us three would be the winner traveling at this speed, if there were no unforeseen accidents. As we continued speeding downhill and toward the next curve, I wiped my eyes again to remove the snowflakes and obtain a clearer view. I looked straight ahead, and the second curve, which was more difficult, was coming upon me quickly.

When I fell into the curve's potentially harmful grasp, I made a sharp turn to the right and rolled most of my body to the right side of the sled. If all went well, this would prevent the sled from possibly tipping upward and over. It worked, and the sled kept its tight hold on the ground as I negotiated through this dangerous curve successfully. I felt good about the maneuver I had just performed and was not worried about the speed I was traveling.

I would now have to negotiate the most dangerous and treacherous ninety-degree turn, which was coming up momentarily. If someone could get through this turn successfully, they would make it to the front of the White Tower with no problem. Joseph and Charles were still slightly ahead of me. Their sleds were on the far right side of the steep Pike roadway and going very fast. Like myself, neither one of them had attempted to slow their sleds down. I started to think about what I was going to do now and put my earlier bright thought to work.

I was getting close to the area where the cinders were located that caused some riders to overturn during the trial runs. However, without anyone seeing me while walking up the Pike, they were now covered over! I had carefully scraped up some snow with my hands, threw it over them, and stomped on it with my clodhoppers to get a good hard pack over the cinders!

If I could get over them, it would keep me on the inside of the treacherous turn. Joseph and Charles would be far to the right and heading into the icy patch, along with the other riders. Even with the additional snow we were getting, it would not be enough to pack over the ice yet.

I was now getting a little closer to Joseph and Charles and cleared the snow from my eyes again. Then I screamed over to them, "See you," and quickly turned my sled to the far left. As I did this, one of them yelled out, "You big dummy, you're heading straight into the bare cinders." They kept speeding down the Pike like me, but toward the right side of the railroad crossing. They had not forgotten about them and thought the cinders would slow, drag, or stop my sled completely, and one of them was going to win the race with no problem!

Steering my sled straight into the cinder area, without slowing down, I ran over it and felt a slight drag that slowed me down momentarily. However, the sled continued going straight down the Pike with no problem and still at a pretty good rate of speed. Richard told me later he thought I was nuts as he watched me steering over the cinders, seeing several fiery sparks shoot out from under his sled. He was also concerned this would cause the repaired welded joint on the sled's runner to crack open.

I continued my steep plunge down the Pike and knew that both Joseph and Charles thought I had overturned my sled and was sprawled somewhere on the snow-covered Pike roadway. Looking ahead, I could see several fiery sparks flying in the air, but could not see Joseph's or Charles's sleds, due to the heavy snow. I assumed that the sparks were coming from their metal sled runners going over the railroad tracks. In a moment, my sled runners would also be spitting out the same fiery sparks, similar to the sparks coming off of Mr. Holmes's welding torch while he was repairing something. When I crossed the tracks, I looked over to my right and saw Joseph and Charles standing up and running toward their overturned sleds.

"Great," I said, "my plan must have worked." In their haste to write me off, they had forgotten, hit the icy spot, and started to lose control. In addition, as they steered quickly to the left to enter the tricky and treacherous ninety-degree turn, both their sleds tipped over. As I passed them, they were picking up their sleds, which indicated to me they were going to get back on them and continue trying to win the race.

Now all I had to do was make the same treacherous ninety-degree turn successfully, and I would be home free and on my way to winning the Great Sled Race. Paying attention to what Richard had told me earlier, I let my sled go as fast as I could and steered hard to the left into the ninety-degree turn. While doing this, I shifted my body weight to the left side of the sled, to keep its runners firmly on the snow and me firmly on the sled. I entered the turn, and fiery red sparks flew out from under the sled runners.

The sled's back end slid to the right a little bit, but I managed to straighten it out and steer it into its final downhill run. Excited and feeling very confident about what I had just accomplished, I quietly said to myself, "You made it, Barrie, you made it, Barrie, whoopee." Richard's advice about staying clear of the icy area and how to take the ninety-degree turn was very helpful, but ignoring his advice about the cinders was what got me to where I was now!

I was finally off the steep downhill run on the Pike roadway, and continued down the Penn Avenue extension hill. All of a sudden, I could hear several of the guys screaming out loud, "The other riders are catching up to you." This alerted me that some of the other guys had also gotten through the ninety-degree turn and were still on my tail. I wondered where Joseph and Charles were and if they were getting close again too.

I kept the sled going as fast as I could and sped past old man Rainio's house and Mr. Holmes's welding shop. I maneuvered the sled through the sharp right-hand curve in front of the gas station with all its night lighting, and continued slowly on toward the front of the White Tower. All of a sudden, I could hear Vincent screaming out, "I am going to get past you, Barrie, and win the race." My heart began to flutter as I looked back quickly to see Vincent, who was close behind me.

I could do nothing now but hope that my brother's sled would still be sleek and fast enough on this flat terrain to glide up in front of the White Tower. All I could say was, "C'mon, c'mon, keep going, sled," as I kept nudging it forward. Then Vincent reached out and grabbed one of my clodhoppers to stop me, but it was too late. My sled came to a stop, and the bright lights hanging above the White Tower roofline were looking down on me. I knew I had won the Great Sled Race.

I jumped off the sled and screamed out loud, "Richard, I won, I won. Your sled was the best and fastest one." While I was doing all this jubilant screaming and shouting, Bobby, then Robert, then Tommy, then Charles and Joseph, and finally Jack and Joy went gliding past me on their sleds. Joseph and Charles were the only ones who crashed that night. The other guys, who survived the Pike downhill run, had followed me over the course I took and avoided the icy area also. Everyone was congratulating me when Richard and Willy finally showed up from their walk down the hill from their lookout posts.

Richard took me in his arms, gave me a big bear hug, congratulated me, and whispered in my ear, "Is my sled all right?" He never did say anything about watching me steer into the cinder area. Joy looked at me and said, "Can I be the one to tell Mom that you won the Great Sled Race and Richard's sled was the fastest?" I looked at her and said, "You can tell her anything you want to."

Shortly thereafter, while we were all standing in the middle of the road on Wilbur Avenue, next to the Brannigan's home we could hear the train whistles blowing. We looked up and saw a few white puffs of smoke coming from the locomotive as it ran over the rusty steel-girded trestle directly above us. Had this second locomotive for the evening shown up a few minutes earlier, it would have stopped tonight's Great Sled Race.

Before Joy could open her mouth again, Tommy shouted out, "Let's all go get our bowl of chili now." With this we all started to walk, while pulling our sleds behind us, to the Greasy Spoon restaurant. When we walked by the White Tower, the big clock inside showed the large black hand resting on the 12 and the small black hand resting on the 8. The one lonely Saint Colman's hallway clock and public school clocks used this simplistic numbered timepiece also. There were not many clocks in the Turtle Creek households or local businesses with the fancy Roman numerals. The three little Polacks in this group of children (me, my brother, and my sister) could also tell what time it might be by listening to the whistles being blown, and did not care much about the numbers' significance.

When we arrived at the front door of the Greasy Spoon, we boys cleaned the snow from under our clodhoppers, and Joy cleaned the snow off her rubber galoshes. We all went inside and could see Gus quickly removing the bowls of oyster crackers sitting openly on the counter. Apparently, the only oyster crackers we would get to take home with us would be those Gus would serve with our bowls of hot chili. We ate heartily, and the chili warmed us up real fast.

We finished our meal, got up, and went outside into the falling snow and freezing cold night. Before leaving to go to our respective homes and apartments, we talked a little bit more about the fun time we had. With the way it was now snowing, the weekend would allow us to get in some more sledding. Everyone was very happy about this, and we all smiled, laughed out loud, and said good night to one another.

We started going in different directions while pulling our sleds behind us again, and Willy shouted out, "Let's hope Saint Colman's will be closed next week too." The loud cheers and yelling of "yes," "all right," "I hope so," "that would be great," and "whoopee" could be heard coming from everyone's mouth. In the distance, the same echoing words of delight, could be heard bouncing off of the high stone Westinghouse protective walls, in the rat-infested back alley behind the Greasy Spoon.

A sad note to this story is that little Tommy would die while taking a bath a few years later from carbon monoxide poisoning due to a defective wall heater.

The White Tower, 1950s.

Little Tommy, 1943.

Left to Right: Richard, Joy, and Barrie in Farmer's Alley, 1939.

CHAPTER 11

GETTING TO THE SHOW

How could my brother Richard and I earn enough money to go to the show on Saturday or Sunday? I pondered this thought to myself while sitting on the stone wall across from the old copper mill. I was gazing down at the still unfrozen creek's stream of swift running water and watching the small logs and other debris float by. I had run up to this spot after being dismissed from school and was without my homemade harpoon to try and spear some of them. The cold Pennsylvania winter months were not particularly enjoyable and not a good time to do any serious harpoon throwing.

The current's swirling motions were sucking the debris downward under the water, and seconds later it would reappear and pass in front of me. This made it very difficult to get a steady and fixed aim on something with the harpoon, spear it, and drag it up on top of the stone wall. At times, during the summer months and heavy rainfall periods, the conditions were even worse, but at least it was warm. Not having to wear gloves and getting a better feel of the harpoon improved one's chances of spearing something every time.

There was a chill in the air on this winter day in December 1946. I was eleven years old. Richard was twelve, and I was contemplating that he might be interested in going to the show. He could help us earn the necessary money to purchase the movie tickets. It would also take us out of the cold and someplace where it was warm and allow us to remove our heavy mackinaw coats. There were many things we could do to earn enough money, such as looking around town for empty pop and beer bottles and collecting their deposits from the local stores.

There was no snow on the ground, so shoveling off neighbors' or businesses' sidewalks to earn money was not possible. Although it sounded easy, we were often confronted with many obstacles in finding ways to earn money. Our parents did not have any spare money most of the time, so they could not afford giving us the luxury of a show ticket. Feeding and clothing four children on a steelworker's pay was difficult enough for our parents.

Many other boys our age, and some even younger, were always out and scrounging around town in the same manner to earn money. The competition to earn money was fierce, and one had to start very early in the morning to find any empty and discarded bottles. Empty pop and beer bottles became even scarcer to find during the winter months, since most folks did not drink as much of it then. The summer months improved everyone's chances of finding more of them and in larger quantities.

People always drank more pop and beer to quench their thirst and help them get some relief from the hot temperatures and unbearable humidity. Although there were always several empty milk bottles to be found, they were ignored. Most of us boys, when first discovering milk bottles, collected them hurriedly and with a lot of excitement thinking about how much deposit money they would bring. This excitement disappeared very quickly when we learned they did not have any redeemable value attached to them when returned to a store or milk truck driver.

Could it be that this was done to discourage anyone from stealing the bottles when they were full of milk, drinking it, and then also collecting a deposit on the bottle? The stealing of milk left on a doorstep, porch, windowsill, or the sidewalk in front of a business did occur from time to time. My brother, sisters, and I used to run to the door when we heard the milkman setting down the bottles on the porch. Whoever was lucky enough to reach out and grab a bottle first, was also lucky enough to spoon off and eat the thick chunk of cream that lay under the cardboard tab at the top neck of the bottle.

One advantage that Richard and I had over the other boys was that we had a few residents who would save up their empty pop and beer bottles for us and promised not to give them to anyone else. One particular woman named Veronica, living in one of the apartments above the New Deal restaurant, was nice enough to do this, and we always spoke of her as "our lady." We had collected a few bottles from her during the earlier part of the week, and I knew she would not have anymore saved up for us.

The deposit on the bottles we collected from her got us ten cents, enough money to buy a *Captain Marvel* comic book. We also had several other ways of earning small amounts of money to make other limited purchases. It could be for a candy bar, an Isaly's ice cream cone, or a bag of Wise Potato Chips. At times, if we had an especially good day earning money, we would splurge and go into the White Tower to order a hamburger or buy a bowl of chili at the Greasy Spoon restaurant.

An especially good day could also find us buying two hot dogs from the Koutavas's corner Coney Island restaurant. They came loaded down with all the relish, sauerkraut, onions, ketchup, and mustard we wanted for just ten cents each. Sometimes there was a special sale going on, and two hot dogs could be purchased for fifteen cents.

On other occasions, the money earned might be used to buy parts to repair Richard's red Schwinn bicycle. Keeping the bicycle well maintained allowed us to travel greater distances, even into some other towns, in our pursuit of finding more items we might be able to sell or cash in. At times, we would even tie up the red wagon we had and pull it behind the bicycle. This was just in case we came across a large haul of bottles or metal items we might be able to sell to the local junkyard.

Not many residents were willing to pay us for carrying their heavy grocery bags home. We stopped doing this after being turned down so many times and being told to just go away. On occasion and without asking for any money, we would carry a local neighbor's groceries or other heavy items home for them. It was also a great way of putting our red wagon to use and keeping the wheels lubricated. In addition, it gave us the opportunity to ask them to save their empty bottles for us and any other junk they might not want. This was very beneficial to us, since a lot of times and unexpectedly, some neighbors would call out and tell us they had some bottles or junk for us to come by and pick up.

I kept thinking about other things we could do to make some money, and various ideas flashed through my mind! We could see if there might be any tins of old lard or oil being thrown away by the New Deal and other local restaurants and bars. They would replace it quite often, after deep-frying a lot of fish, shrimp, oysters, crab cakes, and french fries.

We could also look for discarded cigarette packets along the street sidewalk, gutters, and curb. We would then take them home and meticulously peel away the aluminum foil that lay inside. This was a cumbersome task and took many hours of rolling up the foil into a ball that may have weighed less than a pound and selling it to the local junkyard at going prices.

Another unique way to earn money was to look underneath and inside the cellar of a certain candy store in our town. This was a very special area and one that only Richard and I knew about. We called it our "secret place" and would not tell anyone else about it! For years, many of our friends would ask us where we got so much money at particular times, but we would never tell them about this location. Generally we would just say we found a case of empty beer bottles or several pieces of heavy copper to take to the junkyard. It was not unusual to find a full case of empty beer bottles being thrown away, especially after major holidays. In our minds, finding something like this was like striking gold, since the cardboard beer container also had a refundable deposit on it.

We could walk or ride the red Schwinn bicycle along the local sidewalks from one end of town to the other and look for dropped change in the gutters. The dropped change we would find was always close by a parking meter. We got lucky once in a while and would find a few pennies, nickels, or dimes, but it was not always the fastest way of earning money.

It was slow and tedious work and almost as bad as rolling up the foil found in a discarded cigarette packet. This was caused by having to crawl under all the Westinghouse Electric plant workers' and local townfolk's automobiles parked alongside and on top of the sidewalk curbing. Also, this was not a good thing to do after it rained, since the gutters running alongside the curbs became very muddy. Crawling underneath the cars was bad enough, but deliberately getting mud on our clothing and mackinaws would bring severe punishment at home. Thinking about the harsh sting that would come from our father's razor belt or cat-o'-nine-tails often prevailed over our keen intent to look for the coins and crawl around in the muddy gutters.

While we used this agonizing search-and-find technique, some other, bigger boys in town, providing none of the local police were around, would quickly bang the palm of their hand against the parking meters. This was done hoping that the shocking vibration would eject any coins that might be in the meters' designated slots (penny, nickel, and dime). Years later, the meters were changed to also accommodate quarters. The consequences of getting caught doing this unlawful act could be a good scolding from the police and possibly even the guilty boy or boys being taken to the station to see Chief Whalen.

In some cases, if the police took you home and reported what took place, it would result in a physical beating being administered by the parents or being confined to the house for several days. The sheer embarrassment most parents felt by the police having to confront them about what took place often resulted in the razor belt or cat-o'-nine tails being swung a lot harder!

The socially acceptable mentality during this time period, especially among many men, seemed to be that boys could take such punishment so as to make men out of them! What future mental or otherwise disturbing consequences and effects such beatings might have on an individual in later years were never taken into consideration!

Coins were placed in the meter slots by an automobile owner so as to be readily available if time ran out, allowing the police to turn the meter handle and provide additional parking time. Generally, expired time and no money in the meter resulted in the police writing a ticket and placing it on the vehicle's front windshield. One can only imagine the frustration of the automobile owner upon finding a ticket on his windshield knowing full well he or she had put enough money in the meter to cover any extended time.

Would the police believe the automobile owner's story when he or she brought the ticket to the station? Would they perhaps tear it up? Some automobile owners, who had enough influence with the local councilmen (there were no councilwomen), justice of the peace, or squire would have them dispose of the ticket, thus getting it "fixed."

Moneymaking ideas kept racing through my mind, even as cold as it was on this day. Richard and I might even get out our red wagon and go seek out some old galvanized piping, copper, and other metal objects we could take to the junkyard and cash in. The junkyard trek was always a last resort since Richard and I did not like the junkyard owner. He was always very mean and gruff with us, and we often thought his scales were not correct (rigged, one might say). This meant we were being underpaid, but as kids, how could we challenge him as to the accuracy of his scales?

He really got angry with us one day when we questioned his weight scale and told him we had weighed the iron and other items on Jessup's (the local used furniture store and movers) scale and there was a difference in weight. He told us to take our junk away if we did not like the weight reading and the money he would give us. Disgusted and very unhappy, we took the money and walked away. We thought we deserved more for a hard day's work and felt cheated! Thinking about it as we became older, perhaps the junkman had a good reason to set his scales up this way.

He may have done it to compensate for those dishonest people and many other kids who did devious things to make their junk weight heavier. Some of them would fill up the inside of any circular piping and tubing with mud and let it dry to increase its weight. Some individuals would even put rocks and dirt inside metal cans and crush them, so no rattle could be detected. Some people would fold leaves and lawn shavings inside newspapers before bundling and tying them together with strong cord in various stacks. However, it was unlawful, and perhaps he should have hired more people to examine the junk more carefully.

Earning enough money to pay for a show ticket or some other thing we wanted was never easy. What way would Richard and I choose from the various innovations we had developed to earn money? I collected my thoughts, swung both of my dangling legs up to the right of me, turned around quickly, hopped off the stone wall, and went looking for him.

While searching out Richard, I completely ruled out looking for money along the sidewalk curbing, and we certainly would never do any hard banging on any parking meters. Even for the older boys, it was much too cold outside to absorb the shock that was sure to occur on their hands. Hitting a meter like this on a cold day would send a sting like an electric shock up into the lower arm.

I also was not keenly interested in looking for any bottles, since it would keep us out in the cold too long walking up and down the streets and back alleys. It also meant climbing up several sets of stairs inside the apartment buildings and knocking on doors. If no answer we would then have to climb up the outside metal fire escape steps and knock on some residents' rear doors to see if they had left any empty bottles to give away.

Generally, during the summer months, most residents wanting to get rid of their empty bottles would set them out on the porch. However, being very cautious, Richard and I would always ask politely if we could have them. This avoided our being accused of stealing, and we did not want people mad at us for taking bottles without their permission.

Some of the boys collecting bottles would just take anything they saw on a porch or other open area, without permission! This made some people very mad and, at times, mad enough to even stop giving any bottles away to us. We suffered unjustly because of someone else's bad behavior.

We knew better than to do anything like this since, if reported, it would merit our feeling the sting of our father's razor strap or cat-o'-nine-tails!

During the winter months, some residents would take the bottles back to the stores and collect their deposit, and some would just throw them in their trash. Leaving no stone unturned, Richard and I would often find ourselves inside the main garbage Dumpster, located outside of the apartment building, looking for them. Hopefully we would find some. Looking through the Dumpster trash was no fun, since it meant having to jump into piles of highly stacked, noxious garbage loaded with rats.

After doing this, we would begin the task of picking through, turning over, tearing up, and looking through multitudes of paper bags, boxes, and other loose artifacts of garbage. During the winter months, it would be done wearing a pair of old socks to keep our hands warm. Funny, but the thought never came to us that wearing them also prevented us from touching the garbage. During the summer months, wearing a pair of socks or gloves as protection against the garbage never entered our minds, and we waded through the garbage very cavalierly.

We also had our fair share of competition, in that the Dumpster rats were looking for something to eat! In addition, we often would find scrap metal items that could be sold at the junkyard. It was a dangerous task, and we stood the chance of being bitten by these very large sewer rats, as they jumped about or were uncovered during our rooting through the piles of garbage.

The first time Richard and I saw the rats, we became very frightened and jumped quickly out of the Dumpster! However, after a while and in our quest to earn some money, we worked up enough courage to jump back into the Dumpster together. This was after we argued quite awhile as to who would be the brave one to jump in first!

On occasion, we inadvertently suffered a cut finger or hand, or scrape to some other part of our body from a broken piece of glass or other sharp object in the Dumpster. Even after being cut, especially if we were finding a lot of bottles, we hated to leave the Dumpster. Finding two small bottles might bring four cents deposit, but finding three large bottles could bring a nickel deposit each, almost enough to buy one show ticket.

If we did find a large bottle, then how many more might there be in the Dumpster? Finding a large bottle only increased our desire to look even more through the Dumpster trash and garbage, rats or no rats. We found ourselves running home at times to have hydrogen peroxide, iodine, or Mercurochrome applied to the wound and then be bandaged up by our mother.

Before leaving the Dumpster, we collected all the sellable and deposit items we found, and took them home with us. In some cases, if we had not finished rooting through all of the garbage, back we would go, bandages and all. We wanted to finish up and sort through the remaining bags and boxes we had not covered. Like digging for gold, we never knew when we might hit a major vein of bottles and strike it rich!

After a few years of rooting through the garbage, there was a peaceful coexistence that would occur inside the Dumpster. The rats ignored us and we ignored them, and not once were we ever bitten. They got what they wanted, and we got what we wanted! Although we were never bothered by them, I am also sure that the large, domestically owned cats we saw on the fire escapes by the Dumpster got what they wanted also. Rats were around town everywhere, especially by the creek and any protruding sewer piping. They even found their way into many homes, businesses, and the local theaters.

When I took what would turn out to be my future wife, Arleen, to the Olympic theater at a very young age, she did not believe me when I told her rats were always running around on the floor looking for food! To prove it, I dropped a pretzel stick on the floor; after we heard the rattle of paper and some light scratching, a big rat showed up!

Arleen saw its eyes even in the dim theater lighting and screamed out loud. She picked her legs up and placed them on her seat crossways. I kept telling her to remain calm during the picture show, but she couldn't; she kept making unusual "yuk," "aah," and "ooh" sounds. She was terrified, and to this day, I do not know what possessed her to not get up and leave. Perhaps she was too enamored with the suave Polish boy she was with?

Eventually the show ended, the lighting came on, and she breathed a sigh of relief as we got up to leave the theater. She did not wait on me but flipped her seat up and quickly ran up the aisle and out of the theater into the daylight. I do not believe she ever went back into that theater, even as a grown adult. I did not enjoy the movie that day, nor can I recall what it was about, due to all the distraction she was making. The good thing about it and what I can remember is that she bought her own show ticket that day!

I continued thinking about ways of earning some money and getting to the show, and thought perhaps we might go into the back alleys, where all the bars and restaurants threw away their tins of oil and old, hard lard. This was not a major task, but would require taking along our red wagon. The cans holding the oil or lard could be quite heavy at times, with some weighing over ten pounds. There were relatively few of them, and all in close proximity to one another. It would take no more than about a half hour to look around by their back doors for any signs of the tins.

To save time, we would visit only those places that did a lot of deep-frying, such as the Friendly Tavern, Conn's Bar & Grill, and George's New Deal. If we were lucky enough to locate and find some oil or lard, we would always ask for permission to take it away. We would then haul it off to the local Atlantic & Pacific (A&P) market and sell it for six or seven cents a pound. Finding a full tin of lard, which could weigh up to ten pounds, was like striking gold. We did strike gold a few times at these places.

Cleaning the spittoons out in a local card club, where one could also shoot craps on a pool table and place bets on a chuck-a-luck wheel, was another option for making money. The owner or manager of the club would pay us twenty-five cents for every spittoon we cleaned, and any coins we found inside them we were allowed to keep. Although we had cleaned the spittoons on many occasions, it was one of the last things, along with going to the junkyard that we wanted to pursue.

In addition, the cleaning of the spittoons could only be done on a Sunday afternoon. Giving it a lot of consideration, after waiting around to be paid, it might not leave us enough time to see a movie. I sure hoped that it would not come down to this! I quickly put the thoughts about the lard, oil, and dirty spittoon cleaning out of my mind. I felt somewhat relieved in not having to pursue any of these options. Then my thoughts drifted back to the candy store, its large floor register, and our "secret place."

The candy store was owned by Gus Bargas, one of the local Greek merchants. The store was situated on the lower floor of a row of six upper apartments that Gus owned and rented out. He, along with his wife and two small children, occupied the largest apartment. Inside the store, patrons could buy newspapers, ice cream, comic books, magazines, cigars, and cigarettes. They could also play the numbers, take several chances on a punchboard, or play the pinball machines.

In its heyday, the store was in a prime spot, since it was located directly across the street from the Westinghouse Electric main "I" gate. This gate, staffed with several guards, one of them being Turtle Creek's own Jack McCarthy. The gate during peak employment allowed 10,000 people, working three shifts daily, to enter and leave the plant. Additional gates and guards were located along the East Pittsburgh plant's long stretch of brick walls, at intermittent locations, to accommodate the entering and leaving of several more thousand people.

The punchboard was nothing more than a game of chance, and it contained tiny pieces of paper inserted into the punchboard, with an aluminum seal approximately one eighth inch in diameter placed over them. Punchboard chances came in various monetary denominations and could cost someone anywhere from a nickel and up for a single chance. There were some one, five, and ten dollar punchboards available for those willing to gamble that much taking a chance on punching out a winner.

The larger the amount one paid to take a single chance, the dollar amount paid to a winner could in some cases be much greater. The number of punches inserted into a board could also vary. As an example, they could range anywhere from twenty-five, fifty, seventy-five, one hundred, two hundred, five hundred punches, and up.

A simple punchboard and its chances could be based on a poker or other card-playing game. Someone lucky enough to punch out three aces on a nickel board could possibly win ten dollars. Another board could be based on a concept of using various fruits and three cherries; it could win you twenty-five dollars for a dollar chance. Another board could have several thoroughbred race horses embossed on it. The winner would be paid an appropriate winning dollar amount based on a "win," "place," or "show" appearing on the punch. Anything other than a win, place, or show punch would pay the bettor nothing! The more chances people bought, the greater the percentage chance they had of winning! However, even after buying multiple chances, many people did not win anything.

When playing the slot machines, blackjack, and any other game of chance, one has to always remember that the odds are against you to win. The owner, or "house," is always favored to win, in other words, to take more money in from a player than they will have to pay out to a player! Like the numbers game, only adults were allowed to play and take chances on these boards. Even so, it was and still is against the law to have such punchboards, just as it was against the law to book numbers!

Inside the candy store, stacks of coins being handed to a patron to play the pinball machines would often find some of them slipping through a patron's hand and falling into the large floor heating register. Sometimes coins dropping down into the register may have been the result of a simple purchase and the exchange of money between Gus and a store patron. What choice or choices would we make to earn some money, and would Richard and I be interested in going to the show or not, and on what day?

Maybe he might even suggest something new that we had never done before. I was confident he would want to go, since the show offered a nice warm place to be in. Sometimes it was even warmer than the inside of our house, when there was not enough money to buy more coal. After all the thinking I had done, I became very excited and ran all the way home to look for Richard. If and when I found him, I would ask where he wanted to start and what he would suggest we do first to earn enough money to get to the show. I definitely was not in the mood to dig through the main garbage Dumpster or clean out any spittoons.

It took me awhile, but I finally located Richard, playing with a bunch of other local boys and friends in the back of Farmer's Alley. They had a bunch of old recapped tires that they were playing with. Old tires were easy to come by, since the Divens brothers owned the tire recapping shop adjacent to the alley. They were all playing a game whereby several of the boys would line up with a tire alongside of them.

At a given signal, they would begin to run, while beating and pushing hard on the top of the tire with one hand as fast as they could and see who got to the other end of the alley first. The first boy to get to the end of the alley and a drawn chalk line mark with his tire still upright was declared the winner. I said hello to all the boys, since they were my friends also. After this, I lifted up one of my hands above my shoulders and signaled for Richard to come over to me.

He greeted me, said hello, and like always, gave me a big bear hug, wrapping and squeezing his arms around my back. As I grunted from the hard squeeze, which often took my breath away, he looked at me and said, "What's up?" Since I did not want the other boys to hear what I wanted to say, I whispered quietly and asked him if he was interested in going to the show.

I winked at him at the same time, and he knew this was a signal to not let the other boys know about it. If they figured out our plans, they might begin looking for ways to earn some money also! I did not want any competition in whatever we were going to do! Richard looked at me and whispered, "What day do you want to go to the show?" and I said to him, "How about Saturday or Sunday?"

I also told him I preferred going to the six o'clock Rivoli theater show, since it was a double feature. Two shows for the price of one ticket did not happen often! He said "that either day was okay with him". Putting the show off until Saturday or Sunday also gave us the rest of the day to start looking for something to sell and earn some money. I had hopes!

Richard asked me if I knew what was playing, and I told him, "Two of our favorite cowboy movies. The double feature will star Roy Rogers in *Rainbow over Texas* and Gene Autry in *Call of the Canyon.*" He looked at me and said, "Wow, I can't wait to see them." "Me too," I replied back to him. Going to the five o'clock show, with movie previews, a cartoon, and news events, would keep us inside the theater until around eight o'clock. By the time we got home from the show, coal or no coal to fire the furnace, it would still be somewhat warm underneath our heavy bed blankets.

It would also still leave us enough time to finish our Saint Colman's and Sisters of Mercy homework assignment. We hoped. That is, if during the short intermission, someone did not get up on the stage and start talking about upcoming civic events or raffling off a prize. During the war, there were always people getting up on the stage at intermission talking about the importance of buying war bonds.

Sometimes the theater's manager would appear on the stage with a large wire basket full of the other half of your ticket. From it, he would draw out a few tickets and call out their imprinted numbers. The person lucky enough to hold a winning number might get a free show ticket, several tickets, a candy bar, or some other item, such as a bag of popcorn, ice cream bar, or several long stick-type penny pretzels. Some kids, including myself, often forgot about the possibility of there being a drawing and found ourselves scrambling about under the theater seats looking for the ticket stubs we had thrown away.

At the time, I believe I had all of a nickel on me, and I asked Richard how much money he had. He looked at me and said he was stone broke, and did not have a single penny on him. This meant we were going to have to work extra hard to come up with money for the show and a few pieces of candy or long pretzel sticks. With enough money, we might even be able to buy a box of gumdrops or jujubes. He looked at me and asked if I had any ideas as to what we might do. I replied no, and followed up by telling him I was not interested in cleaning spittoons or rooting through garbage bins. He laughed at me and said, "I agree."

I also said it was too cold to do anything outside, and our chance of finding enough bottles to pay for the tickets was very slim. He agreed again and said to me, "How about we try our secret place under the floor register at Gus's store?" I looked at him and said, "Great idea! I was thinking about it also, and I am all for it." Richard knew what he had proposed would keep us very warm, but we had to be careful and not burn our hands or lower arms!

Richard still wanted to play with his friends, which meant we would not do anything with the rest of the day to earn money! I stuck around and got into the tire-rolling game also. After a couple of hours of playing this game, we quit and went home. We entered the house, removed our warm clothing, and sat down at the kitchen table to eat a hot bowl of our mother's bigos, or Polish peasant stew, and we were ready to call it a day for playing in the snow. Without any heavy snowfall, there was not much more one could do at this time of the year since the evening darkness appeared quickly.

We went down into our coal cellar and played with our chemistry set for a while. Then we set off some .22 caliber bullets, slipped into a metal tube, held in place by a steel vise. The bullet was fired by our striking it with a small ball peen hammer and sending the projectile slamming into a dirt wall. After this, we would remove the shell casing and load the "pipe" up again.

We went to bed that evening agreeing to start out early in the morning and go into the cellar under the candy store to look for any dropped coins. The cellar was located underneath and at the back of Gus's building. Richard and I had often wondered what might be inside the cellar and were always curious to get inside. We counted the number of stair steps leading to the door and memorized that there were six. We ran up and down them on many occasions while playing hide-and-seek with the other kids.

One day we went down the steps and tried to open the door with several skeleton keys that Richard and I had found. "Yippee," we cried out and giggled to ourselves when one of the keys unlocked the door. The next morning, after a hearty breakfast cooked by our mother and consisting of some home fries, eggs, and kielbasa, we set off for our journey to the candy store cellar. When we arrived, we took care to look around carefully and make sure no one was watching us go down the stairs and enter the cellar.

We had to be especially careful about Mr. Knee. He was one of the apartment tenants, and he was always sticking his nose in everyone's business and making inquiries as to why they were around the building. During our pop and beer bottle searching, if he saw us going or coming up the back stairs to the apartments, he would chase us away from the building as if he owned it.

He knew better than to do this when our father was around. Our father confronted him one day when he heard him hollering at us for playing around the area. Using the Polish word *dupa,* or ass, he told Mr. Knee in no uncertain terms what he would do to him if he ever did it again. The other tenants, who liked us, would also tell him it was none of his business if we wanted to go up the stairs to their apartments and look for bottles. By this time, inserting the skeleton key and turning the lock to open the cellar door came very easy for us.

We walked into the dark cellar, a little bit afraid. We closed and locked the door behind us. We did not want to use a flashlight to see around, so as not to attract anyone's attention! There was one small glass window framed into the foundation, but after years of neglect and never being washed, it was covered in mud and not very visible to the public's eye. Because of its filthy condition, we both thought no one would ever see the light coming off a flashlight in the darkness of the cellar. We both decided not to take a chance, though, on using a flashlight at this time.

One day we were going to clean off the window to take a peek at what might be inside the cellar, but decided against it since Gus or someone else might see it and become suspicious as to who may have cleaned it and why. The only light we had to somewhat see by was the hot gas flames rising up from the floor furnace grates. Sometimes the only light we had to guide us would be that coming from the flicker of the small pilot flame.

Gus was one of the few people able to afford to convert over from a coal-fired furnace to a natural gas heater. If only the pilot was burning, this meant that the thermostat had not reached a set temperature that would cause the burners to ignite, in a sudden way, and spew out a whoosh of hot flames. We could never understand this phenomenon, and it was several years before we learned about how thermostats worked.

Underneath the hot flaming burners of the overhead floor furnace was what I will describe as a long, lower, half-circle-shaped piece of sheet metal, integral to the design of the furnace. I now know that this metal sheeting was a safety design feature and meant to prevent someone from inadvertently coming in contact with the hot burner grates. When Richard and I first saw the furnace, it looked as if it had fallen partially through the flooring and was suspended in midair. The lower part of the furnace was hanging about four and a half feet above the cement floor of the cellar.

Upon further examination, we could see that the furnace was secured firmly to the rafters and flooring above us. We had to stand on our tiptoes to take a better look and examine exactly where the flames were located, while at the same time attempting to maintain our balance. Being a little taller, Richard could see a lot more of the flames and other furnace parts than me. Standing like we were was a little agonizing, and taking a quick look, we noticed several coins lying on the bottom of the half-circle metal piece.

We relaxed the strain on our toes, ankles, and feet by planting our shoes firmly back on the cellar floor. Several minutes later, we rose up again on our tiptoes to gaze excitedly at the coins again as they glistened brightly, below the light of the glowing burner flames above them. Taking the time to look a little longer and placing even more strain than before on our toes, feet, and ankles, we could hardly believe what we saw. We were in awe at the dollar amount they represented in our minds. Dropping down quickly to the cellar floor and easing the throbbing pain we both felt, Richard said, "There must be twenty dollars worth of coins inside there."

I was flabbergasted, could hardly speak, and stuttered back to him, "ya, ya, yes, Rich." Talking even faster, I stuttered again and said to him, "There has to b, b, be more than that." While looking at the coins, after a third time of rising up on the tip of my toes, the thought of a pirate's chest full of coins entered my mind! I mentioned this to Richard, and we could not understand why Gus the Greek had never found this hidden chest! Or had he?

Since the red and orange flames were burning hot and bright, we had to figure out a way to retrieve the coins without possibly burning our extended hands and arms! There was an open chamber of about six inches between the bottom of the furnace grates, its upper hot flames, and the protective metal sheet. We thought this would allow us to slide our hands and lower arms into the chamber and grab some of the coins quickly. We questioned each other as to how far and for how long a period of time we would be able to reach into the chamber without the heat burning us.

Due to our limited time at being able to get a real good look, we wondered if there could be more coins lying farther inside the chamber and on the metal sheet. We did not want to have to come back to get them. We did not want to miss any coins, and we could not take a chance on Gus finding them or us in his cellar! We decided to leave the cellar in a hurry and go find a box to stand on to give us some additional height and a better look into the metal chamber.

We did not want anyone else to find our secret place and hidden treasure this day. Especially Mr. Knee. We unlocked the cellar door, opened it slowly, and after seeing that no one was around outside, we exited and locked the door back up. We darted up the short row of cellar steps and ran as fast as we could to locate a box. Breathing very heavily and full of excitement about our find, we ran to the rear door of the Giant Eagle Market. There were large piles of cardboard boxes stacked in an orderly fashion waiting to be picked up by the trash company.

Another area had a row of steel garbage cans, lined up to hold those meat parts and bones that could not be used and stuff swept up off of the sawdust-laden floor inside the store. Other cans were used to dump spoiled vegetables, broken jar products, bad cans of food, and other perishable items. Looking at another storage area we were quite familiar with, we saw the large pile of wooden boxes that came in all shapes and sizes. We grabbed a two-part empty orange crate with a picture of a female picker pasted on its side.

There was some cursive handwriting on its side, showing the oranges came from California. The two-part boxes had a heavy solid board in the center, which made them much stronger. We had used this type of box quite a bit to place inside our red wagon and store any bottles or other junk we found inside it. One would think that people might ask what we were going to do with an empty orange crate as we lugged it down the main street in town, but no one did. This was not an unusual scene in our town, especially for Richard and me, who were always pulling, dragging, or carrying something around with us.

Perhaps they might have thought it was to put pop bottles, beer bottles, or other junk in to haul away in our red wagon. The people who did see us that day just said good morning and went on about with what they were doing. One day, Richard and I found an old 9x12 Persian rug. We walked down the street carrying it on our shoulders to Jessup's used furniture store to see if they might want to buy it. The only thing people said to us was, "That rug sure looks awful heavy. Hold onto it tightly, and be careful not to hurt yourself."

With box in hand, we returned quickly to our secret place, again making sure no one was around. Then we walked down the steps, lifting, not dragging, the orange crate behind us very carefully. We did not want to make any noise or attract any attention to ourselves. I unlocked the door, entered the cellar, and followed the glowing flames to the furnace area. Suddenly, Richard stopped quickly and said to me, "Barrie, you big dummy, you forgot to lock the door." After setting the box on the cement cellar floor, I went back and locked the door and returned to the furnace area.

Richard was standing underneath the furnace with the box, and I stood alongside him. We both placed the box on the cellar floor and stabilized it, to eliminate some unevenness. Then we took turns standing on it, to make sure it would hold our weight without breaking up or tipping over. To our delight, it did the job!

The furnace flames were still burning brightly as I stepped up carefully and stood on top of the box first and looked into the metal chamber. I became extremely happy as my eyes came in contact with piles of additional coins that I had not seen earlier. The extra height provided by the box was great; it provided more visibility and kept Richard and me from having to stand on our tiptoes ever again. I jumped off the box all excited and told Richard to take a look at what I had just seen. Without any hesitation, he stepped up on the top of the box quickly and looked intently into the chamber. He uttered, "Oh boy!"

He jumped off the box onto the cellar floor and said to me, "Wow! Barrie, there sure are a lot more coins here than we could see before. I am sure glad we went out and got this box." From what we could both see while standing on the box, there were numerous pennies, nickels, dimes, and quarters lying around. There was nothing larger in the coins we could see, such as half or silver dollars. We assumed that the upper floor register openings were not large enough to let them fall through. "Shucks," we both said as we looked at one another.

We thought in our imaginative minds and state of joy and excitement that there could be even more than twenty dollars in coins. Whatever the amount, it was more found money than we had ever seen or would have in our possession at one time. Taking turns while standing on the box, we started to retrieve with our hands only those coins lying close to both outside edges of the hot metal chamber.

We realized that attempting to push our hands and lower arms any farther into the chamber took too much time, and we would begin to feel the heat of the burner flames on top of them. Attempting to reach farther into the chamber very quickly did not work either, and we had to withdraw them to avoid being burned.

While retrieving the initial coins, we could hear Gus's voice and many of his patrons' voices talking loudly above us and echoing down through the register openings. We began speaking very softly to one another after this, afraid they might also be able to hear us and possibly even see us through the floor register! We were in a dilemma and had to figure out how we were going to get the rest of the coins and not burn our hands or arms! We also had to do it quietly and without attracting attention to ourselves. We did not want Gus or anyone else to find the coins or learn about our secret place.

We had worked hard up until now, and no one else deserved this treasure chest. It did not take us long to figure out what to do. The answer to our problem was very simple as we both said, "Let's find a long stick." With the stick, it would be easy to have Richard or me stand on top of the box and push the coins out of the center of the metal chamber into one of our hands. The initial coins on the edge were not too hot and easy to handle, but we were not sure about the ones buried deeper inside the chamber.

Sticks were easy to find around town, and we had plenty of old mop and broom handles lying around our house, which was located right behind the candy store. It was also right behind Mr. Knee's apartment, and we did not want him to see us. Rather than both of us running off to get one of the old handles, I told Richard I would do it and be back in five minutes. He said he was too scared to be left alone by himself in the darkness and wanted to come along too.

We both knew from experience that there had to be a lot of big sewer rats lurking around on that cellar floor and perhaps even in the wood rafters and flooring above us. It was not uncommon to see them running around the outside of many of the buildings in town. At times, one could even see them running around on the five-and-ten store floor. The store sat adjacent to the local creek, and the rats generally came in through the sewer pipes that emptied into it! It was the favorite spot of a lot of the boys in town to take their BB guns and shoot at them.

Without arguing about it, we both left the cellar together and closed, but did not lock, the door behind us, since we would be back quickly. We looked out and saw no one around. We made a mad running dash to the front door of our home, located about fifty feet away. We picked up an old broom handle and returned to the cellar immediately to begin our task of retrieving the remaining coins. Once back in the cellar and our secret place, Richard got back up on the box and told me he was going to push a single coin out of the center part of the chamber into my hands to see if it was too hot for me to hold.

He said to me, "Are you ready?" and I replied, "yes." I was already squinting my eyes in pain, anticipating that the coin was going to be very hot and burn both my hands, which were cupped together. Moving the stick about in the deep chamber and placing it in front of a coin, Richard pushed his arm forward and said, "Here comes the first one."

I heard the stick scraping the metal, and shortly after that, felt a coin drop into my hands. It was not hot! I told Richard he could push more coins out, which he started to do immediately, and they were not hot either. All the coins I had caught were warm, but not hot, and I was enjoying stuffing them into my mackinaw pocket as quickly as they fell into my hands.

It took around ten minutes for Richard to push every coin out that he could see. While filling my mackinaw pockets with each bunch of coins as they fell into my hands, I kept wondering how much money we might have found. Finally, Richard said to me, "I think we have all the coins; I can't see any more." He jumped off the box and down onto the cellar floor. He asked, "Where are the coins?" and I told him, "They are in my pockets." He then said to me, "Let's get out of here."

We picked up the box and left the cellar as quickly as we could, being sure to lock the door behind us. We looked around again when outside to see if anyone was around who might see us. We both walked up the cellar steps holding onto the box and stick. We wanted to be extra careful since we did not want to alert Gus, Mr. Knee, or anyone else that someone had been in the cellar. We wanted to protect our secret place. We ran all the way home without stopping, and threw the box down hard on the outside dirt ground.

We went upstairs to our bedroom, removed the coins we had, and threw them on our tightly stretched bed blanket. Just looking at all the coins lumped together, we knew there was more than enough to buy a double-feature show ticket. We could even buy a lot more theater tickets, or anything else we wanted, for quite awhile. We divvied up the coins between us and began sliding them along the blanket, counting up how much we had while doing it.

When we finished, I asked Richard how much he had counted. He looked at me and said, "Four dollars and sixty-three cents." I yelled out loud, "Oh boy." Then he asked me how much I had counted up, and I told him, "Three dollars and fifty-eight cents." The arithmetic lessons taught to us by the Sisters at Saint Colman's was being put to good use now! We were both disappointed that our expectations in the beginning of perhaps finding twenty dollars or more in coins did not come to fruition. Nonetheless, we were quite pleased with our find that day.

We split the eight dollars and twenty-one cents and hid it away behind a loose rock in the foundation of our house. Richard told me to take and keep the extra penny that day. From time to time, we would go back to the cellar looking for coins in the furnace chamber, and on occasion find a few more. But there was never a major accumulation of coins like our first treasure chest discovery. At times, we found nothing!

When summer came and the gas furnace was shut off, Richard and I wondered if perhaps there might be some more coins lying on top of the cold burner grate that had not fallen down onto the metal chamber. Without the burning flames, a pilot light, or a flashlight, we would not be able to see anything. One day while standing outside the building, we wondered if anyone, especially Mr. Knee or Gus, could see any light coming from inside the cellar through the one old, solitary glass window.

The window, encased in its rotted wood, battered frame, and embedded into the foundation concrete blocks, had become encrusted with mud and dirt over the years and was hardly recognizable. We believed that Gus and the previous owners of the store just ignored it and did not want to take a chance of it falling apart if someone were to attempt to clean or fix it. Discussing further what we might do, we developed a plan whereby one of us was going to have to go into the cellar with a flashlight, and the other would have to remain outside by the building.

After flipping a coin in the air, I called out tails, and when it landed in the dirt head side up, I knew I was the one who would have to enter the scary cellar by myself. A short while later, I returned with a military-style flashlight in my hand. The color of it was military olive drab, and it held two D-size batteries in its rubberized case. It was weird looking, since its circular glass face light was bent over.

When I was a Boy Scout, we used the same style flashlight on a lot of camping trips. It looked like an "L" when turned upside down or while lying on its side. It was not long and straight looking, with the circular glass at one end like most flashlights.

Bravely I walked down the steps, unlocked the door, and entered the cellar, while Richard was outside the building, kneeling down in the dirt trying to see through the dirty glass window. I turned on the flashlight and closed, but did not lock, the cellar door behind me. If someone came around and discovered what we were up to, I wanted to be able to make a quick escape. Richard had a better chance of getting away than me! I held the flashlight up in the air in front of me, and swung its light back and forth to locate where the window was.

I found it and quickly walked up and stood in front of it. Without saying a word, I directed the bright light on the window, and held my breath for a few seconds. Richard said nothing! I turned around, left the light on, and walked all around the cellar, looking at different things. At one point, as the light came in contact with the closed cellar door, I noticed a light switch next to it. If there was a switch, there also had to be a light somewhere. I continued to scan the cellar and located a lightbulb hanging from a wood beam in the center of the cellar floor.

I called myself and Richard stupid for not discovering this light switch during our earlier, frequent visits to the cellar. However, thinking about it, I don't believe we would have ever turned the light on. I made a mental note to inform Richard about it and to see what his reaction would be.

While shining the light all around in various places, I saw I was correct about there being big rats in the cellar. I saw several of them running around. Some of them sat motionless and stared at me with their yellowish eyes. As I moved forward to get a closer look at them, they scampered off quickly.

Some of the rats ran down a grated sewer drain, and some of them ran up the low cellar walls into the wood floor rafters. I tried to remain calm and not become frightened or scream out, since I thought they might come after me. I placed the light coming from the flashlight on the cellar door, and ran over to it in a hurry. Although it was only a few feet away, it seemed like it took me forever to reach it! I left the cellar, locked the door behind me, and ran up the steps and over to where Richard was.

He saw me coming out of the cellar, and I ran up to him and told him how scared I was about seeing the big rats. He told me he was starting to worry about me and wondered why I did not turn on the flashlight inside the cellar! I looked at him with a big smile on my face and told him, "I did turn it on." At that point, we both knew our plan had worked, and no one would be able to see any light in the cellar when we turned on the flashlight. I also proceeded to tell him about the light switch by the door and the lightbulb hanging from a wood beam in the center of the cellar. He looked at me with a shocked expression on his face.

His expression turned quickly into a big smile, and he said to me, "Barrie, how stupid we were in not finding out about it much earlier. But I don't think we should ever turn it on." I looked at him and said, "I agree." Walking home and talking some more about how our plan had worked, we both suddenly realized how stupid we really were! During the many occasions we were in the cellar, we never saw any daylight coming through the window, meaning no light could be seen coming from inside the cellar. We chuckled about our stupidity the rest of the day, but never told our friends about it.

Several days later, we both entered the cellar again. I carried the flashlight in one hand, while Richard carried the wood box for us to stand on. No stick was needed since the furnace flames were out and we could feel around in the chamber without getting our hands or arms burned. He also had the skeleton key in his pants pocket and was in charge of unlocking and locking up the door when we were done searching for more coins. Shining the light all around and being very quiet, I pointed out to Richard everything I had seen.

As usual, we could hear Gus and several other voices and people walking around on the wood and linoleum flooring directly above us. Hopefully they were all far enough away from the register that none of them might see the glare from the flashlight.

Our plan should have also included Richard going into the store and looking down through the register to see if he saw any light while I was down in the cellar. Since we did not do this, we were both taking a chance with what we were now doing. Hopefully, just placing the light inside the chamber and nowhere else would prevent anyone upstairs from seeing it.

Minutes later, I was standing on top of the box. I placed the light coming off of the flashlight on the burner grate and placed my free hand into the chamber. Then I reached up and placed it on the top of the burner grate and began to move it around slowly. As I was doing this, I felt what seemed like a coin and pushed it off the grate, not caring where it fell. It made a loud clanging noise, and Richard became alarmed, thinking that maybe Gus had heard it also. Would he become curious and look down the register, or come down into the cellar to investigate the noise? We hoped not!

We became very quiet, I turned off the flashlight, and we waited to see what might happen. After waiting several minutes and not noticing or hearing anyone say something as to "What was that noise?" or "Did you see that light?" I turned the flashlight back on. "Now what are we going to do?" we whispered to one another. Richard looked at me and said, "I have an idea." I gave him a curious look and said, "What is it?" Without saying a word, he removed his T-shirt and motioned for me to do the same thing.

I stepped down off the box, removed it, and gave it to him immediately. Without saying another word, he got up on the box and placed both shirts into the metal chamber, to muffle the sound of any coins that might fall down onto it. "What a smart brother," I said to myself. I always looked up to him, as younger brothers generally do. Then he signaled for me to hand him the flashlight and proceeded to turn it on. After this, he moved his hand back and forth across the top of the burner grate. With this movement, several more coins came plummeting down and fell quietly into the T-shirts.

After a while, he could feel no more coins and stepped down off the box. We quit looking for anymore. We pulled our T-shirts out of the chamber very carefully, to keep the coins in place without spilling them on the cellar floor. We had no idea as to what the coins were or how much money they represented! I picked up the box, and Richard turned on the flashlight to guide us back to the cellar door. We went outside, and Richard carefully locked the door back up. We looked around, could see no one, and scurried up the steps, with box in hand, and ran home.

On this day, we had found six quarters, three dimes, seven nickels, and eleven pennies. Not a bad haul, and the $2.26 was split evenly. It was more than enough for both of us to see the show at least six more times. That is, if we did not buy any pretzels, candy, or Popsicles. Being very frugal with the money and not knowing how long it might last, we often split a Popsicle.

As the years went by and as much as they begged us, Richard and I never did share our secret place with any of our friends. We also knew that they had never found any secret treasures like ours. Or did they, and not share it with us? I doubt it very much.

As time passed and Richard and I became older, we eventually shared with Gus, who liked us a lot, what we used to do in the cellar. To our amazement, he looked at us and said, "I knew what you guys were up to down in the cellar, and I also knew you had a key to the door." We both looked at him dumbfounded and did not say anything back to him. We talked about it later and decided he must have seen us going down his back steps one day and did not say anything.

He knew we were good boys, and a little mischievous at times, but like most of the other people in our town, he knew how hard times were. He also had a pretty good idea as to what kids would do to make some money. Apparently he too had to begin learning about ways to earn money at an early age.

Richard and I talk quite often, and we now believe that Gus overlooked a lot of things we were doing since he knew how hard it was during these days gone by. In addition, we also believe he was not interested in the coins falling down the register, since he, like Johnnie, was doing very well with his numbers and punchboards business, like most of the other local candy store owners.

Getting to the show, especially when a cowboy movie was playing, was very hard at times, especially for us boys. But looking back, it was all worth the laborious effort we, and many other children our age, put into making enough money to pay for a theater ticket!

CHAPTER 12

THE POOLROOM

I had my first exposure to a poolroom at the early age of nine, in 1944. At the allowed age, I went into one and visited them for several more years thereafter. Due to a great deal of exposure and knowledge as to what goes on inside them, I have always been amazed as to what some people's thoughts were and still are about them. This was especially true with many teenage girls and what they may have been told, especially by their fathers and mothers, as to the evil, sinister things that might take place inside them.

What misconceptions may they also have had about the boys and adult men who went inside them quite often? Were they told to stop hanging around with individuals like this to avoid unsavory comments that might be made about them and destroy their reputation as being a nice girl? I believe a lot of the unknowns about poolrooms and disreputable stories about them are based mostly on one's own perceptions, imaginary thoughts, lies, and rumors.

Some fathers and mothers felt uncomfortable with their young sons going into a poolroom and the influence it might have on them! My parents never objected to my brother or me going into a poolroom. In fact, one of the first jobs we ever had was mopping up the Cima Brothers' poolroom floor and cleaning the spittoons on a regular basis. However, my parents would never allow my sisters to go inside one. The poolroom seemed to be all right for us boys, but a place that was taboo for the girls. When my sisters, Joy and Judy, would ask my parents why they felt this way, their answer was always "because ladies do not go inside or hang around poolrooms."

The curiosity and perceptions of some individuals, who may never have been inside a poolroom, also tend to escalate a lot of the negativity about them. Some of the outrageous things I have heard people say over the years about a poolroom and its influence on individuals who hung around them were:

It will turn them into gangsters.

It will promote their becoming a bookie.

It will lead to dropping out of school.

It is a sure path to cigarette smoking.

It will promote the use of drugs and alcohol.

It will cause them to go from good to bad.

It will lead to disrespect for law enforcement.

It is a sure path to jail.

It will lead to rebellious behavior with teachers and parents.

Good things and bad things happen every day in different business establishments within America. So I often ask myself why poolrooms were singled out by some people as being the den of evil and the first step toward wrongdoing. I cannot say with certainty without having any statistical data that some poolrooms were not instrumental in leading some individuals astray in life. I must also point out, however, that taking the right path in life is one's personal choice and responsibility.

The poolroom I am going to write about and provide an insight into is what I will describe as a "class act," along with its owner, a well-respected hunky named Joseph Evanovich. His nickname was Pinky, and the business name etched boldly with large lettering into the front window of his poolroom, which opened in 1948 in Turtle Creek, Pennsylvania, was "Pinky's Poolroom."

The original location of the poolroom was demolished, along with many other Turtle Creek businesses, over the years, but Pinky's was relocated to another part of the town. As of this writing in 2011, it is still a focal point to hang out for many of the surrounding area's men and teenage boys. In addition, a few teenage girls and ladies are now visiting Pinky's to play some pool, accompany their boyfriends, or just socially "hang out together."

My best remembrances about Pinky's were during the years 1951 through 1957, when I frequented it quite often. Although it was not a place where one might learn the Ten Commandments, or study his or her Catechism lessons, it was a favorite place for grown adult men and the local high school or teenage boys to hang out.

As I recall, small children and most kids under the age of fourteen were not allowed inside Pinky's unless accompanied by a parent or another adult. This was permissible under Pennsylvania law. I am quite sure, however, that some of our puritanical town locals, seeing a young child going into a poolroom, frowned upon it.

Inside the poolroom, there was always money changing hands due to the betting going on between pool players and numbers being booked. Money also changed hands between individuals over the outcome of a horse race and basketball, baseball, or football games being bet on. Paying off someone in cash who had a big winning score on a pinball machine, was a daily event. All of these things, I might add, were and still illegal under Pennsylvania law.

The booking of a number was never done by Pinky or any of his employees. However, the booking of numbers was generally the only gambling law ever enforced from time to time. Because of this, those individuals doing illegal things always had to be careful that an undercover detective, or "county dick" as they were called, was not planted inside the poolroom or some of the local candy and cigar stores!

Punchboards, which promoted a game of chance and the possibility of winning several hundred dollars, although very popular at the time, were illegal and never allowed inside Pinky's. Also, to my knowledge, no drugs, alcohol, or promiscuous ladies were ever allowed inside or around Pinky's by its owner. He just would not tolerate such illicit things, which could corrupt the morals of young people.

I cannot begin to list the notable lawyers, scholars, ministers, scoutmasters, war heroes, teachers, and many other professionals who walked into and out of Pinky's and made great contributions to our society. Some of them I have mentioned in this book. Perhaps their experiences and interaction with friends while hanging out inside Pinky's were very beneficial in their continued academic education (including street smarts) and business success.

Many of them were familiar with the gutter-type language that sometimes could be heard echoing off the walls of the poolroom. On occasion, some of them, in their younger and exuberant years, may even have blurted out a few choice foul words themselves. However, due to the strict educational and moral discipline promoted at home and in the schools (both Catholic and public) during this time, every one of them turned out just fine. They also had an excellent command of the English language and always behaved as gentlemen while in the presence of others.

Some of these teenage boys and young men, even after spewing out a few foul words from time to time, were also capable of carrying on a professional dialogue with a US Senator or working out a complex mathematical problem. A few guys, however, had no sensitivity as I describe it, and looked down with disdain on the unfortunate and uneducated.

The majority of the guys, and many who served during World War II and Korea, were true gentlemen. Some went or were still going to school on the GI Bill, and they always looked up with envy upon the educated and their success in life.

One might ask if some of the swearing, and gambling going on inside Pinky's may have created some bad people or led them astray. If they had, then in theory, every state in the union today creates bad people. This is because they all now have "legalized" some of the gambling I have described in one form or another, such as the Lotto.

Here in California, where I live and the state is suffering from a severe deficit, just about anything goes to bring in money and balance the budget. In good humor, I often say, "The innovative things our legislatures do to increase our GDP and revenues are amazing." I do not mean "gross domestic product," either. Our GDP laughingly refers to gambling (casinos and lotto), drugs (legalized marijuana), and pretty soon down the road, perhaps even legalized prostitution!

Will this den of sin, as I describe it, lead to young people taking a bad path in life? What do people who do not gamble, use marijuana, or are against prostitution think of people who do, and what negative thoughts might they have about them? What might they think of those individuals visiting the Mustang Ranch in Nevada and seeking out a prostitute? People's perceptions of this scenario will vary greatly, just as they do with the good or bad seen by individuals about a poolroom!

Heavy cigarette and cigar smoking also went on inside Pinky's, along with the chewing of tobacco. As I recall, Mail Pouch was the preference of most guys and especially Yunko. On occasion, some filthy four-letter words would ring out loud from some adult, but very seldom from any of the teenage or high school boys, over a missed pool shot. Irish Frank and Lou the Puerto Rican were some of the younger exceptions.

Listening to the radio inside Pinky's, hearing that Duquesne University's Dick Ricketts or Sihugo Green had missed a game-winning basketball shot would always bring about a lot of foul swearing. This same foul language could also ring out when Pitt's notable all-American linebacker Mike Ditka failed to tear an opposing player's head off during a football game tackle or kickoff return!

This was a time when, on occasion, star high school athletes and some students who were straight "A" and "B" students could also be heard swearing out loud. One of them was a gentleman in every way and the son of a local minister. This boy also liked his beer drinking and carousing about town. Eventually he settled down, went on to college, and today, like his father, is an ordained and practicing minister. The poolroom culture never left any permanent undue influence scars on him!

To really highlight the mysteries and perceptions about a poolroom, there is one story about Pinky's that brings back a lot of memories for me. I was seventeen years old when Connie, a sixteen-year-old high school sophomore, told me about a conversation that took place one day between her and her mother, Vivian, about Pinky's Poolroom. Connie, along with many other high school girls and women, often wondered what really went on inside Pinky's.

Some of these girls in addition to Connie told me personally that out of curiosity they also wanted to be able to go inside and look around Pinky's. I personally believe it was because they fantasized about the boys who went there! Perhaps they found pool players more interesting and daring and better dressers and dancers. Perhaps some of them may even have thought they would also make great lovers!

Arleen, the girl I was dating at the time and who would become my wife years later, told me she was horrified and scared to death the first and last time she ever went into Pinky's. Her choice of going there was not an easy decision. One could even say as an excuse that it was done under severe duress, bribery, and what is frowned upon today as harassment. It was part of an initiation process to become a member of the Nine Little Darling Bachelor Girls (NLDBG) club.

At the direction of the senior NLDBG girls and with the fear of not being accepted into the club, she, along with other applicants to the club, were told they must go inside the poolroom dressed in very funny clothes and beg for money! She did this and suffered a great deal of embarrassment in the process! As the adult men and boys inside the poolroom dropped coins in her cup, some of them made ridiculous comments, but none that were sexist, off-color, or distasteful, and laughed at her.

Scuffling about and running from pool table to pool table, she finished her collecting of coins, and after what seemed like an eternity, ran outside crying very hard over her ordeal. She told me later that, other than Pinky's being filled with smoke and having very dim lighting, she could not remember what the place looked like inside. Nor could she remember whom she had seen and begged money from. She was more interested in keeping her head down very low, so as to avoid any boys from school recognizing her.

Some of the girls who accompanied her in this money-begging ritual were her twin sister Eileen, Bernadette, Cornelia, and Janie. They too felt very embarrassed and humiliated by what they had to do. However, when it was all done and over with and they were all far away from the poolroom entrance, they all began to giggle and laugh out loud. Their tears were erased quickly and replaced with bright smiles, since they were done and would now become members of the prestigious NLDBG club.

It is only because of my hanging out at Pinky's, these casual conversations, observations, and Connie's story in particular, that I am able to write this story and tell you what generally took place during a typical day or evening inside Pinky's Poolroom.

On Friday, August 29, 1952, the temperature reading of 89.2 degrees Fahrenheit was one of the highest ever recorded. Businesses all over were very busy, since the Labor Day holiday was beginning. It was also the last weekend before the end of summer and the start of the new school year for all of the kids. After an early morning shopping spree at the Famous department store in Braddock, Connie and her mother caught the # 55 electric streetcar to return home to Turtle Creek.

During the streetcar ride, Connie talked about the new clothes bought for her to begin school on Tuesday, September 2. She told her mother about how excited she was. She could hardly wait to wear one of her new blouses and poodle skirts to the upcoming Wednesday night dance in the high school gymnasium.

It seemed as if they had just boarded the streetcar when they heard the bell clanging, and the car coming to a halt at their stop in front of the New Deal restaurant. Every now and then, they would go inside this restaurant, like a great deal of other people in town, and order a tasty hot sausage or fish sandwich. At times and depending upon the amount of money she had, Vivian might even splurge on a superb shrimp platter, which came loaded with handmade french fries.

Rising from their seats, they picked up their shopping packages and carefully stepped off the streetcar onto the sidewalk. It would be a short walk from this location to a local bus stop. They would board the bus a short distance away in front of the Murphy's five-and-ten. It would drop them off in front of their home. With packages in hand, Vivian told Connie, "We are not going to walk past Pinky's Poolroom!" Pinky's was just a few feet around the corner from where they had left the streetcar.

With the start of the long weekend, the streets and town of Turtle Creek were bustling with people inside the local butcher shops, bars and grills, grocery stores, and retail outlets. The next day, Saturday, August 30, would be even busier, since many people did not have to work. This was because of the long Labor Day holiday, which gave them an extra day of rest and time to shop. Most husbands would stay home and it gave a lot of mothers a chance, to get away from the kids, after a week of being cooped up with them and relax a little.

The long weekend would also bring a lot more guys and high school boys to the poolroom to plan out what they might do. There would be a lot of activity going on outside and inside Pinky's on this day. Some of the guys, especially Freddy of Italian heritage, might be yelling and throwing their fingers at each other while playing and betting quarters on the outcome of the Italian game of morra, which can be traced back to Roman times. Vivian felt for sure that today would be no different. She just did not want Connie or herself having to walk past them. What were her hidden fears and perceptions about Pinky's?

To this day, I ask myself why she felt this way, since no female had ever been molested or sworn at indiscriminately in front of the poolroom. In addition, females were never spoken to in a disdainful manner or had lewd suggestions thrown at them by any one of the adult or high school boys hanging around Pinky's. I should also point out, at least to my knowledge, that no whistling or catcalling toward any female ever took place in front of or inside Pinky's.

Was Vivian's fear based only on rumors that she may have heard about guys who hung around poolrooms?

On this particular day, it was possible that Mike, a former batboy for the Pittsburgh Pirates, might also be hanging around Pinky's. If so, he might even be lending out money to various adults and some of the teenage boys. The borrowers would have to pay twenty-five cents or one quarter interest on each dollar borrowed. They even had to give him something of value, such as a watch, ring, or perhaps even their driver's license. This was his form of additional security until the loan was repaid.

At times, some of the boys could make a few extra dollars by doing a little extra, special work for Mike as "spies." Mike would pay them several dollars, or perhaps even forgive their loans, to follow, spy on, and report back to him the activities of a young lady named Sandra. Listening in on the conversations and gossip between Sandra and Melba, the owner of the local beauty parlor, and reporting on what was said seemed to interest him the most!

He was insanely in love with Sandra, a prominent model, and always interested in whom she was dating and what her social plans might be. However, she had no interest in him whatsoever and avoided him like the plague as much as possible, since she found him to be somewhat of a boor. This hidden love and spying by Mike went on for quite awhile, but eventually, after Sandra married someone, his jealousy and infatuation over her came to an abrupt end. I might add that the earning of any extra money by the spies also came to an abrupt end!

One boy never got close enough while sitting on the steps outside Melba's to hear any detailed conversations that Sandra might be having with other people. However, he would make up some story to pass on to Mike, just to get his spy pay or loan debt erased. I leave it up to you to wonder who this very young spy might have been!

Rather than go past Pinky's, Vivian took Connie by her hand, squeezed it tight, and said, "Let's cross right here and go to the other side of the street." Apparently, this action would ease Vivian's apprehensions about walking past Pinky's and allow for more protection of her daughter.

Connie, being headstrong and a little rebellious at times, looked at her mother and said, "Mother, I do not mind walking past Pinky's. I might see some of the guys that I go to school with and say hello to them."

In Connie's thoughts, she was hoping that some of the boys might take notice of her also. One boy she liked in particular had asked her earlier in the week if she was going to the first school dance. Connie responded to him with an excited cry of "yes," and he told her to "save one for me." Connie not only wanted to walk by Pinky's, but secretly, she had a strong desire to go inside the poolroom.

Many of Connie's girlfriends were already dating some of the guys who played pool and hung around Pinky's quite a lot. Some of the guys took the automobile shop courses and mechanical drawing, while others majored in the college preparatory classes. A few were players in the band, existing and former altar boys, and Boy Scouts. In addition, the boys from the high school athletics football, basketball, baseball, and track programs were always hanging around Pinky's. Then you always had a group of guys who were just your average individuals; no one particular thing they did could be identified to make them real standouts.

Vivian became quite perturbed with Connie's comment and said she did not want her daughter to associate with any boys who hung around poolrooms. Vivian continued by telling Connie she did not want her to begin smoking after she dated someone who might go in a poolroom. Then Vivian said, "Everyone who hangs around or goes inside a poolroom will eventually begin to start smoking." She followed up her unsubstantiated remark by also telling Connie, "Poolrooms have a terrible influence on young people."

Connie challenged her mother's remarks, which she found to be a little offensive since they placed a stigma on the nice boys she knew. She told her, "The boys I know who go into Pinky's do none of the things you talk about."

Ignoring what Connie was saying to her and outraged by her talking back, Vivian made another impetuous and explosive comment. She informed Connie, "The poolroom guys are after only one thing, and afterward they will have no more to do with you." Vivian continued spurting out even more absurd things and followed up with a final statement, "Most of them do not go to church either!"

Connie's lower jaw fell open as she looked aghast at her mother with a bewildered and blank stare on her face! Then she said, "Mother, what exactly are you implying? What awful things to say please tell me. I don't know any boys like that, nor do any of my girlfriends. The guys we date, even those who go into the poolroom, are all gentlemen, study hard in school, go to church, are very polite, and are nice to talk to and be around. There may be some other guys who think this way, but none of my girlfriends or I would ever associate with them. Why don't you just come out and tell me what you mean when you say the guys are after only one thing? I believe I know what you are implying."

Hearing Connie's outburst and talking back to her, Vivian looked Connie in the eye and began scolding her harshly. With an outcry of anger, she blurted, "To get you to have sex with them."

Connie looked bewildered again at her mother and said, "Mother, this is what I thought you were implying, and it is an unbelievable and ridiculous thing for you to say. It also tells me you have no faith or trust in me!" With this, Connie gave her mother an odd look, not believing what she had just heard her say. She dug her shoes into the concrete sidewalk, stood fast, and held her body back reluctantly!

Her mother tugged on her hand to get her moving and said to her, "Stop with your attitude right now, young lady." Juggling the packages in her arms and almost dropping one of them, Vivian continued by telling Connie "not to make a scene, or she would not be allowed to go to the upcoming high school dance."

To draw a parallel to this story and the misconceptions some folks had regarding Pinky's Poolroom, and to show how ugly rumors and innuendos can feed on people's minds, one must ask, "Where were all the teenage girls and adult ladies hanging out at the time?" Why, it was the local Pullen's Drug Store, located directly across the street from Pinky's. A little farther down the same street, many of them could also be hanging out inside Mraz's Drug Store.

While they were inside these establishments, sitting around in one of the cushy leather booths, was it true, or just speculation, that many of the girls drank Cokes and dropped in a couple aspirins to give them a high? (Or so they thought.) I never heard of any parents forbidding their daughters from going inside these drugstores because they might have a bad influence on them. In addition, I do not believe the parents told their sons not to date or hang around with these types of girls lest they corrupt them or try to have sex with them.

After hearing about this, some of the guys let their sexual imaginations run wild and openly discussed it inside the poolroom. They became delighted with the possibility that a mixture of Coke and aspirins might have some sort of aphrodisiac effect on the girls. Perhaps they may have even participated in or encouraged the girls to do it if it could improve their chances of getting a date and making out with them. Another myth at the time was that if the girls drinking the Cokes spiked with aspirin also wore ankle-top gray suede shoes, it indicated they were more than likely to become sexually promiscuous with a guy.

Connie and her mother continued to argue, but a mature parent always seems to be able to say the right thing, even though sounding very cruel at the time, to an immature child, to make them think and change their minds! Connie screamed back at her mother, "You wouldn't," and her mother replied, "Oh yes, I would!"

Connie callously, with cold eyes, stared her mother in the face and said to her, "Why don't you just take all these new clothes back also? I don't want them." Starting to cry while making these remarks and thinking about the upcoming dance, Connie gained some self-control and told her mother she was very sorry for what she had just said.

Releasing her solid stance and lifting her feet off the cement sidewalk, Connie stepped forward quietly and followed her mother to the sidewalk across the street. When they reached the other side of the street, they stopped in front of the Olympic Theatre before continuing on. They would have to walk up this side of the street just a little bit to pass by Pinky's. Then they would pass Faller's furniture store and cross back over to the other side of the street to catch their bus home. If it had not been for Vivian's apprehensions about walking past the poolroom, they could have continued in a straight line, rather than taking this zigzag course.

After sulking quite a bit, Connie lifted her drooping head, looked at her mother, and told her, "I love you, Mother, I know you are always trying to protect me, and I am truly sorry for what I said. Please do not take my new clothes back, and please allow me to go to the dance." Apparently what her mother had said earlier was beginning to make Connie think a little more clearly, and she was fearful that her mother would follow through with her threat.

Vivian, still upset with her daughter's antics, ignored her and continued walking at a fast pace along the sidewalk. She finally looked at Connie and told her, "Hurry up, or we will miss the next bus."

Connie desperately wanted to go to the dance and meet up with the guy she was subconsciously hoping to see in front of Pinky's. He was one of the high school shop guys and owned a hot-rod automobile that he built himself and drove quite fast. Connie had heard stories about how exciting it was to go for a drive with him. Again she found herself daydreaming about sitting in the hot rod alongside him! She was also thinking if he asked her for a date that he might even drive her up to Speelman's Lane, a local teenage lover's hideaway, to park and make out awhile.

While standing in front of the Murphy's five-and-ten store waiting on the bus to take them home, Connie and her mother became very civil with one another again. Both of their moods had mellowed quite a bit. The black and white bus that would take them home stopped in front of them. There was a loud swishing noise that could be heard by everyone around the bus stop.

This was the sound emitted as the bus driver pushed forward on his manual hand lever and the two metal, rubber, and glass-encased bus doors swung open to allow them to board the bus. Along with the other waiting passengers, Connie and Vivian boarded the bus, paid their fares, and walked down the aisle to take the closest seats.

Connie liked the open window view, and it also would offer more outside air to help cool her down a bit. She chose the window seat and sat down quickly. Her mother, just wanting to get home and end today's bitter argument, also sat down quickly, on the aisle seat next to her.

The driver looked around carefully, checked his rearview mirror, and after seeing that all the passengers were seated, manually pulled the lever toward him to close the bus doors. Then he checked his rearview mirror again and the exterior side-mounted mirrors on the bus to make sure no vehicle traffic was coming his way. Once everything was clear and no pedestrians were crossing the street in front of the bus, he pulled away from the sidewalk slowly. While doing this, he gave a signal with his left arm and proceeded to move the bus along the roadway.

After Connie and her mother had taken their seats on the bus and carefully placed their bags and shopping purchases on their laps, they both sat back, closed their eyes, and relaxed a bit. The bus driver would have three more, short-distance traffic lights on his route and one more bus stop location, in front of the Bell Telephone building.

If the bus driver got lucky and caught a green light at each signal and had none or few passengers to pick up at the next stop, the journey home for Vivian and Connie would take no more than five minutes. Having to stop for any red lights or several passengers at the next bus stop would delay them for another five to ten minutes. In either case, they would arrive home safely to enjoy the cooling air from a large Westinghouse electric fan in their living room.

People could not count on such a quick trip like this during the bitter months of winter, when the bus drivers had to cope with snow and icy road conditions. At times when the bus became stuck in the snow, many passengers would just get off the bus and continue their journey home on foot. Soon, both Connie and her mother could hear the noise of the brakes and the bus coming to a stop.

They opened their eyes and saw they had stopped in front of their home. The narrow bus doors were opened, and they got up from their seats. They gathered up their shopping packages and walked down the aisle to depart the bus. Both of them planted their feet carefully on the single bus step, and then stepped onto the sidewalk before them. Without looking back, they could hear the swishing noise of the bus doors closing. The last thing they did, like most of the other passengers getting off the bus, was pinch their nostrils closed with a thumb and index finger. Hopefully they could do it without dropping any shopping bags. This was generally done to avoid the obnoxious diesel smell being emitted from the exhaust pipe as the bus pulled away. If someone were standing too close to the exhaust and ignored or forgot about the bus fumes, they might begin to cough and gag. The smell alone could be overwhelming.

Holding onto a homemade, red, two-inch galvanized pipe handrail, they walked up a flight of three concrete steps. After this, they stood momentarily on the front porch of their home. Vivian unlocked the front door to the house, and they went inside and placed their shopping packages on the living room couch close by. The cool breeze coming from the Westinghouse electric fan felt good!

After putting the packages away and without talking, Connie poured herself a glass of iced tea and Vivian made herself a gin-and-tonic! Somehow, during the summer, a gin and tonic always seemed to have the psychological effect of cooling a lot of people down. When I say cooling off, I mean in mores way than one!

Connie and her mother relaxed some more after this, and had a little more civil conversation about the poolroom that evening. Vivian expressed her concerns and views, and told Connie "that she was only doing what she thought was best for her, and how much she loved her."

Connie, wanting to diffuse the situation, said "she understood and agreed with everything her mother was saying." However, she secretly objected to and disagreed with just about everything her mother had to say about the poolroom and the guys. Especially the ones she went to school with who hung around Pinky's.

Connie, thinking more clearly now, was not going to jeopardize her chances of going to the dance. Hopefully, she would be asked to dance by the guy she liked. In addition, she might even get to enjoy a nice ride and a drive up to Spellman's Lane in his hot rod.

While Vivian and Connie were walking past Pinky's on the opposite side of the street, the poolroom was alive with a great deal of activity that day. Vivian was right, and a lot of boys were hanging around outside Pinky's, and several adults could be seen entering and leaving the poolroom.

Harry's hat cleaning/blocking and shoeshine parlor next door to the poolroom was also a hub of activity. A lot of people were picking up their dry cleaning, blocked hats, and repaired shoes. Some men could even be seen sitting down in a large black leather chair having their shoes shined and new liquid dressing applied to the outer sole and heel edges with a small toothbrush. If you wore brown shoes, it would be brown dressing. If you wore black shoes, it would be black dressing. In either case, Harry was always the best when it came to shining shoes.

The younger boys polished their own shoes and very seldom got a shine at Harry's, except for a special occasion. The special occasion might be going to the prom, a big dance event, graduation ceremonies, a wedding or reception, or a big date night at the movie theater in downtown Pittsburgh.

The adult guys and boys standing outside the poolroom, some of them being the local high school jocks, were chatting about the upcoming football season. They were providing their input as to who might win the double AA WPIAL championship. Of course, they were all hoping it would be Turtle Creek, although Aliquippa, Clairton, Central Catholic, Scott, and New Kensington were the heavy favorites.

Directly across the street, where Connie and her mother had taken drastic steps to avoid Pinky's, the high school girls were hanging around outside or inside Pullen's drugstore. Connie did not see any of her girlfriends as she walked past the drugstore that day. In addition and unknown to her mother, she did not see that special guy she had on her mind. Without her mother noticing it, she secretly looked across the street and stole a side-eyed glance at the guys standing outside Pinky's. She knew many of the high school boys would be hanging around the place.

She was hoping she could get permission to leave the house and go into town tomorrow and hang around the drugstore! It was the best place to meet up with the school guys, next to meeting them at the gymnasium dance! To get there, however, she knew she would have to promise her mother to stay away from Pinky's and return home by 7:30 p.m.

She was planning to spend the night at one of her girlfriend's house, if allowed by her mother. The girlfriend she picked was Doreen, whose mother and father allowed her to stay out until 9:30 p.m. when there was no school the next morning. This would give her some extra evening hours to check out the guys. Connie knew that her mother would be calling Doreen's parents to confirm she would be staying at their home overnight, and would insist on her being back by seven thirty.

The guys' sports conversation would eventually work its way into how well the Pitt Panthers, the college football team, would do. With Mike Ditka playing, they were the pick to win the big East championship. The opening game this year at home would be against Nebraska, whose star quarterback John Bordogna, a former Turtle Creek High player, would take the field against Pitt.

Many other Turtle Creek players, like fullback George Cifra and tight ends Andy Lohr and Will Brown, would also be playing in this game. All of these individuals were fortunate enough to be recruited by Ralph Fifes, an ex-coach at Turtle Creek High who was hired by Nebraska. They also received scholarships.

Of course, but of less importance at the time, the Pittsburgh Steelers professional football team would be talked about. No one placed much hope on them ever being a championship team. Without a crystal ball to see what the future would hold for the Steelers, no one knew they would become Super Bowl champions for many years, led by Terry Bradshaw, mean Joe Greene, and the "Iron Curtain defense."

The Pittsburgh Penguins were never talked about much either, since hockey was not a popular sport or played at most of the area high schools. Again, if only someone could have seen what the future would hold for the Penguins and their Stanley Cup wins!

When anyone not familiar with Pinky's entered on Friday or Saturday afternoon or the evening, they would temporarily roll their shoulders up a little into a small hump and place both hands over their ears. Their face would take on a grimacing expression until they got comfortable with the loud noise level inside the place. It was even worse on a Friday night after a big football game, win or lose. The noise level was generally bearable and somewhat subdued during the weekdays, when the teenage boys were in school and the adult guys were working. The summer school break brought a much calmer tone inside the poolroom also.

Extra help was always needed at Pinky's on Fridays and Saturdays, and at times it would consist of Andy Carter and Ray Sangelo or even Pinky's brother, Frank, or "Yunko" as he was known. They would work behind the glass showcase counters selling things like cigarettes, cigars, various candies, Wise potato chips, Planters nuts, and cheese crackers. Pepsi, Coke, Hires Root Beer, Vernors Ginger Ale, and Cream and Mission Orange sodas could also be found for sale. The glass pop bottles could be found floating loosely in a red Coke dry cooler, filled with ice and melted water.

On very hot and humid days during the summer months, some of the guys would even dip into the cooler with a glass and drink the ice-cold water to quench their thirst. I know it sounds awful to do this, but the fear of possibly getting sick from doing it never seemed to enter anyone's mind. It was the lesser of two evils when someone had no money, and was forced to drink only the warm, slow-running, and ungodly tasting tap water inside Pinky's. In addition, this warm water came out of a rusty and tarnished sink spigot inside the small, one-toilet bathroom at Pinky's. This bathroom, although kept very clean, would never win any Good Housekeeping awards after being punished by the guys continuously going in and out of it!

At times just before leaving the poolroom, some of the younger boys, without wanting to be seen or heard out of sheer embarrassment, would quietly ask to buy a pack of Trojans, or rubbers. They were always neatly hidden behind closed doors underneath the glass counter display cases.

There were no options at the time to buy anything else but a standard brand. It was quite different as compared to today's mind-dazzling and openly displayed array of erotic condoms! Sort of like buying a car with the color you like and the proper engine size.

Prearranged stacks of nickels, dimes, and quarters were neatly stacked on a wood ledge behind the glass counter showcases. These coins would be exchanged for paper money from individuals wanting to play any one of the different and exciting pinball machines. One or all of the people employed at Pinky's would also rack up pool balls on a table, if requested, for the start of a new game.

Pinky did not work inside the poolroom at all, since his main business was the selling, installation, and repair of pinball and other machines in various social clubs and other business establishments.

If someone did not want Yunko, or one of his employees to do it, the honor system was always in place with pool-playing customers at Pinky's. This meant that you personally kept score of how many games of pool were played, or "racked up." Customers doing this always paid what they owed, before leaving the poolroom. To make it simple, at twenty cents a game after playing ten games, you owed two dollars. I would not swear to it, but this I think is what a game of pool cost in the 1950s.

The noise level inside Pinky's was caused by the half dozen pinball machines being played and their ringing, clanging noises. The guys playing the pinball machines were always hyperactive (perhaps a trait left over from their public and Saint Colman's school days?) and constantly yelling or screaming at the machines or to themselves!

They did this while standing on their tiptoes clenching and banging the side of the machines tightly with both hands and moving or twisting their body about. This technique, body language as it was called, hopefully helped them to direct the small, round, steel chrome ball inside the machine to go where they wanted it to. Hopefully, it would roll into a high-scoring, lighted object, known as a "thumper bumper." This bumper would automatically push the ball away after being hit and record the number of points it was worth. The higher the number of points recorded on the machine over a certain amount, the more money the player would receive after the game ended.

By definition, the pinball player's body antics helped them to improve their chances of winning on the machines. That is, if they did not overly do it in mishandling the pinball machine, causing it to rock about and turn off. Located inside the machine was a very thin metal rod, about a quarter inch in diameter and four inches long. The rod hung down and swayed about inside a small circular metal ring, about one in diameter and charged with a small amount of electricity. If this hanging rod came in contact with the inner part of the ring, it created a short circuit, sending out a signal to display "Tilt" on the machine.

241

When this happened, one may or not hear sayings of "Oh shit," "god-dammit," and "son of a bitch." Often, four-letter foul language came spewing from the mouth of the person at the pinball machine. Sometimes you could even hear one of the pinball machine players chastising himself and saying out loud, "Oh you dumb shit you, quit handling the fucking machine like a god-dam gorilla."

I often wonder how much money someone could really make standing around and playing a nickel, dime, or quarter pinball machine for several hours. Was it worth the time, or wasn't it? In 1952, winning ten dollars on a machine was considered a good hit, but losing the same amount could be considered a disastrous ending. I personally preferred doing a little hustle on the pool tables, since I found my odds of winning a hell of a lot better there most of the time.

There was a blond-haired Italian kid by the name of Louis, who often went home with no money left in his pockets after being continually beaten at an eight or nine ball pool game by the Polack. It was even worse when, during a game to help prevent him from losing, he would talk away at a "shooter," hoping to make him "choke up" and miss the shot. Sometimes Louis would even say it would be impossible for the Polack to make such a difficult shot.

He soon ate his words after the Polack pointed his cue stick and gently pushed it forward, to send the white cue ball on a collision course with a winning nine or eight ball, which easily fell into the pocket.

Louis's verbal anger, but never any swearing over losing, was overheard by everyone watching the game as he screamed out, "This is it! I am not going to lose any more money to this lucky hunky. I quit, I am never going to play you again, and I am going home." Everyone around laughed out loud at this hilarious statement, since they knew the Italian kid would be back very soon to try and win back some of his losses.

His second greatest fear, next to losing a game of pool to the Polack, was his father catching him inside Pinky's, since the father looked unfavorably down on poolrooms.

His third greatest fear was to have his white cue ball fall into a pocket as a "scratch," after he had successfully sunk an eight or nine ball to win a game. For you non-pool players this meant he lost the game!

Winning a game against the Polack and replacing some of his previous losses always seemed to elude him. However, at times, he was able to beat some of the other players to minimize or cover his losses.

The loud music coming from a multicolored, neon light Wurlitzer Jukebox, loaded with rock 'n' roll and hit sentimental records, was always set to the highest volume level. The boys standing around the jukebox and singing out loud to Bill Haley's "Rock Around the Clock" only elevated the noise level. It was even worse when some of the boys tried to sing along with Al Martino and hit his high-pitched notes from the record "Here in My Heart."

From time to time, Andy an employee would step out from behind the counter to dance strangely. He pretended to be holding an imaginary girl in his arms! He would dance around with her in front of the jukebox as records were played. He performed this ritual quite well, and some of the guys called him Fred Astaire Junior.

Meanwhile, in the background, smashing white cue balls slamming against freshly racked pool balls only added to the noise level and turned the poolroom into a giant echo chamber. The numerous pool players talking loudly or yelling and screaming at one another over a missed or completed shot, which meant winning or losing a few dollars, also contributed greatly to this echoing noise level.

After learning how to cope with these loud noise levels, individuals in the poolroom could stare straight ahead into the main area at a barrage of pool tables. They were all lit up by round, green-colored, metal light fixtures hanging above them. Scattered about on the pool hall floor were several wood benches for the pool players to sit on while taking a break from the game. They were also used just to chat with someone or read a newspaper or magazine.

Hanging on the walls and strategically placed by each table were cue racks, which held cue sticks in various lengths and indicated weight to suit each player's choice. Hanging high above each table, there was a long, thin-stretched piece of wire. The wire held fifty each, ivory and black plastic disks about the size of a quarter, threaded onto it. This high wire could only be reached by pool players lifting and pointing a cue stick tip at it. Then they would carefully slide the disks to one side and keep track of their score count as the game progressed!

If two individuals were playing a game of twenty-five or fifty balls, one player would select the color disk he wanted to keep score as to the number of balls he had "sunk"! The remaining color was taken by the opposing pool player, to keep score of the number of balls he had sunk. The first pool player to reach the twenty-five or fifty mark would win the game. This game, like any other pool game, could be played just for the fun of it. It also provided a measurement of a player's shooting skill and positioning the cue ball for his next shot.

The game could also be played for money, which was generally the case, and there was no limit as to the amount of the wager. In the late fifties, when money was scarce and good jobs hard to find, I personally witnessed fifty-dollar and hundred-dollar games between individuals. Teams of two individuals each could play this game also. Another string of disks would be used by them to count their combined sunk balls. The two-man team sinking the first twenty-five, fifty, or one hundred balls would win the game and share the dollar winnings equally.

Scattered about on the poolroom floor in various locations, one could also see several brass, lightly dented, tarnished spittoons. They were available to capture the spit-out tobacco drippings from the pool players' or other individuals' mouths. Some guys were fairly accurate with being able to spit directly inside the spittoons, and some were not. Those who missed only added to the multitude of brownish tobacco stains the surrounding floor planks were covered in.

A tobacco-chewing spitter's accuracy was not all that important, since the spittoons and poolroom floor had to be cleaned on a regular basis. After being cleaned, the spittoons were filled up with a Lysol and water mix to absorb the tobacco smell, and a lot of other stench collected inside the poolroom.

This liquid mix was also used for sanitary purposes and left a strong medicinal smell, like one would find when entering a hospital. You older pool players and graduates of Pinky's and other poolrooms know what I am talking about! I often asked myself why the need for the sanitary stuff, since surely, no one would ever be eating or drinking from these spittoons! From time to time, the lonely bathroom commode inside the restroom at Pinky's was cleaned and washed down with the Lysol. Even so, still, no Good Housekeeping award was ever presented to Pinky or his brother, Yunko.

After surveying the main poolroom area carefully, which was often engulfed with clouds of cigarette and cigar smoke drifting about, one could begin to see all the individuals playing pool. Some were standing around by the tables, and some were sitting on the benches, waiting their turn to "shoot." If the place were really busy, Carmen, one of our former "good" altar boys from Saint Colman's, might be seen running around and racking up pool balls for the start of a new game. He did this at no charge to help out Ray, Andy, or Yunko.

Yunko, in particular, was loved by everyone around and could be relied upon for a loan of small amounts of money to the high school boys. I am talking about three, four, or five dollars, which was more than enough to fill up a gas tank and go out on a date.

At the time, walking to the picture show when you had a date with a girl was favored in most cases. This was because the majority of the high school boys in town did not own a car. However, when they got permission to use their parents' car, most of them opted for the drive-in theater. In most cases, they only wanted to be alone with their girlfriend on a date and were not interested in taking along another couple! However, there were always exceptions, and four persons might attend the drive-in together.

On occasion, some of the boys would see how many people would fit into their car or truck. In addition, many would also place people in the car's trunk and sneak them into the drive-in. This was not necessary when Eddy was driving, since his father, a councilman from another borough, was provided with a free pass to the Blue Dell Drive-In. No matter how many kids were in the car, everyone was admitted free of charge.

The money might also be needed to buy a ticket into the Blue-Dell swimming pool and mix with the girls! Sometimes money was needed to buy a corsage or a new tie for a prom or other special event. In all cases, the loan money was always paid back, and there was never any charge for interest. In addition, no one had to give up their watch or ring as additional security.

Good-paying full-time jobs were not around for most of the boys until summer recess, and one had to be known as being dependable and a hard worker to get them. The better-paying jobs were helping plumbers by doing ditch-digging for new gas lines and miscellaneous assistance. Helping out the skilled carpenters and roofers was a good-paying part-time job. Another well-paying part-time job was carrying a hod. This required the individual to place a trough over his shoulder and carry heavy loads of bricks and mortar to the brick masons.

A young high school boy, although in great physical shape, carrying a hod for the first time would always develop a large, sore blister on his upper shoulder. The short wood pole that held the hod would twist and rotate against the skin and bone as items were being carried. Those who were fortunate enough to get this job never complained to the boss or anyone else about their pain. However, the boss and all the experienced workers knew what was happening.

A dark-colored stain, located on the upper shoulder part of a worker's T-shirt, was the first sign of a blister forming and the oozing bloody residue. Eventually, scar tissue buildup and the formation of a hard callous would eliminate all this initial bleeding and pain. Working for a plasterer, even though mixing was required, was a little easier work, since plaster was not carried in a hod, but shoveled onto a flat wooden plank.

Another job that did not pay much, but had a lot of side dating benefits with the girls, was being a lifeguard at one of the local swimming pools. This required taking many classes and tests and obtaining the required lifesaving credentials! I and most of the guys I hung around with were not interested in this and followed the best money jobs. A few low-paying part-time jobs were always available year-round in some of the local retail, drug, and grocery stores and gas stations. However, you or someone else had to have an "in" with the merchants or know them very well to obtain such jobs.

Looking about inside the poolroom, one might see a sharply dressed individual known as Mitzi standing at the far end of the poolroom. He would make sure to be out of the way of pool players as he took football bets from some of the guys. He was a regularly employed carpenter and a Korean War veteran, and did his bet taking as a side way of earning a few extra dollars.

On Saturdays, when betting was very heavy on the college football games, you could also see the feisty, blond, curly headed boy called "Jimmy", who now had his Saint Colman's school yard "chipped tooth" repaired, and helping out Mitzi.

It was all good, or what some called "gravy, when Mitzi was on the winning end of his business. However, he also took his lumps due to game upsets and point spreads making him a loser in any given week. Another adult individual by the name of Al, a part-time bartender at the local Speelman's café, could also be seen booking number bets from several adults and a few high school boys.

Looking at the younger players scattered around the pool tables and elsewhere, the typical dress one would see, looking through the crowd and especially on the high school guys at the time, was a pair of Levis and a T-shirt. On cooler days, a V-neck sweater might be worn over the T-shirt.

Very few belts were ever worn with a pair of Levis, and the shoes worn were a leather-type oxford or sandal style, or a very fancy dress style, such as a "Bostonian" (you know, the ones that looked like they had a thousand little holes drilled into the leather) in brown, black, or cordovan color. Some of the boys might have on a pair of work boots, after working at a full—or part-time job, required by their employer as protection.

Tennis shoes were rarely seen about town and seldom seen inside Pinky's. If someone did wear tennis shoes, they were sometimes classified as a "fruit." or homosexual. Tennis shoes just were not in style with most of the older guys and boys. It got to the point, if you were caught wearing tennis shoes for any reason, especially white ones, you could be called a sissy. Of course, one was always very careful who they said this to, depending on their size and personality.

Another option for pants one might see was gabardine slacks. Long-sleeve shirts with button-down collars and short-sleeve polo-style shirts were usually worn with the slacks. A leather belt was generally sleeved through one-inch "tunnel loops," as they were called on the slacks.

In addition, the slack pant legs were tapered down and had tightly "pegged" cuffs at the bottom. In some cases, you might see a cuff with only a four-inch opening at the bottom of the pants. Panama Putt was well known for his tightly pegged pants. When the cuffs were this tight, most guys had to remove their shoes to get their slacks off. But if this was what one wanted, they had to put up with a little inconvenience.

I myself had a greenish-color pair of gabardine slacks at one time. I bought them at the local Carlton's men's store, and they came with a small leopard-skin-type material sewn into the seam of the outside legs. With my one-inch tunnel loops and tightly pegged pants, I became the center of attraction for a brief period of time. This was especially true during the Wednesday-night YMCA summer dances held above the Mellon Bank building.

My brown suede shoes highlighted the pants even more, and brought out many sly and silly comments from my buddies. However, I was not alone in this type of stylish dress, and many others tried to copy it. Hardly anyone notices how some guys and girls dress today and the weird color combinations they wear.

I do not say it disparagingly or to single out anyone in particular, but most kids today do not even iron any of their clothing before going to school, and if they have a piece of clothing that should be ironed and it isn't, so what? Recognized high fashion stores are not on some of today's youthful agenda when out shopping, but Goodwill stores are!

A first-time visitor to Pinky's Poolroom might think he were at a show, seated in front of a stage with many actors and ballet dancers prancing about. Looking at one pool table, you might see a guy with his chest, arms, both hands, and a cue stick spread out on the top of a pool table's green cloth. One of his legs would be planted solidly on the floor, while his other leg was up off the floor and extended straight out into thin air behind him. This was all being done to get into the perfect position to make a difficult pool shot.

The shot and proper connection with the balls may or may not have been all that difficult to make. However, the player with cue stick in hand felt comfortable doing it this way to make the shot. When he was done with the shot, he congratulated himself and pushed his body up from the table. Then he twirled away, holding the cue stick in his arms as if it were a lady he might be dancing with, and kissed it lightly. Sort of like Andy would do in front of the jukebox.

Looking at a different pool table in the room, another individual could be seen yelling, smiling, and jumping up and down with joy. Then he would dance all about gracefully, on the tips of his shoes, like a prima ballerina, congratulating himself. From the same area, one could also hear in the background the bitter mumbling coming from losing players.

One of them would suddenly shout out, "That was a lucky fucking shot; you gotta have a horseshoe up your ass." Tommy was the winning player's name, and he had just made a very difficult side pocket, single bank shot, to win a nine-ball game and several dollars.

Looking at another pool table, where a game of eight ball was being played, Wimpy, with his back flush up against the table, could be heard moaning as he bent over slightly backward. He could be seen holding a cue stick behind his back, getting into a comfortable position, and carefully sliding it back and forth in an attempt to make the shot. His cue tip struck the white cue ball dead-on and it connected with the eight ball, but he was unsuccessful at making the shot count.

Rather than cursing, Wimpy laughed out loud a bit. Then he did a quick pirouette on his shoe tips and pushed away from the table. He looked at the other players who were in the game and could see they were elated that he had missed his chance at "the money shot." He smiled at them and said out loud, "Maybe next time."

Confident Tommy, who moved into this game after winning an earlier game on another table, was the next shooter. He stepped up to the table, and with two quick slides of his cue stick, moving between his fingers, drove the white cue ball into the eight ball, which dropped into a corner pocket.

At the far end of the poolroom at the last pool table, another player looked as if he might have been a dancer in a show. He had a difficult shot to make and was going to need a "bridge stick" to do it. Like Gene Kelly dancing about, he shuffled and skipped along the poolroom floor until he reached the cue rack holding the bridge stick. He grabbed it and spun around on the heels of his shoes twice, and continued his shuffle and skipping dance back to the pool table.

Whistling all the way back to the table, he took the bridge and cue stick he was holding and raised them both in the air, in a triumphant victory motion. Then he lowered the bridge slowly and placed it on the table for his shot. He carefully extended his arms, placed his cue stick onto the bridge stick, and took a slow but solid aim at the shot he had to make.

The show he was putting on was almost complete now, as he bent forward in a bowing motion. This was all being done for the audience of guys standing around and watching the pool game.

Suddenly he stopped what he was doing and quickly lifted his cue stick off the bridge and turned away from the table. One could sense there was something wrong, and perhaps he might be rethinking his strategy on how to do the shot! "Whoops," he said to himself, as he realized at the last minute he had forgotten to do something very important!

He wiped his forehead off with his handkerchief to clear away a few beads of sweat. Then he reached over, grabbed a cubed piece of blue pool chalk off the rail, and listened to the screeching noise it made as he rubbed it against the tip of his cue stick.

Still whistling with confidence, he placed the tip of his cue on the bridge stick again with his right hand, and then he lifted the rear of the bridge stick up slightly with his left hand. With his right hand, he slowly slid his cue stick back once, twice, three, four times, before he let it slide forward to meet the white cue ball for his shot.

Suddenly he stopped his whistling, and his earlier joy of dancing and happiness disappeared. He sprang up and away from the table quickly, as if it might be the finale to his dancing routine, and screamed out, "You no good fucker." He had missed the shot!

Some guys will do anything to make a difficult pool shot. Jumping up on the top of a pool table was one of them. Sitting on the table rails on one's ass is another one. Some guys could get closer to the cue ball with their stick while doing it! This was also done in a particular situation, such as wanting to make the cue ball jump over a ball, or several balls, to get to the next sequential ball number in a game of "straight" pool. You know, where you sink the 1 ball first, then the 2 ball, then the 3 ball, and on.

I cannot tell you how many times I have seen the Gorgeous George wrestler-type guys hold on to the table rail and do a few knee squats to eye up their shots. After doing this, they jump up on the pool table (no shoes were allowed to touch the green cloth) and place both knees on top of it to make a shot. One of our well-known town weight lifters, Tony, did this one day.

He was going to attempt to make his 6 ball jump over a 9 ball. It was blocking his shot to get to the 7 ball, which was hanging on the edge of a corner pocket. With both of his knees on the top of the pool table and his shoes dangling over the table rail, he placed his cue stick between his left finger and thumb and took aim.

He counted quickly while pushing his highly elevated cue stick tip down hard, and struck the white cue ball at a very low level to make it jump. "Holy shit, Jesus Christ, you whore bitch," he screamed out loud when he barely touched the white cue ball and saw his cue tip rip a large tear into the green felt pool table cloth. Tony was a longtime pool player with a lot of experience, and this should never have happened.

To keep things like this from happening, Yunko and Pinky had one special table set up for beginners or amateurs and the younger kids to practice on. Once they could demonstrate they were ready, they could play on the "good" tables. This practice table was very recognizable from the rest of the tables, with its patchwork of black tape pieces holding together the various rips or tears put into the green felt cloth.

Tony, acting like a wrestler who had just been beaten in the ring, bounded off of the table grunting and moaning, onto the poolroom floor. Looking up, he could see Yunko walking quickly toward him with a look of disgust on his face, and as usual,—chewing on a wad of Mail Pouch tobacco. Tony knew his mistake was big-time and was going to cost him, at least, a twenty-dollar bill to replace the torn felt.

Yunko would do the repair work himself, and if Tony were lucky, he might get a reduced price if he helped with the labor in taking the table apart and putting it back together. Tony had the bulk, but not the smarts, to do this very easily and to meticulously place, tightly stretch, and tack the new cloth down properly.

The conversations taking place among the high school boys inside the poolroom could drift from schoolwork, to joining the military, to passing their driving test and getting a license. They would also talk about jobs they had or missed, the new shoes or clothes they were wearing, and some new clothes they would like to buy.

Other discussions would take place from time to time as to who was the best pool player in town. Names like Nick, Boston Blackie, Big Mac, Joker Jack, Panama Putt or Patsy the Shoe would be tossed about. Sometimes this discussion would turn into an argument, and you could hear some of the boys telling someone else they were "full of shit" when they disagreed over a mentioned name. Everyone had their favorite!

Some adults and boys would also be talking about what wedding receptions were coming up on Saturday, and their VFW, American Legion, local firehouse, and Polish, Slovak, and Italian Club hall locations. The local *Independent News Paper* would have a complete published listing of all of them, making it very easy to check out.

Some of the guys and boys would be going to a few of them via an invitation, and some of them, even though not being invited, would attempt to sneak into the reception. There would be a lot of free food and drinks for everyone. In addition, there would be a lot of dancing, and girls to meet up with and possibly set up a date.

When most of the boys talked about their girlfriends, they were very respectful of them and very discreet as to what was going on between them. Discussions went on as to what shows they were going to and where they might be parking or going after a football or basketball game or a dance. They would discuss their long conversations on the phone with a girlfriend and the time spent at her or his house.

They might even talk about walking them home and kissing in the park. There were many dark alleys around town where one could kiss and make out, but the nearby creek and its horde of river rats were avoided during the evening hours. Besides, if one had a car, Speelmans Lane was preferred over anything else!

Some boys would talk about the girls they had dated, "felt up," or attempted to get a "free feel" from, and perhaps even discussed the possibility of having sex with them. The character of these few individuals spoke for itself. However, most of the adult guys and teenage boys with steady girlfriends for any period of time, out of respect for them, would never discuss details of their intimacy, if any, with anyone.

Several fights broke out on occasion when a gentleman-type guy or boy would get fed up with someone taunting them or saying disrespectful things about a girl they might like or be going steady with! Such taunting could even include making lewd and subjective sexual gestures with their hands and pointing to various male parts of the body.

In summation, I would say that discussions about females by some of the adult guys and boys inside Pinky's Poolroom were no better and no worse than those said in a high school gymnasium, public bar, social club, or local swimming pool!

I will not be a hypocrite or attempt to make Pinky's into a holy monastery or place of divine worship. Nor was it like sitting down in a pew at your local church, where everyone was very civilized and quiet. (Except for the young infants crying out from time to time) It was just a poolroom, where one could socialize and that was frequented by a bunch of youthful, exuberant guys and boys. One had to take a look at each boy or adult who went in and out of Pinky's individually, and judge them by their character, not what someone thought of them.

I have described the backgrounds of several of the people who walked in and out of Pinky's Poolroom. The majority of them became fine gentlemen and professionals of every sort in life. To my knowledge, I do not believe any one of them ever became gangsters, burglarized a home or business, held up a bank, or sexually assaulted a female on the streets of a wonderful town like Turtle Creek, because they went inside or hung around a poolroom.

For those individuals who saw Pinky's Poolroom as a place one should not go into lest it corrupt them, it is their loss, since they missed out on a great deal of Turtle Creek history. What other establishments in town had a tarnished image such that these individuals might not venture inside? Could it be the liquor stores or bars due to such narrow-minded and biased perceptions?

I saw Pinky's as a place of learning, where one could acquire all the social interaction needed between young boys and individuals. I also saw it, in addition to a good formal education, as a stepping-stone to help them go on to a successful, humble, and gracious lifestyle. I also found it helpful in developing a flexible and friendly attitude with friends and neighbors and being able to easily interact socially with individuals in the workplace.

Daring to explore means daring to be brave! Exploring all of the adventurous, exciting, unknown, and mysterious places one can find while young, full of energy, and growing up is a must in my opinion. I personally recommend that a poolroom like Pinky's should be found and included in such exploration.

Note: Connie did get to go to the dance on that Wednesday evening. The boy she was interested in asked her for several dances, and later on they went for a ride in his hot rod. When asked, Connie would not tell me if she also took a drive up to Speelman's Lane.

CHAPTER 13

THE SAFE

It was a hot summer day in 1947 when Bobby, Vincent, Richard, and I were walking home from a day in the nearby woods. We discovered an old abandoned Wells Fargo safe in some very tall foliage and piles of dry, fallen tree leaves. It was located just a few yards off the macadam road we were walking on, very close to the ice plant on Brown Avenue.

I was surprised that no one else had noticed it while walking on the sidewalk or visiting the ice plant. Our collective thoughts were that it had been hauled there by someone in a vehicle and dumped off during the night. Apparently someone just wanted to get rid of it, and not take the time to bust it up and remove all the concrete or plaster poured into its inner walls as fireproofing material. Selling it as scrap was difficult at the time, since safes of this size (38" high x 27" wide x 23" deep) weighed around 500 hundred pounds and were hard to move around.

Most junkyards were reluctant to take them, since it was a very laborious job to separate the concrete or plaster from the true weight and value of the safe's steel. There was very little profit to be made after doing this. Safes like this were also very hard to sell to most people and businesses, including used furniture stores, since it would cost extra money to have a locksmith to open it. In addition, the locksmith would charge additional money to provide the combination for the lock tumbler needed to open the safe. Transportation costs and the heavy labor required to move it would also cost some money.

I now have a Diebold Safe made for Salt Lake Hardware, Co, Dealers in my home, and it is very similar to the safe in this story. It has been a task moving it about, even with its steel roller wheels. It is not too bad when moving it around on solid concrete surfaces, but it is hell moving it into and out of trucks and up and down steps. I moved it from Glendale, California, to Simi Valley, California, and then to my present central California home. I personally will never move it again and have passed this task on to my granddaughter Erin and her husband, Eric.

Upon seeing the safe, all of us boys started to run toward it, while shoving and pushing one another out of the way to get to it first and claim it as "mine." There was never a written rule at the time, but anyone who found something and touched it first, it automatically belonged to him or her. With luck on my side, I got there very quickly and touched it first. Immediately thereafter, Bobby and Vincent began shouting, "You have to share it with us—and what's inside also." Richard knew he did not have to say anything to me, since we always shared everything we found.

After listening to Bobby's and Vincent's bellyaching, as we called it, and knowing Richard and I were going to need help moving it, I reluctantly caved in and agreed to share its contents with them. As part of my commitment to sharing its contents, I asked each of them to swear to absolute secrecy and not tell anyone else where it was hidden. Thinking about the jewels, coins, dollars, and other treasures it might contain, they had no problem agreeing to this. After placing more leaves and old brush on top of my find to hide it even more from public eye, we left the woods and walked home at a hurried, excited pace.

As we walked back toward our homes talking with one another regarding what treasures could be inside of the safe, our imaginations began churning away. Prior to covering up the safe some more and leaving, we had attempted to open it by spinning its tumble lock for quite a long time. However, being novices in safecracking techniques, we knew a difficult job lay ahead of us.

"How will we ever get it to our workplace, my backyard?" Richard asked the rest of us. Vincent chimed in, "We will also need some tools to open it up with." I told everyone, "Don't worry, my dad has all kinds of tools, and he lets Richard and me use them anytime we want, as long as we put them back where we found them."

I began thinking about the many movies I had seen and the various methods used by crooks and other people to open safes, and dynamite was one of them. I said to myself, "Where can a bunch of boys like us lay our hands on some dynamite sticks if needed?" In addition, we would need some blasting caps. My knowledge about dynamite and blasting caps came from my father, who used both to blow out pieces of slag coal in several abandoned mine shafts. It was harder to burn during the winter, but was better than having no coal at all during hard times. I also learned about dynamite and blasting caps by watching the movie shows and seeing the cowboys, gold diggers, and coal miners use them from time to time.

Absolute secrets were never kept even when promised, and after a few days, we told four other boys (Robert, Willy, Joseph, and Charles) we played with about our find on the roadside near the woods and close to the ice plant. We were reluctant to tell them about the safe at first, but we knew a gigantic task lay ahead of us; Vincent described it as being "something like having to move a pyramid." We decided to cut them in for a share of the safe's contents if they would help us.

After the deal was cut, they all volunteered to help get it out of the woods to Richard's and my backyard. Every one of us also had to figure out a way to open the safe. The initial task was to figure out how to move it! How would we do it? Drag, push, roll, and pull on it with some strong bull rope were the initial suggestions. Loading it onto a wagon was another suggestion. This suggestion was quickly dispelled since most of us kids knew from the safe's size and weight, not one of our Radio Flyer red wagons would support it.

After awhile Willy came up with an excellent suggestion. He said we could borrow the large wagon from the junkyard owner over on Church Street, which we had done on other occasions. The wagon frame was about eight feet long, four feet wide, and sixteen inches in height. Its T-shaped, long, heavy handle, flat loading surface, and wheels approximately one foot in diameter were all made of steel. There was a two-inch solid piece of rubber wrapped around each wheel.

The junkman would let us use this wagon when we told him it was needed to bring him a heavy load of scrap items we had collected. However, we could not use it when his workers needed it to haul items around inside the junkyard. Generally two of us boys could pull the wagon along fairly easily, with each of us sharing, the "pull" needed on the handle to move it along. At times, other boys would help push it along from the rear, when our junk load became very heavy.

The distances we traveled with the wagon were not long, and we knew we could never pull it up a steep hill with a heavy load. We also knew, because of our experience with our own smaller wagons, that attempting to pull it downhill would be disastrous; it would ultimately become uncontrollable and run, or "get away," from us. This is why we always brought the heavy pieces of junk we all collected to my yard.

From here, we only had a short distance of no more than a quarter of a mile to pull the wagon and get to the junkyard. Pulling the wagon from the junkyard to where the safe was located, loading it onto the wagon, and taking it to my backyard would be a half-mile trek. We boys figured out that, including the trip necessary to take the wagon back, we would have a mile of wagon pulling to do.

The owner also expected to see quite a few salvageable items loaded on the wagon when we returned it. He advised us he was not interested in anymore newspapers or crushed cans. Before borrowing the wagon, we would have to collect and stash quite a bit of junk metal to take back to him when we returned it. Even though he would not have taken it, we did not want to tell him we had found a safe! We wanted to keep it and its contents a secret!

The plan we put into effect was that after borrowing the wagon, we would pull it along the flat brick and cobblestone streets. After passing over them, we would hit a short stretch of concrete roadway on Brown Avenue. From this point, we would pull it up and onto the small macadam road and adjacent to where the safe was located. The macadam road was really part of the ice plant parking lot. There was a minor uphill grade getting onto the macadam road when pulling off the concrete roadway, but we figured we could handle the wagon with ease among all of us. The safe was approximately another sixty feet away.

Once we loaded and got the safe home into Richard's and my backyard, we would all push or pull it off the wagon. When this was done, we would load the wagon up with all the scrap iron and other salvageable items we had collected, and return it to the junkyard owner.

After weeks of collecting, the eight of us had accumulated a large load of old galvanized piping, rusted railroad spikes, copper wire, automobile hubcaps, and a few discarded tire rims. We decided we had enough items and weight to borrow the wagon. From time to time, we came across an old iron-claw bathtub that someone had thrown away. This in itself would bring us around three dollars. The junkman did not care about the enamel inside it, since a good smack with a thirty-pound sledgehammer would remove it quickly. However, we did not come across any tubs during our weeks of collecting!

Vincent was the one who walked along the railroad tracks for several days collecting the old spikes. We assumed the railroad maintenance workers, "gandy dancers," had inadvertently left them. This would happen often when they were pounding new spikes down through metal plate track supports and into the wood railroad ties. Robert was successful in finding a bundle of copper wire. Our load of junk would be a win-win situation for everyone. We would get the safe home to begin our tedious task of getting it open. The junkyard owner would get his wagon back, along with a hefty load of scrap; and we boys would all share in whatever money the load of delivered scrap would bring us.

Richard and I went to the junkyard on Saturday morning and asked the owner if we could borrow his wagon to bring him a heavy load of scrap items. He advised us that he would be using it all day until quitting time. Then he told us we could have it then, if we still wanted it, and to bring it back the next day, Sunday. Our town's junkyard, along with every other junkyard around, seemed to be open every single day.

They opened very early, but closing time was generally around 6:00 p.m. However, if they were quite busy with customers who had a lot of scrap, they would not close up shop until everything was moved inside. Just like the Goodwill drop-off centers of today, items dropped off in front of the junkyard might not be around in the morning!

I cannot tell you how many times we found items of scrap late in the day that would bring us enough money to buy several packs of BB's, for our Red Ryder guns and a few candy bars, hoping the junkyard would still be open. Sometimes it was and sometimes it wasn't. After rushing to get there, our biggest disappointment would come when we had enough items to buy a theater ticket and we found it closed! Sometimes even before six o'clock.

The other boys were all excited and happy to hear the good news about being able to use the wagon on Sunday. All six of them said they did not have anything to do, and it worked for them! However, being able to use the wagon on Sunday, especially this particular Sunday, was not good news for Richard and me. We often wondered why our Jewish friend Robert never mentioned having to go to a synagogue or having to do something special on Easter.

We looked at one another dejectedly, without saying a word. It would be Easter Sunday, and we knew we would not be able to skip Mass, read our missal to find out what the Gospel was about, or look into church and steal a peek as to what color vestments the priest was wearing. Our facial expressions said it all as we looked at each another. They clearly were saying, "What are we going to do?"

This was one of the times where our mother and father insisted that we all go to Mass together. Afterward, we would have to sit down to our traditional Polish meal of homemade black forest mushroom soup, kielbasa, *golomki*, pierogi, pickles, homemade beet/horseradish, deviled eggs, ham, rye bread, and unleavened communion. After dinner, desserts would probably be some of everyone's favorites, like *paczki* (a donut-like pastry filled with creams and jams), *kolaczki* (cookies), *babka* (sweet coffee cake), and *chrusciki* (fried dough sprinkled with powdered sugar). In addition to coffee and tea, there would also be some Corby's whiskey shots, cold vodka shots, and Iron City Beer chasers (Again hunky highballs as they were called) being drunk by our father and other male and female invited relatives and friends.

Our parents had said they were thinking about going to the twelve o'clock Mass, the last of the day. How terrible, we thought to ourselves. This would kill half of the day, and dinner was always served early on this special day, starting around four o'clock. There just would not be enough time for us to retrieve the safe. We certainly were not going to let the other boys go get it without us and see the treasure that lay inside it. That is, if they could get it open!

It was around noon, and Richard and I advised them we had to go home and check with our parents about possibly getting away on Sunday. We also asked them to meet us in front of the White Tower around two o'clock, and we would let them know if we could be available to help out on Sunday.

We said good-bye to them quickly and took off running to get home. When Richard and I got to our front door, he looked at me and said, "What story should we tell them as to why we do not want to go to church?" I said, "We certainly cannot tell them we are sick, since that means we will be sent to bed and never be able to leave the house. How about we try and convince them to go to an earlier Mass? Daddy is off work today and tomorrow, and will be a little mellow after drinking some of his whiskey; he may just listen to us."

We went inside the house and greeted our parents, without mentioning a word about the safe to them. They inquired where we had been and what we had been up to. We informed them we had ventured into the woods with our friends for a few hours, come out, and played some kick-the-can. They asked if we were hungry, and we both told them that we were starving. We sat down at the table, and our mother pulled out a big tray of her homemade macaroni and cheese. Then she sliced off two huge pieces and placed them on plates in front of us.

Both Richard and I could see by the gleam in our father's eyes and from his robust and jolly humor that he had been drinking a little bit. I thought to myself that this might just be the right time for us to broach the subject of going to Mass tomorrow. Perhaps we might even be able to convince them to go to an earlier one. I winked at Richard, and he knew what I was thinking and winked back at me. We certainly did not want to upset our parents and possibly get into an argument and maybe even a good beating by challenging what Mass they wanted to attend.

While continuing to eat my macaroni and cheese and pouring gobs of Heinz ketchup all over it, I told my mother what a wonderful cook she was and how lucky Richard and I were to have both of them as parents. Our father looked at us and said, "Barrie, you are absolutely right about that." After this, I was about ready to approach the possibility of changing the Mass time from twelve o'clock to an earlier time, hoping it would not cause an argument.

Suddenly my mother looked at me and Richard and told us that she and my father had decided to go to the nine o'clock Mass in the morning, since it would allow her more time to get her food cooked and prepare for the early dinner. Even with all the help she was going to receive, she felt more comfortable going to the early Mass. Our father spoke up and said that it would also give him more time to do some extra things.

Richard and I had already figured out what the extra things would be, but hesitated to say anything. Since it would be Sunday and he knew that all the bars and liquor stores would be closed, he would be able to go to the Valley Business Men's Club and get a few shots and some beer chasers there. The club opened at 9:00 a.m. and would not close until midnight. We both knew that he would be going there shortly after Mass let out and he walked home with the family.

Elated over the good news we had just heard, we both knew this would provide us enough time after Mass to help get the wagon and retrieve the safe with the other boys. Richard then asked "if we could go out and play after Mass was over". Our father looked at us and said "we could go out and play, but he wanted us home in time to clean up and not be late for dinner."

Richard and I got up from the table ready to leave, and our mother said, "Where are you headed off to now?" We told her we would play some more in the woods. She then told us to be careful and stay safe with whatever else we might do, adding, "I love you." Then she said, "Richard, you take care of your younger brother also."

Heading for the door to leave the house, we told her and my father that we loved them both very much. We ran out the door screaming "hooray, hooray, hooray. Let's go meet the other boys and tell them about our being able to help out tomorrow."

By now it was close to two o'clock, and we got to the White Tower fast. Sure enough, the other boys were there and waiting on us to show up. We explained to them what had happened, and they all screamed out, "yippee, yippee." We started planning and talking about some items we would need to bring with us to get the safe on the wagon. We also discussed what time we would all meet and go to the junkyard. For Richard and me, it could not be before ten o'clock, since Mass would not be over until around nine forty-five. We set a firm time of ten o'clock for all of us to meet again by the White Tower.

Joseph and Charles said they had a long, heavy piece of bull rope to bring, and we thought that would be great. Charles even said, "I will bring my knife, in case we have to cut some off to tie the safe down on the wagon." Richard said "he and I would bring our father's long steel dig bar to help move it around." Vincent volunteered to bring along some two-by-four timbers to help move it along also. Finally, Vincent said "he would bring some wooden blocks to place in front of and behind the wheels if needed." No one ever suggested bringing gloves, since we all knew none of us had or could afford them!

Richard and I woke up early Sunday morning, anxious to get to church and get it over with as quickly as possible. Hopefully the priest would keep his sermon short. It would not take us more than ten minutes to rush home, change our clothes, and meet up with the guys. Thinking ahead, we took the dig bar out of the tool shed when we came home that evening and placed it on our front porch. This way it would be right in front of us as we left the house, making it hard for us to forget it!

Richard and I did not sleep well that evening, and we talked about what we might find inside the safe once we got it open. Our first thoughts were that it would be filled with paper money and coins or maybe even some war bonds, since that seemed to be what everybody who could afford them was still buying. We also thought it might contain some jewelry, like rings and watches. I thought we might even find a couple of guns inside it, since the movies always showed a gun in most safes being opened up by wealthy people, gangsters, or crooks. I stole a quick glance to check and see if the dig bar was still around, and it was. We did not want to leave this behind and had to make sure we did not forget it.

The morning came early, and we both got up, washed, brushed our teeth, and headed downstairs. No food would be eaten by anyone this morning, since we were all going to receive Holy Communion. We left the house around eight forty-five, which gave us plenty of time to walk to church and be in a pew before the priest entered the main sanctuary. As usual, the ranking members of the parish and their families were already seated. People were still coming into the sanctuary and church rails could be heard being lifted up and falling back down as they went into the pews to take a seat.

Richard and I were on our best behavior this Easter Sunday, April 6, 1947. We did not fool around or punch one another while in the pew or going up to receive Holy Communion at the altar rail. We wanted nothing to interfere with our opening up the safe! Mass seemed to be going pretty fast. During the priest's offertory before communion, the passing around of the wicker donation, or money collection basket even went fast. Our father dropped a dollar in the wicker basket, and each one of us four children dropped in a nickel. In addition, today's Gospel, Mark 16:1-7, "The Resurrection of the Lord," was very short, only half of a *Continuous Sunday Missal* page long.

On the other hand, the Palm Sunday "Prayer before the Gospel" the week before, Matthew 26:36-75 and 27:1-60, "Passion of our Lord Jesus Christ," or also known as "the agony in the garden" was a real killer. We had to continue standing and follow the readings of eight pages from our missals as the priest read them out loud. It was a tortuous ordeal, and you could see many parish individuals picking up one leg to let it rest a bit, putting it down, and picking up the other leg for a short rest.

You could also see and hear impatient groans of uum, uum, and agh, agh, coming from the mouths of some teenagers and small children. Some were also stretching or bending forward, backward, and sideways, to relieve the pain in their lower backs and feel a little more comfortable. In addition, many others extended their arms and elbows back and forth so as to stretch out even more. We kids called it a "Catholic Endurance Test" and it did not end with this reading!

After this long versed reading the Gospel reading, even though only one missal page long, still had to be read! This one and only Mass torture day of the year during Easter was bad, but never as bad as having to say a rosary during long kneeling periods on the bare oak floors at Saint Colman's parochial school.

This was one Sunday's Mass where you better be some of the first people to get out of church early, to avoid being trampled to death by people wanting to get out of church quickly. In the English language, there is a way to abbreviate many things and still leave them understandable to most people. This is what I had hoped the Catholic Church would do when it came to reading "The Prayer before the Gospel" on Palm Sunday.

Today's Mass was over by nine forty-five, as we had thought it would be, and we were delighted. Richard and I were allowed to run home and get our old play clothes and clodhopper shoes on. We exchanged our clothing very quickly, ran downstairs, and cut two large pieces from the leftover macaroni and cheese that was in the refrigerator. We wrapped it up in wax paper, stuffed them in a brown paper bag, and left the house.

When we reached the outside, our parents had just arrived home, and our father said, "What are you boys up to?" I looked at him said, "We are going into the woods to play with our friends, like we told you last night." Then our mother said, "But you haven't eaten anything yet." Pointing at Richard, who had the paper bag in his hand, I told her, "That's all right. We made a lunch out of the delicious macaroni and cheese you made." Everybody in our household loved cold macaroni and cheese.

After this brief encounter, we started to run away, but our father hollered at us and said, "Wait a minute, slow down, boys. I want to remind you that you better be back home in time to clean up and be ready for dinner." Richard and I both said to him simultaneously, "We will, we promise, and can we leave now?" He looked at us sternly and said, "Yes, you can, but be careful and stay out of trouble."

We started to take off running again, and I suddenly remembered about the dig bar and ran back to get it. My father looked at me and asked, "What are you going to do with that?" I replied, "We found some junk metal by the ice plant and need it to help us dig it up." He told me, "All right, but make sure you bring it back home."

Due to all the questioning, we did not get to the White Tower until ten minutes past ten; the other boys were waiting. They were happy to see us since they had thought we were not going to make it. In checking before we departed for the junkyard, Joseph and Charles had brought their bull rope, and Vincent had two two-by-fours and two small, short pieces of four-by-fours. With the dig bar I had in my hand, we thought we were all set to go get the safe.

We walked at a fast pace and arrived at the front of the junkyard's big sliding doors in five minutes' time; it was only ten thirty. This would give us five hours to get the safe and return the wagon and load of scrap material back to the junkyard. We asked the junkman if we could still borrow the wagon. He looked at us and said, "Yes, but I want it returned by five o'clock. It is in the back, where the guys are working on an automobile."

We thanked him, took off running, found the wagon, and shortly after that loaded our tools (dig bar, rope and wood on top of it). Willy and Joseph, the two biggest boys, took the wagon's long steel handle in their hands and began pulling it away from Church Street. Then we crossed Railroad Street, turned left onto lower Monroeville Road and followed it to Brown Avenue extension, the ice plant area, where our safe was hidden away.

With an unloaded wagon, we made good time; it was only eleven o'clock now. We pulled the wagon up the slight macadam grade, turned it around, and placed the back of it up as close as we could get it to the safe. Vincent placed his two wood blocks under the front wheels to keep it from moving. After this, we started to remove all of the brush, leaves, and branches that had been covering the safe.

The safe lay on its side, with the combination tumbler pointing upward toward the sky. It was on a hilly mound of dirt, and with the dig bar and long two-by-four boards, we began the tedious task of rolling it over toward the wagon. The safe moved, but rather than roll over as we thought it would, it just slid off the mound onto the hard macadam road. It was just a few feet away from the wagon.

Robert said to all of us, "What do we do now?" One part of the safe was still off the ground partially, and Joseph said to Vincent, "Put your long boards in front of it, and we will roll it up and onto the boards with the dig bar." The dig bar slid easily under the open area between the ground and the safe, and four of us lifted on it and rolled the safe over onto the boards. We all got very excited with how well it was going, and Bobby said, "This is going to be easy."

Little did we know we were in big trouble! Even though we had the dig bar, all of our timber pieces could not be used anymore. The two-by-fours were under a couple hundred pounds of safe, and the four-by-fours were keeping the wagon from running down the slight macadam downgrade. What we needed was a few more pieces of wood blocks that we could roll the safe over again on. This would place the side of the safe at the height of the wagon's steel plate. From this point, we thought, like Archimedes (give me a lever and I can move anything), that by using the two freed-up two-by-fours and dig bar, we would be able to roll it up onto the wagon.

We stopped for a while to think about it some more, and in the interim, Richard and I ate our cold macaroni and cheese pieces. The other boys had already eaten a big breakfast.

We went back to work and searched for some more large pieces of wood or blocks, but with no luck. "What are we going to do now?" Vincent blurted out. With this, Richard said, "I will run down to the back part of Divens' garage and get something from there. They always have stuff like this laying around by their tire recapping shop." Charles said, "I will go with you," and they both took off running. Five minutes later, they came back, each one carrying two large wood blocks.

We placed these blocks right behind the rear of the wagon wheels and, using the dig bar, under the rear of the safe, now resting on the two-by-fours. After this, four of us boys and without crowding one another, were able to pull up hard on the dig bar, and roll the safe over again onto the new wood blocks. We now had the safe sitting really close to the wagon's steel plate and slightly higher. We did not know what to do from this point. Richard spoke up and said, "Let's try to move the rear of the wagon a little closer to and underneath the safe part sticking up. From there, we can tie the bull rope around it, and pull it all the way onto the wagon."

By clearing away some dirt and other debris from behind the wagon's rear wheels, we were able to do this. With bull rope in hand and tied around the safe, four of us boys struggled to pull it forward, while the other four boys pushed hard on it from the rear! It just would not move. After awhile and the making of quite a bit of noise, two neighborhood men came by and asked us what we were doing. I spoke up and told them we were trying to get my safe to my backyard.

With this, one of them said, "We will give you a hand." With them helping to pull on the rope, we edged the safe forward until it fell on the wagon's steel plate! With this, we all screamed out in delight, with some saying, "whoopee, whoopee" and others saying, "we did it, we did it." We thanked the men, removed the blocks of wood from the front and rear wagon wheels, and carefully moved the wagon slowly down and off the macadam road onto Brown Avenue.

Willy was wearing a watch and able to keep track of the time for us. It was now 1:15 p.m., and Richard and I were wondering if we were going to get back home in time for dinner.

We turned the wagon left on Brown Avenue and started to pull it down to and across Penn Avenue extension. From here we would head straight into Farmer's Alley and the rear of my house. This was a very short distance to travel and would normally take only ten minutes or less walking time. However, with the heavy load we now had to pull, it would take a little longer. Willy and Joseph took hold of the wagon's handle and began pulling, while the remaining six of us boys, three on each side of the wagon, bent over slightly and began pushing.

The wagon moved along slowly and without too much difficulty, since we had a little downhill grade, until we reached Penn Avenue extension. All we had to do was watch out for vehicle traffic and hope the drivers saw us also. We crossed this street and kept pulling the wagon into Farmer's Alley, which was nice and level. Finally, we reached the back of Richard's and my house. We were all pretty tired by now, and there was not much joy or celebrating coming from our mouths as we sat down and rested.

It was two o'clock by now, and we still had to roll the safe off the wagon, load it up with the collected scrap junk, and get it back to the junkyard owner. The pressing time now was for Richard and I to get home in time to clean up, somewhere around three thirty. There would be no problem getting the wagon back by five o'clock. The other boys could do it and collect the money we had coming for the scrap; we would split it up accordingly tomorrow.

Using the dig bar again, placing it under the safe and lifting up on it while the other boys pulled on it with the rope, we tipped it off the side of the wagon and onto the dirt. It did not have to be moved and was not in the way of anything. What would our parents say when they saw it? I thought to myself. Maybe it would not be too big of a surprise to them, since Richard and I were always bringing all types of junk home. But this was the first time for a safe!

We all pitched in after this and began loading the scrap iron on the wagon. We finished around two forty-five, and the other boys told Richard and me that they could handle everything from this point; they would take the wagon and junk back, collect the money, and see us tomorrow. We thanked them and said good-bye as they pulled the wagon away and headed to the junkyard, all on flat streets. It would be an easy pull for them. The very last, and most important thing, I thought about before going into our house was to put my father's dig bar away.

After I did this, I looked at Richard and said, "Race you to the bathroom." We both took off running, and he shoved me aside and made it into the house first! Our parents heard us come in, then they saw us, and our mother said, "You are home early. Did you have a nice time in the woods, and what did you do?" Richard said, "We will tell you later about a piece of junk we found," never mentioning the safe, and then we ran upstairs to our bedroom. We both took a bath and changed back into our good clothes for Easter dinner.

After dinner, we helped our mother, along with our two sisters and visiting Polish relatives, clean up. Our father, grandfather, and two uncles were busy talking and drinking their three-finger shots of whiskey and vodka. They were all in a very jovial mood, and Richard and I thought this would be a good time to approach our father and tell him about the safe. Richard looked at me and asked, "Which one of us do you think ought to tell him?" Not being the dumb brother, I replied back quickly and said, "You should!" He hesitated a little bit over my response, displayed some nervousness, stuttered somewhat, and said to me, "Al-al-al-all right, okay, I will do it." After this, we discussed how we might tell him about the safe and it being in our backyard. After a while, we decided that we would just tell him, "We found a safe and think there may be some money and other valuables in it." Hopefully it would work and keep him from getting mad at us.

We walked over to the room where our father and the other relatives and friends were having their drinks. Just before dinner we decided between us, that Richard would not be the dumb brother this time, and I would tell our father about the safe. We waited for the opportunity to speak to him without interrupting anyone. Before I could say anything, my father looked at us and asked, "What do you boys want?" I said, "We have a piece of junk we brought home and would like to show it to you."

Gruffly he asked, "What kind of junk?" I told him, "We found a safe, and we think there might be some money and other valuables in it." He said. "Let us go take a look at it." Our grandfather spoke up and said "he wanted to see it also." He said, "Have you tried to open it up yet?" I told him, "We tried turning the tumble lock for a long time and different directions, but could not get it to open." He looked at us and said, "That is why it is nice to buy a safe from someone who has the combination to it."

We all walked toward the rear door of the house and stepped outside. Our father said, "Wow that is a big safe. I kind of expected something a little smaller. How did you boys manage to get it here?" He was not mad, and this made us very happy. We explained to him how we found it and were able to move it. In a way, he seemed delighted and proud to learn we were able to come up with the innovative ways to get it where it now lay. Then our father asked us, "Now, how do you plan on getting it open to show me all the money and valuables inside it?"

Richard replied to this question and told him we would try to chisel it open as a start, and asked permission to use his tools. He said to Richard, "That might be harder to do than you think, but go ahead and use the tools you might need. You boys do it as soon as you can. I do not want that safe laying around and cluttering up the yard very long. You have one month to get it open, and you better make plans to move it away after that."

We thanked him for being so nice and promised him we would get it open as fast as we could, share with him what we found, and have it moved away quickly. Moving it away would probably require us to borrow the wagon and start scrounging around again collecting more scrap metal. Opening the safe would be our first priority, and we would have to work on this after school and the weekends. We would inform the other boys of what we had to do when they returned tomorrow with our share of the scrap money.

Joseph and Charles brought our share of the scrap money to Catholic school the next day. The load brought us six dollars, and each boy's share came to seventy-five cents. After school, we caught up with Willy, Vincent, Bobby, and Robert, and informed them also of what we had to do. After school the next day, we would try breaking into the safe with some of my father's tools.

The next day came. With the heavy safe on the dirt ground, we placed a large chisel into the miniscule seam that separated where the door closed and locked in place. While one boy held the chisel in place, we other boys took turns pounding on it with a small sledgehammer. More boys wanted to swing the sledgehammer than hold the chisel, and you surely must know the reason why.

After days of doing this, the only thing we had accomplished was putting a lot of nicks in the safe's surrounding seam and taking several steel chips out of my father's chisel. Would he be mad about this? You bet he would. The next thing we tried was a bigger sledgehammer and chisel, all to no avail. Even on the weekends when we had more time, we barely made a dent in getting the safe door to open.

The next couple of days, we tried chiseling and knocking off the safe's two hinges, but we did nothing but put more dents all over the door and hinge areas. We attempted to place small sheets of tin into the miniscule opening and wiggle it back and forth, in hopes of sliding the lock back. This also did not work, and we had no dynamite to help out.

We did not want to pound on the safe's tumble lock, since all of us kept trying to be safecrackers from time to time and get it open. After three weeks of all this chiseling and pounding, we decided to knock the tumble lock off. If we could do this, perhaps we could slide the lock back or move it up and down with a screwdriver to open the safe. We placed a two-inch-square piece of steel about a foot long on top of the safe door and up against the safe's tumble lock. Then we decided that even though Willy was the biggest boy, Robert was the heaviest of us all, and he was chosen to swing the sledgehammer and knock it off.

Robert had to swing the sledgehammer from an awkward sideway position, hoping to provide enough force to do it. He informed us he was going to do it on the count of three. He counted out loud, "one, two three," and swung the sledgehammer as hard as he could, but the tumble lock never moved. He attempted this same maneuver six or seven times, but the round movable tumbler would not break off; it was only scarred and dented.

We gave up on this, got out the chisel again, and attempted to get under it and pry it off. This did not work either. Robert went back to hitting it sideways with the bar and sledgehammer, and after several tries, he was successful in knocking the tumbler off the safe door. From here we could see bare metal rods and pieces, but attempting to move them around proved fruitless.

Three weeks had gone by, and as Richard and I suspected, our father asked us "how we were doing in opening up the safe." We told him, "Not too good." He said, "You better get moving. You only have another week, and I want it gone by then." Being older and wiser today, Richard and I often tell each other that our father knew there was nothing in the safe. Why would someone throw valuables away?

No matter what we did, we just could not get the safe door open, and we knew we had to get it moved away from our house. We had also been collecting more scrap metal, as a bargaining chip in asking to borrow the wagon again. We could not get the safe open and asked our father "if he would help us load it on the wagon." He said, "Yes, let me know when you are going to get the wagon, and I will make arrangements to be here." Then he added, "Next Saturday around noon would be best for me."

Off we went the next day after school, which was a Tuesday, and asked the junkyard owner "if we could borrow his wagon on Saturday to bring him some more scrap." He said "yes." We then asked him" if we could get it around ten o'clock," and he said, "Yes, that would be fine, but when do you plan on returning it?" We told him by five o'clock, since this would give us plenty of time to figure out what we were going to do with the safe. He then told us "that would be fine." Thinking about something, I took a chance and asked him" if he was interested in a safe—we knew where one was." He said, "I do not want any safes ever. I do not have time to cut them open and remove the cement or plaster from their inner walls."

Saturday came, and all us boys got the wagon from the junkyard and brought it home. Our father finally showed up and asked Richard and me, "Where are you going to take it?" Richard told him "we did not know yet." With this, our father, trying to help us out since he wanted to dispose of it as much as we did, said, "Why don't you dump it in the dirt path behind the Westinghouse recreation building?" This was an area that for years was a local dumping spot, since no homes or any other structure could be built on it.

There was just one problem! The path, though easily accessible, was all soft dirt and very bumpy! With the weight of the safe on the wagon, even with its large wheels, it would become bogged down quickly. We all kept thinking about what else we could do. Richard said, "We could pull it up to the top of Penn Avenue extension and push it over the hillside down onto the path." Our father looked at Richard and said, "That is a wonderful idea. I will even help you get it up the extension. I think we will need my dig bar to help put the safe on the wagon and will go get it."

After a while, with our father's help and body strength, we were able to pull the wagon and safe up the Penn Avenue extension hill. Then we pulled the wagon up the road onto the very edge of the dirt hill overlooking the rear of the Westinghouse building. We rolled the safe off the wagon, and it hung precariously on the top edge of the hillside. Our father then looked at, and told all of us boys "he thought we could handle the safe from here, and he left the area."

Looking down the steep hill, I saw a huge chunk of concrete, and my brain started to work. I did not want to give up on trying to open the safe one more time, and shared what I was thinking about doing with the other boys. Pointing my index finger toward the area, I told them, "Why don't we roll the safe over and down toward that big chunk of concrete, and maybe on impact, it will open the door." Everyone was all for doing this, and we all assembled around the safe to give it a big push with all the strength we could muster.

We would do this on the count of three, and soon you could hear, "one, two, three," and a lot of grunting and groaning. The safe moved over the edge of the steep hillside quickly and rolled over once, twice, three times, and stopped suddenly! It had become bogged down in the center of the hill and would roll no farther. Our final attempt at opening the door had failed, and we all left disappointed and without any money or other things of value to show for our efforts.

In the coming years, Richard and I would walk and play along this path and still see the safe laying undisturbed. We wondered why some of the younger boys around town had never attempted to open it. We also wondered why no one ever attempted to roll it farther down the hill. Who knows? Perhaps they had heard the tales about eight young boys who had attempted to do it years earlier and failed! Eventually, during the redevelopment phase of Turtle Creek and putting in a new highway, the safe disappeared.

Although we never did get this safe open, I have obtained a great deal of satisfaction from the old Diebold safe I bought in 1968 in Glendale, California. First of all, I received the combination, making it easy to open. When I opened it, I found a green canvas bag, containing over one hundred Indian head pennies, in a locked compartment. The key to open this compartment was in the lock, and I left it in place. Over the years, I have found additional satisfaction in cleaning up those pennies that had a young person's birth year on it and giving it to them as a present.

Diebold safe, circa 1879.

THE BOYS HAVING A GOOD TIME IN THEIR CLODHOPPER SHOES.

LOOKING AT PHOTO TO LEFT IS WILLY, VINCENT (CENTER) AND
BOB STRADDLING THE TOP OF HIS SHOULDER AND BARRIE.

CHAPTER 14

NATIONAL CASH REGISTER

Richard and I wanted a bright shiny brass National cash register to play with and ring up imaginary sales of grocery items. We wanted one like we had seen on display one day in Jessup's used furniture store, located on Braddock Avenue. It was sitting on top of a glass display case on the lower floor of his two-story building. Harry Jessup, the son of the owner, would let us pretend to ring up a sale on it from time to time.

Entering several keys, especially the $ keys, and watching the amount appear inside a framed glass window fascinated us. After ringing up a sale, we would each take a turn at rotating the cash register's polished steel, hand-crank lever, with an oak wood grip. The cash register was an item for sale, and Harry did not use it in his everyday business dealings. He did keep several pennies, nickels, dimes, and quarters in it, though, which also caught Richard's and my attention.

One day we went into the store, and the beautiful brass National cash register was gone. Harry told us "he had sold it," and we went away discouraged, since we had both hoped that someday we would have enough money to buy it.

The year was 1944, Richard was ten years old, and I was nine years old the first time we saw the cash register. We decided we wanted one just like it in our bedroom to play with. Time went by, and we both forgot about it until one day a year or two later. Then, out of curiosity and with no intention of stealing anything, we found a way one day to enter the second story of Jessup's furniture store.

The trucks entered the upper floor by driving over a gravel laden ground entry. Even though the two large outside double wooden doors were always locked, we found a way to get through one of them. The doors would sway back and forth toward us as we pushed on them from the bottom, and we could see they left a little opening on the side. However, this opening closed quickly, and we did not want to place our hands inside it.

The thought of having the door swing back hard on our hand or arm and possibly break either one scared us. In addition, the thought of a hand or arm becoming wedged inside the opening and our not being able to break free frightened us even more. We did not want the police or fire department to rescue us and ask questions.

After thinking about it for a while, I told Richard, "If I lay down on the dirt driveway outside the door and push on the bottom of it with my clodhoppers, you might be able to slip through the wider opening." "Let's try it," Richard replied. I put my back on the ground, placed my hands firmly on the dirt, raised up my bent knees, straightened out my legs, and pushed firmly on the door with them. Grunting and groaning and pushing on the lower part of the door as hard as I could, a wider opening appeared. With this, still keeping forward pressure on the door, I told Richard "to see if he might be able to slip inside the building." "Hurry up," I screamed out, since I did not know how much longer my legs would last, or how much longer I would be able to maintain the wider opening."

Richard was already on the ground, and after wiggling around a little bit, he was able to slip through the opening and enter the building. He did this just before my legs collapsed from pushing on the door, and the opening closed quickly. Now the question was, "How do I get inside to join up with Richard?" Richard, who was much stronger than me, said "he thought he could pull on the lower part of the door with both of his hands and hopefully create enough room for me to slip inside also."

Richard told me, from where he was inside the building, "On the count of three, I am going to pull hard on the door. When I do this, get close to the area I got in from, and slide through the opening if you can." I lay down on the ground close to where the opening might be, and listened as Richard started counting "one, two," and at the sound of hearing him say "three" and seeing the crack appear, I was able to wiggle about and slide my body inside the building also. This was the first time we had ever done anything like this and as time passed, we would one day regret what we had just done.

I stood up quickly, and we hugged each other and giggled about our success. "Shush," Richard said, "we do not want to let anyone know we are in here." "Okay," I replied, and as we looked around, we could see the second story was used to store additional furniture and park their two large moving trucks inside. After looking around some more, we could also see that small statues, moving blankets, record players, jukeboxes, and a lot of beds, mattresses, dressers, chairs, and couches were placed on this level. It had to be an excess of the furniture on the lower floor. A large area was left open for the trucks to pull into when not in use or stored for the night.

Off to the left-hand side, we saw a flight of ten to fourteen stairs, which led to a single door and what we thought might be a small office. Out of curiosity, we walked up the steps to the darkened area at the top to see what might be inside the room. Richard turned the doorknob to open the door, but it was locked. "Shucks," I whispered to Richard, and he said, "I sure would like to know what is in there."

We both turned around, and due to very little light at the upper part of the steps, we walked carefully back down them. We continued to walk around inside the building and look at some more items for a long time. Then, without touching or taking anything, we left through the door opening the same way we entered. After learning how to get inside the building, when we became bored with all the other games and things we were doing, we would sneak back into it on occasion. We would look at the new pieces of furniture brought in by the trucks and unloaded.

We would never enter the building until we knew the trucks were gone. This meant they would be out on the road, delivering or picking up furniture items, and would not return for quite a while. We never once entered the building in the evening hours, due to it being pitch black inside and for fear of being bitten by any rats running around. This Jessup building was located just a short distance away from Gus's candy store and his big cellar rats.

One Saturday afternoon, Richard and I were playing on the TRI-BORO coal slide, which was located directly across the street from the second story of the Jessup furniture building. It was also the place where the big doors we would slip through were located. From where we were sitting, we saw the workers and two moving trucks driving away, and the doors were locked. This meant the truck's drivers and movers would not return for quite a while!

Leaving the coal slide, we played on the railroad tracks and threw crab apples inside a switching track and watched them being crushed as the track closed. Shortly after this, a train being switched over went by the same area a few minutes later. Sometimes we would throw a broom or old mop stick handle between the switching tracks, and watch and listen to them emitting a snap, crackle, and pop noise while being crushed.

We became bored after a while, and I asked Richard "if he wanted to go look around inside the furniture store. Now would be a good time to do it, since the trucks are gone." He did not say anything and started to run away, as fast as he could, from the railroad tracks up over a small hill and toward the furniture store doors. From this action, I knew I had gotten his attention.

He stopped at the Penn Avenue extension roadway, and I caught up to him. Making sure no vehicles were coming, we ran across and over to the furniture store doors. When we got very close to the doors, we looked around carefully to make sure no one was watching us and worked our way inside.

We had not been inside the building for a few weeks and wondered what new items might have been brought in. After looking around for a while, we saw a lot of new and beautiful used furnishings we had not seen before.

Not once was it ever our intention to steal anything. We were just being overly adventurous, mischievous boys looking for something different to do and see. With all the new and different items we saw from time to time, it was like walking around inside a museum. Stored in different locations, we could see large rugs and wall tapestries, couches, chairs, tables, jukeboxes, slot machines, pinball machines, poster beds, stoves, refrigerators, and tub-style washing machines. Large and small pictures hung from the walls and knowing what I do today, as taught to me by my wife, several of them were done in oil and ink pen or charcoal.

As we continued to look around on this day, we came upon an item sitting on a bedroom dresser that shocked both of us. It was a beautiful, large, brass National cash register. It was very similar to the National cash register Harry had let us play with from time to time. Richard and I both looked at it in awe, and then Richard said to me, "How nice this would look in our bedroom!" I said, "Why not? We already have a pinball machine in there."

I looked at Richard and said to him, "Where and how could we ever earn enough money to buy it?" There just were not enough pop and beer bottles around town anymore to help us make a large purchase like this. We both wanted this brass National cash register very badly and would do just about anything to get it. That is, anything except steal it! We had never forgotten how much fun and excitement we had with the National cash register Harry let us play with.

With our past experience at ringing up sales on Harry's National cash register, we began to take turns playing around with this one. After punching in various register keys with our fingers, turning the handle, listening to the "ca-ching, ca-ching," sound and watching the drawer spring open for a very long time, several hours had passed and we quit. We decided to leave, go home, and think how we could earn some money to buy the brass National cash register we had just played with.

I told Richard as we were leaving that we had to go see Harry and ask him how much money he wanted for it. Richard gave me a dumbfounded look and said, "We can't do that, you big dummy." I said, "Why not?" Then Richard said, "Barrie, I am surprised at you. Think about what you just said, and the questions that Harry would ask us."

Suddenly my mind came back to me, and I said out loud, "How could I be so stupid? If I did that, Harry would know we were in his building." Both of us were morons in what we were doing by entering a building without the owner's permission!

We talked a little bit more and thought perhaps Harry might move the cash register downstairs and put it up for sale. Since we often went into the store, if by some miracle he did have it on display, we could ask him then how much it cost.

All of a sudden, we heard a lot of noise, car engines running, and voices! The movers, trucks, and drivers had returned. We really did lose track of time as we became so absorbed in thought playing with the brass National cash register. Whispering to each other, Richard and I both said, "What are we going to do?"

I looked at him and whispered, "If we get caught in here, they will put us in jail. I do not want to go to jail!" He whispered back, "I don't either." Shaking nervously and holding onto one another, I told Richard, "Let's go up the stairs and hide!" I did not think we would be safe hiding behind any furniture items. We took off running toward the steps, and when we reached the bottom stair, we walked up the rest of them very quietly.

Richard and I sat down on the top step very close to one another, holding hands and shaking nervously. Then a voice on the outside hollered out, "Hurry up and get those doors unlocked; I do not want to spend all day here." Another voice said, "Neither do I." "Well, step on it," the first voice replied. Shortly after this exchange, we could hear some rattling noises coming from the door and thought it might be someone opening the lock.

One door began to swing outward, and the second door followed. Both doors were now moving forward together, and the outside light was beginning to slowly peep into the inside of the building. The more the doors were opened, the more light came in, and I was really afraid. Like Dracula, as often seen in the movies, I felt that as the light shone on my face, I would start to burn and turn into smoke and ashes! Richard and I held onto one another even tighter, shaking fiercely and breathing very heavily.

Suddenly the first voice, which we recognized by now, spoke up and said, "Let's hurry up and get those trucks inside and unloaded. I want to get home as soon as possible, but without damaging anything." Someone else said, "All right, boss."

By this time, I began to cry a little, and my knees began to knock together. Richard took one of his arms away from me and placed an index finger up to his closed lips, telling me silently to be quiet. I nodded my head up and down silently agreeing!

One of the trucks was driven inside the building and parked. The second truck followed shortly after and parked alongside the first truck. The contents loaded onto the trucks were covered with canvas tarps and tied securely with heavy rope. Both drivers turned off their ignitions. opened their cab doors; moved forward, swung their legs out sideways, and jumped to the floor. Richard and I had a panoramic view to see everything the men were doing. We kept hoping none of them would see us.

A total of four men were now inside the building, and the two drivers walked to the rear of the trucks they had driven in. They each removed the two-pin chains that locked the truck's tailgate in place. Then they took the heavy tailgate in their hands, pulled it toward them, and let it drop down slowly. The tailgates moved back and forth a little bit after this, but suddenly they stopped. The boss spoke up and said, "All right, let's move the stuff out of the trucks and store it."

The two drivers jumped into the rear of their trucks and started to untie the ropes and remove the tarps. The other two men, one of whom was the boss, stood directly behind them. Alongside them stood a truck dolly, with two wheels and a strong web belt to hold things in place as they were being moved about. A short square wood piano mover, secured to four large steel roller wheels, sat beside the dolly to help the men out.

Several dressers were moved to the edge of the truck bed by the men inside. As they were lowered down slowly, the men standing outside lifted them off carefully and placed them on the piano mover. After this, they moved them to a storage location. The next items that appeared were refrigerators, and they were also lowered down the back of the truck slowly and carefully. The two men standing outside the truck would guide them down carefully onto the truck dolly to be moved away.

This unloading and moving various pieces of furniture and appliances to their storage locations went on for about forty-five minutes to an hour. All during this time, Richard and I were in a muse-like state, praying none of them would look around and see us sitting at the top of the darkened stairs. We were also praying that none of them had to come up the steps, open the door, and go into the office. If they did, it was going to be a little difficult, since Richard and I were blocking their way.

The next thing we heard was the boss telling the other men, "You guys did a great job unloading and moving the stuff. Let's get the hell out of here and go home." Then he said, "Lock the trucks up and hide the keys. Harry knows where they will be if he needs them."

Richard and I looked at one another when the boss said this. From the expression on each of our faces, you could see a sense of great relief and happiness, and we stopped shaking so hard. We saw the two drivers open their respective cab doors, reach in, take the keys from the ignition, and lock the doors. Then we saw them walk toward several covered furniture pieces, lift the cover up, and drop the keys onto something.

The boss asked "if anyone had to use the bathroom and looked toward the steps we were sitting on." Richard and I became very nervous again when he asked this and wondered what we would do if someone came toward us. We started to shake all over again. Then suddenly we heard one voice say, "Not me," and then two more voices simultaneously said, "Not me either." The boss said, "Let's leave. You close the doors, and I will lock them up." With this, a sigh of relief came from both Richard and me. We continued to sit very still and be quiet, and watched as the doors were being pushed forward to close up the building entrance.

Then we heard the same rattling noise from the doors and hoped it was the lock being put in place. The noise disappeared quickly. I do not remember how long Richard and I continued to sit on that top step, but finally he looked at me and whispered in my ear, "Do you think they are all gone?" I whispered back to him and said, "I think so. Why don't we walk down slowly to the doors and see if we can hear anyone?" He replied, "All right, let's get away from these steps now."

We walked down the steps slowly, and carefully, holding hands just as we did while walking up them. We walked straight to the two big doors, got as close to them as we could with our ears, and listened for quite a while. After hearing nothing, Richard said to me, "I don't think anyone is around anymore, and I think we should leave now." I told him, "All right, I will pull the door back for you to slide outside." He looked at me and said, "No, Barrie, you have a lot of strength in your legs when pushing on the door, but you do not have enough strength to pull it open." I want to do this, so lie down, get ready, and on my count of three, I will pull on the door and you slip outside."

Listening to Richard as I generally did, I placed myself on the floor quickly and got ready to move on his count. I heard him say, "one, two, three," the door came toward me, daylight appeared, and I slid outside. I was free! Looking around, I could see no one and lay down on my back. I brought my knees upward and placed my legs against the door, and pushed on it as hard as I could. The opening appeared quickly. Richard saw the daylight and also slid outside. He too was now free!

With smiles on our faces and a sense of joy and relief, we both jumped up off the ground quickly and started to run home. When we reached our back porch, I told Richard, "I have never been this scared in my life." He looked at me and said, "Me too." We went straight up to our bedroom and played a couple of games on our pinball machine to relax.

Richard and I never told our parents about what we had done on this day, fully knowing they would have punished us severely. However, we did learn a valuable lesson for life: "Never enter someone else's premises without their permission!"

As the years passed, I never forgot about the National cash register, just as I had not forgotten the safe. I just had to have a cash register like the one Harry let us play with from time to time. Harry eventually displayed the cash register for sale. Richard and I went back often to the store to look at, but one day it was gone. Harry had finally sold it.

As I became older every time I went into a store carrying old items and antiques, I would look around for one just like it. I finally found one that looked very similar, located in an antique store known as the Penny Pincher, in Simi Valley, California, in 1971. It was a National cash register, Model

442, manufactured in September 1911, and sold out of San Francisco. After a little negotiating with the store's owner, I bought it!

As the years passed, nothing gave me more pleasure than watching my granddaughter, Erin, punch on its keys and play pretend, ringing up grocery sales. My greatest joy would come when she would look at me and say, "One pound kielbasa, Pap, at $1.29 a pound, right?" I would say, "That's right, Erin," and she would turn the crank to hear the nice-sounding ca-ching, ca-ching, which I as a little boy had heard years before her. Then the drawer would pop open, and she would hand me coins from the small coin compartments I had placed pennies, nickels, dimes and quarters in. Several one-dollar bills were also placed in the compartments designed to hold paper money.

I often wonder why Harry never put any dollar bills in his brass National cash register for Richard and me to play with. Did he not trust us? I say no, it was simply because hard-earned money during these days gone by would never be left lying around unattended! Especially by a good person, a friend, and a hardworking individual like Harry!

Brass National cash register, 1911.

AUTHOR'S NOTE

With a few exceptions, every individual mentioned in this book, whether it be by only a first name or by both first and last name, is a real person. The childhood antics I have described did take place, and all the games identified were real, along with some of the savagery that occurred while we boys played them.

At first, with a feeling of guilt, I gave considerable thought to not writing about some of the harsh incidents and the discipline administered by a few Sisters of Mercy at Saint Colman's school. I decided, however, they had to be told. I did it not to demean them during their times of overly aggressive punishments, since I also brought to light their lack of specialized training, which teachers of today are put through. These episodes did not diminish the good work of the other Sisters. Those Sisters who were overly aggressive with their discipline and punishment have been assigned fictitious names.

One has to remember that this was during a time when strict discipline policies were in effect in just about every Catholic school. Harsh paddling and manhandling of students was also present in many, if not all, public schools. Although not right, it seemed to be an accepted practice, by parents, law enforcement, and many other government and social service agencies at the time.

The Catholic Church has banned all paddling, and I believe as of my writing, all but thirteen states have banned corporal punishment and paddling. It is believed by many professionals that it impairs self-image and is the foundation for even more disruptive behavior.

Today the rules have changed, and there is greater legal oversight as to the way children are treated, even in their own homes. Child abuse is unacceptable in today's society, whether it is physical or verbal, and the punishment for such is harsh. It will be carried out by a judge handing out warnings, fines, or both a fine and imprisonment.

Lastly, there is not a day I do not think of the wonderful times I had while living in Turtle Creek. Attending school at Saint Colman's was a wonderful privilege and experience. Therefore, to the Sisters, priests, teachers, and my classmates, both living and deceased, God bless every one of you.

CPSIA information can be obtained at www.ICGtesting.com
Printed in the USA
BVOW04s1858091213

338613BV00003B/186/P